Scots and the Spanish Civil War

Solidarity, Activism and Humanitarianism

Fraser Raeburn

T0333645

EDINBURGH
University Press

Edinburgh University Press is one of the leading university presses in the UK. We publish academic books and journals in our selected subject areas across the humanities and social sciences, combining cutting-edge scholarship with high editorial and production values to produce academic works of lasting importance. For more information visit our website: edinburghuniversitypress.com

© Fraser Raeburn, 2020, 2022

Edinburgh University Press Ltd
The Tun – Holyrood Road
12 (2f) Jackson's Entry
Edinburgh EH8 8PJ

First published in hardback by Edinburgh University Press 2020

Typeset in 11/13 Foundry Sans and Foundry Old Style
IDSUK (DataConnection) Ltd, and
printed and bound by CPI Group (UK) Ltd,
Croydon, CR0 4YY

A CIP record for this book is available from the British Library

ISBN 978 1 4744 5947 1 (hardback)
ISBN 978 1 4744 5948 8 (paperback)
ISBN 978 1 4744 5949 5 (webready PDF)
ISBN 978 1 4744 5950 1 (epub)

Contents

Tables

Acknowledgements

There are far too many people requiring thanks, and the remaining permissible word count far too small, for me to recount them all. Friends, family, colleagues and supervisors have all left their direct and indirect marks on this text, and I will be forever grateful for their advice, feedback and support along the way. One person in particular, though, has had to put up with the entire decade of studies, research and writing that has led to this point, and I'm immensely thankful that she was there for all of it.

Note on Translation and Abbreviations

All translations, unless otherwise noted, have been undertaken by the author. Source titles remain in the original language of publication throughout.

Initialisms and acronyms are the bane of almost all writing on the Spanish Civil War, and the present text is no exception. The following are used in text throughout the book:

AEU	Amalgamated Engineering Union
BUF	British Union of Fascists
CPGB	Communist Party of Great Britain
FCKMU	Fife, Clackmannan and Kinross Miners' Union
IBA	International Brigade Association
IFTU	International Federation of Trade Unions
ILP	Independent Labour Party
ISF	International Solidarity Fund
JC	Joint Committee
LBC	Left Book Club
LMU	Lanarkshire Miners' Union
MFGB	Miners' Federation of Great Britain
NUR	National Union of Railwaymen
NUSM	National Union of Scottish Mineworkers
NUWM	National Unemployed Workers' Movement
PCE	*Partido Comunista de España*
PCF	*Parti communiste français*
POUM	*Partido Obrero de Unificación Marxista*
SAC	Spanish Aid Committee

SSP	Scottish Socialist Party
STUC	Scottish Trades Union Congress
TC	Trades Council
TLC	Trades and Labour Council
TUC	Trades Union Congress
UMS	United Mineworkers of Scotland
WADC	Wounded and Dependants' Committee
YCL	Young Communist League

Introduction: 'Unforgotten'

It is difficult today to imagine how marginal Spain once seemed. Before tapas spread across the world, and the world spread across Spanish beaches, the first decades of the twentieth century saw Spain occupy a marginal position in the global imagination. Slow progress in industrialising, neutrality in the First World War and the persistence of traditional social, religious and cultural institutions all marked Spain as a state that modernity had largely passed by. Whilst Spain had once been the continent's foremost power, it had long since ceased to matter greatly in the foreign ministries of Europe, save perhaps as an object lesson in imperial decline. Although some interest was piqued in leftist circles by the founding of the Spanish Republic in 1931 – as one of very few European states to move towards rather than away from democratic governance in the interwar period – Spain generally remained marginal to European political life. Even today, Spanish football remains far better observed abroad than Spanish politics.

Yet for a few brief years in the late 1930s, Spain's anguish captured and held the attention of the world. In a decade not lacking in international crises and flashpoints, the Spanish Civil War remains distinctive in the scale and intensity of the responses it inspired across the globe. While the sheer drama of the military uprising against the recently elected left-wing Republican government and the subsequent popular resistance accounts for some of this interest, Spain's true appeal was political. It was an ideological Rorschach test writ large, a mirror in which a great many people could see their own beliefs and struggles being reflected. For those on the right, Spain was a new front in the struggle against godless Bolshevism, a stand by noble generals led by the 'Christian gentleman' Francisco Franco on behalf of Western civilisation. For the left, the Spanish Republic was the latest victim of militarism, authoritarianism and fascism – yet, unlike other democracies that had seemingly succumbed meekly to these forces across Europe, in Spain fascism's opponents finally appeared willing to stand and fight, and perhaps even win. The most apt comparison, perhaps, is with the Vietnam War of the 1960s and 1970s – a regional conflict that was transformed into a global phenomenon thanks to its diplomatic and ideological context.

Scotland, like much of the rest of Europe and the world, was immediately fascinated and appalled by events in Spain. Fuelled initially by a trickle, then deluge, of first-hand accounts and reporting in the popular press, interest in the Spanish Civil War has since been maintained through representations in film, art and literature, many of which – from Orwell's *Homage to Catalonia* to Picasso's *Guernica* – have remained cultural touch-stones. Yet for a great many Scots, this was not a conflict to be experienced at a distance. Like countless others across the world, Scots sought out ways to make their own personal interventions felt in Spain. Huge numbers gave money, food or clothing for the Spanish people, and often the most generous contributions came from the parts of Scotland that the interwar slump had hit hardest. Many thousands of Scots gave their time and voices to pro-Republican solidarity campaigns, marking a first political awakening for many lifelong activists, growing into a nostalgic, hopeful memory that only grew more cherished in later years of Cold War cynicism and disappointment. Perhaps most strikingly, over five hundred Scots journeyed to Spain to fight in defence of the Spanish Republic. Nearly a quarter of them are still buried there.

This is a remarkable story, yet one that has remained surprisingly marginal in academic history writing in Scotland. The history of the political left in interwar Scotland is hardly neglected, yet most such accounts shy away from dealing with the impact of the war in Spain. This does not necessarily reflect a lack of interest on the part of historians – names such as Victor Kiernan, Ian Wood and Ian MacDougall are familiar to many in the Scottish historical profession, and each has or had an enduring fascination with the conflict. Yet none attempted to write their own history of Scotland and the Spanish Civil War, in marked contrast to the many scholarly tomes discussing the ways in which Britain – not to mention Ireland and Wales – responded to the war in Spain.[1] In the vast majority of these accounts, however, Scotland has remained entirely marginal. At best, distinctive features – such as the disproportionate number of Scottish volunteers among the British contingent in Spain – have been noted, but never explained. Other aspects, such as the impact and basis of pro-Republican solidarity campaigns, have been addressed within British or English frameworks, but never with particular regard for Scottish sources and perspectives.

In light of this, it would perhaps be expected to claim that this book deals with 'forgotten' history – the uncovering of a neglected Scottish past that otherwise would remain obscure and unknown. Yet this could not be further from the truth. Scottish involvement in the Spanish Civil War has never been forgotten, even as numbers of surviving participants slowly dwindled, and historians at Scotland's universities focused elsewhere.[2] Local history has been preserved and remembered, with exhibitions, concerts and plays still regularly organised in the honour of Scotland's contribution to the struggle.[3] Since the 1970s, memorials to the conflict, and the Scots who died there, have been built across the country, from the banks of the Clyde to Princes Street Gardens, from plaques in Ayrshire villages to trades union offices in Aberdeen.[4] Such memorials could sometimes be controversial – in Edinburgh, Tory councillors attempted to block council funding because the inscription was not dedicated to 'both sides' that died in Spain, a position memorably compared at the time to asking 'the Luftwaffe to do a fly-past at Churchill's funeral'.[5] Yet with the passage of time, not only has conservative opposition to commemorating Scottish involvement in the Spanish Civil War faded, the memory has been embraced by an ever broader segment of the Scottish left. At commemorative events, it is not unusual to find an incredibly broad cross-section of leftist positions represented, from the trade union movement and Labour Party to the remnants of Scottish communism, Trotskyism and anarchism, achieving a tenuous unity on the issue of Spain that eluded their forebears in the 1930s.

The story has found its own chroniclers from within these celebratory circles, from local studies and biographies to a popular book written in 2008 by Daniel Gray, which was also made into a two-part STV documentary, *The Scots Who Fought Franco*.[6] Yet Gray's book, like many of these efforts, reflects the ambiguities of the commemorative scene from which it emerged. Firmly celebratory of any and all pro-Republican efforts, the fragile unity of contemporary commemoration necessitates a delicate approach to conflict within the Republican camp. That is not to say that difficult subjects are ignored entirely, for they are certainly not, but rather that there is a sense that past differences are reconcilable, and that Scottish involvement in the Spanish Civil War reflects a collective achievement of the Scottish left. Yet, as explored in these pages, understanding the nature of Scottish involvement in the conflict requires appreciating the ways in which these responses were often fragmented and partisan. Closing these doors not only risks misrepresenting this past, it also imposes an analytical straitjacket on explaining it.

Gray's book – as with several local studies – is nonetheless well-written, making use of neglected Scottish sources, and provides an indispensable narrative of Scottish involvement in the conflict. A reasonable observer might well ask: what then is the point of this book, or indeed academic history writing more broadly, if this story has already been remembered and preserved in a relatively complete form? Two answers suggest themselves. The first is that, like some British historians before him, Gray was able to note exceptional features of Scottish involvement in the Spanish Civil War, but was less able to explain them. A key purpose of this account, then, is to provide those explanations – why did the Scottish response to Spain take the forms it did? In what ways did it diverge from the 'British' experience, and why? The answers to these questions can tell us a great deal about the ways in which a distinct Scottish political culture continued to exist throughout the 1930s and 1940s, despite the absence of general elections after 1935 and increasing prominence of international issues prior to and during the Second World War. Rather than reflecting a newfound centrality of national, 'British' politics, the responses to the Spanish Civil War are an indication of how local politics can continue to matter, even in the face of all-consuming international crises. In addressing these questions, this book aims to make a significant contribution to the history of Scottish politics in the interwar period, with existing scholarship not only tending to neglect the Spanish Civil War, but often the second half of the 1930s entirely.[7]

The second answer is that Scottish involvement in the Spanish Civil War is part of much wider stories, stories that transcend the boundaries not only of Scotland but of Britain and even Europe. It is a story that intersects with the histories of socialism and communism in interwar Europe, and the connections and networks formed across borders by those who viewed the world in inherently internationalist terms. It is an important part of the history of how the world responded to the rise of fascism, and how people managed to take action despite, or perhaps because of, the failures of their governments. The Scottish volunteers in Spain also represent a crucial chapter in the history of so-called 'foreign fighters', part of the largest such transnational mobilisation in the twentieth century. For these reasons, this book seeks to explore not only what participating in the Spanish Civil War reveals about Scotland but also what these Scots can tell us about much bigger histories.

There are, naturally, several important things this book does not do. Perhaps above all, in focusing on explanations ahead of narrative, it is not a blow-by-blow chronological account of the ways in which Scots reacted to the conflict, or the military exploits of the Scottish volunteers who served in Spain. Moreover, in choosing to explore certain themes in depth, coverage of certain aspects of Scottish involvement in the conflict are comparatively neglected. Counterintuitively, it is often the most controversial subjects that receive less coverage, for the simple reason that these are the topics which have received the most prior historical attention, and about which there is correspondingly less to say. This includes the infamous death in custody in Spain of the Independent Labour Party (ILP) activist Bob Smillie, or the exploits of the Glasgow anarchist Ethel MacDonald in Barcelona.[8] The Scottish Ambulance Unit, plagued by controversy in Spain, is dealt with chiefly from the more neglected perspective of domestic fundraising.[9] Finally, the focus throughout is on the Scottish left – the labour movement, Communist Party and other progressive parties and institutions around which the bulk of Scottish pro-Republican activity was based. The intent is not to downplay pro-Franco feeling in Scotland – it certainly existed on a substantial scale, particularly among Scottish Catholics – but to acknowledge the reality that such sentiment was not the basis for the same kind of large-scale, sustained mobilisations.[10] If nothing else, with Franco's side seeing most of the benefits of international state-led and corporate-led intervention, there was little practical need for the contribution of Scottish money or volunteers to the Nationalist cause, and Franco himself was leery of inviting the direct participation of foreign ideological allies.[11]

The Spanish Civil War and the International Brigades

The Second Spanish Republic was founded at an inauspicious point in history. The end of the First World War had transformed the map of Europe, resulting in a host of new countries that were, generally for the first time, nominally both nation-states and parliamentary democracies. Yet by the time the Republic was proclaimed in April 1931, the mass retreat of democracy across the continent was well under way. Despite the hopes of many Spaniards, the new Republic faced similarly daunting prospects. It was founded in an explicitly reformist, modernising spirit, seeking to break the hold of landowners, Church and monarchy over the Spanish economy and society.[12] This in itself contributed to the new government's lukewarm reception among traditional elites, many of whom were hostile to the very idea of Republican government and its liberalising agenda, let alone growing revolutionary unrest on the part of many Spanish socialists and anarchists. The latter were unusually powerful – Spain was home to the world's largest anarchist movement – and held little fondness for the new democratic regime, refusing even to participate in elections prior to 1936. The first major test of the parliamentary system came sooner than expected: a conservative coalition won the 1933 elections, and began to roll back reforms amidst strikes and uprisings, culminating in open revolt in Asturias in October 1934, which was put down with considerable violence by troops from Spanish Morocco, under the command of General Francisco Franco. These so-called '*bienio negro*' – 'black years' – were marked by growing radicalism on the left, met with an increasing reliance on paramilitary violence from the ruling government and conservative political groupings alike.

Though a broad left-wing coalition – under the banner of the 'Popular Front' – won the next set of elections in February 1936, political instability and violence continued apace. For many in the military – long a bastion of Spanish traditionalism – the situation appeared to be a descent into revolutionary chaos, with the new government either unable or unwilling to forestall the collapse of traditional society and government. Plotting among certain echelons of the military leadership began soon after the election of the Popular Front, but it was not until the summer of 1936 that they felt confident that they had sufficient political and military backing to succeed, not least from Franco himself, who delayed choosing sides until the final weeks before the uprising. The catalyst came with the murder in July of the conservative parliamentarian José Calvo Sotelo, who was killed in revenge for the murder of a socialist-aligned officer in the Assault Guards, Spain's urban paramilitary police force. Yet when it came just a few days later, the coup did not go according to plan. Not only did large sections of the police and military refuse to join the uprising, the plotters did not count on an unprecedented wave of popular resistance. Left-wing political parties and trades unions armed and organised themselves, and, with the aid of loyalists in the military and police, defeated the coup in most of Spain's major cities. Its partial failure marked the beginning of a war that would last for nearly three years, and lead to the deaths of hundreds of thousands of Spaniards.[13]

Although no civil conflict has ever been entirely divorced from an international context, Spain's civil war happened at a time and place that guaranteed exceptional international interest and involvement.[14] Yet an inevitable consequence of this – despite the self-confident and self-appointed 'experts' that soon filled the pages of newspaper letter sections – was that Spain was understood in ways that sometimes owed little to the realities on the ground. For the Scottish left, the military uprising in Spain fitted neatly into a broader global narrative of fascist expansion. In the words of the

Edinburgh communist Donald Renton, Spain was 'part and parcel of the general offensive by the Fascist Powers against working class rights and liberties all over the world'.[15] Many others shared the Dundonian Tom Clarke's retrospective view that the Spanish Civil War offered an opportunity to defeat this offensive, and 'that if we were able to win there the possibility is you would never have had a Second World War'.[16] These narratives left little place for the nuances of Spain's politics and history, and the complex causes of the war itself. In so far as Spain's particular context was understood, it was through the broad sweep of Spanish history, with the old, feudal Spain of the army, landlords and Catholic Church conspiring to destroy the new modern, progressive Spain.[17] The conflict was rapidly constructed and construed as a set of moral binaries – progress against reaction, civilisation against barbarism and, above all, democracy against fascism.

Viewing the Spanish Civil War as a flashpoint of a global anti-fascist struggle was lent credence by the conflict's rapidly apparent international dimensions. Swift intervention from Fascist Italy and Nazi Germany provided crucial early impetus for the military rebels, particularly in enabling the transfer of the Spanish Army of Africa – Spain's most experienced military formation – to southern Spain. Both also lent direct military support to the rebels on air, sea and land, as well as providing substantial material aid. On the Republican side, initial support from the French Popular Front government was soon withdrawn following British diplomatic pressure, reflecting France's own internal divisions, as well as British alarm at the potential for escalation should Spain become a proxy war between democratic and fascist powers.[18] The impact of what became known as the Non-Intervention Agreement was uneven, only restricting the participation of states that abided by international rules and conventions. This meant that, while Italy and Germany happily continued to provide support for the rebels after signing, only the Soviet Union and Mexico proved willing to aid the Republic on similar terms, to considerably less effect.[19]

For military historians, quantifying the foreign support each side received in terms of guns, planes and tanks has proved an arduous task.[20] Yet for this study's purposes, it is the qualitative differences that matter more. Unlike Mussolini and Hitler, Stalin was both unwilling and unable to send a Soviet army to Spain to fight for the Republic. Instead, using the networks and influence developed through the Comintern, the Soviet Union undertook to recruit and organise an international volunteer army to fight for the Spanish Republic.[21] Although the Comintern had not pioneered the idea of foreigners joining the Republican war effort, its involvement profoundly changed the nature of foreign volunteering. Not only did their resources prove vital in enabling far greater numbers to make the journey to Spain, the establishment of dedicated international units – the International Brigades – marked a departure from the scattered participation of individual volunteers. Their status as independent units lent them a unique and highly visible role in the struggle, both militarily and in propaganda. It was in these units that the vast majority of Scottish volunteers in Spain served, and the International Brigades have remained as a key focal point for commemoration of the conflict, in Scotland and beyond.

Historical interest in their story predates the International Brigades' withdrawal from Spain, with an official archive service – and historian – integrated into the XV International Brigade staff from 1937, and the first 'history' of the British Battalion was published as early as 1939.[22] This eye to future history writing at 'undefined future date' – possibly not 'for 10–20–30 years' – complicates the task of the historian in the present, driving home the reality that much archival material preserved in Spain was collected, selected and preserved with a view to its use in celebrating the International Brigades.[23] These contemporary efforts were subsequently supplemented by memoirs, articles and books – from both admirers and detractors – published since the 1940s, but it was the renewed interest surrounding the fiftieth anniversary of the conflict that stimulated new writing about specifically British involvement.[24] Not only did this decade see a new book on the British Battalion – written by the ex-volunteer Bill Alexander, the long-time head of the International Brigade Association – but the first broad accounts of British domestic responses to the war also began to emerge.[25] These accounts were broadly celebratory, both of the International Brigades themselves and of the Communist Party's role in their organisation and pro-Republican activism more broadly. These claims sparked a more sceptical wave of scholarship in the 1990s and 2000s, which sought not only to question the centrality of the Communist Party to the British response to the Spanish Civil War but also to puncture some of the 'myths' surrounding the International Brigades themselves.[26] These texts, particularly in an American context, were often motivated explicitly by proving communist – and Soviet – perfidy in Spain, for others the subtext was subtler.[27] Only in the past decade or so has scholarship emerged which is not defined explicitly or implicitly by Cold War-era divisions, with new accounts productively, if slightly belatedly, embracing the cultural and transnational turns.[28]

Whilst the approach taken here seeks to build on these methodological developments, it also represents something of a throwback in terms of focus. Particularly in discussion of domestic activism, but also to an extent in new work on the International Brigades, there is a tendency to avoid the Communist Party as the main institutional perspective. On one level, this was a necessary challenge to a heroic Party narrative that acted to mask important nuances and diverse perspectives among participants. Yet in some respects, the pendulum has swung too far: as Lisa Kirschenbaum has recently shown, the cultures of Stalinism permeated the International Brigades, in terms of not just political rhetoric but day-to-day existence and experience.[29] This account seeks to explore some of the implications from a Scottish perspective, not out of a desire to resurrect a triumphant communist narrative, but because recruiting and organising the International Brigades within a defined political sphere had important consequences. Not only does this involve, I argue, rewriting the basic narrative of volunteer recruitment and motivation – a question that several generations of scholarship have never quite adequately addressed; it means reappraising the dynamics of life and politics in the International Brigades themselves.

Scotland has a particular relevance here, as it intersects with another thorny outstanding issue: the so-called 'national question' in the International Brigades.[30] This was an army made up of internationalists, yet one in which national lines remained very apparent. How did the diverse mix of cultures, languages and identities in the International Brigades work in practice? In other words, how far did it matter in Spain that a volunteer was 'Scottish', as opposed to English, or British, not to mention French or German? This book seeks to bring these questions together, positing that the answer to the questions of both volunteer recruitment and the continued importance of existing identities stems from where the volunteers came from, not only geographically but also socially. Recruitment was a local phenomenon as much as a transnational one, taking place within very specific social-political networks, defined most often in Scotland by their connection to the Communist Party. Not only does this help explain the recruitment process – as one in which social as well as political factors played a role – but it also hints at the reality that these networks could survive transmission to Spain. The volunteers' experiences can be understood only by appreciating that political and personal relationships were to a large extent already defined before the volunteers even set foot in Spain. While prior relationships among the Cominternian elite in Spain have been explored in some depth by Kirschenbaum, those that were formed much more locally – and remained defined chiefly by local and national political cultures – have not previously received the same attention.

In a similar fashion, this book seeks to reappraise the role of the Communist Party of Great Britain (CPGB) in terms of domestic activism. Since the landmark publication of Jim Fyrth's account of pro-Republican activism and fundraising in Britain, work by scholars such as Tom Buchanan, Lewis Mates and Emily Mason has consistently shifted the focus from British communism.[31] This shift in perspective is in many ways amply justified: 'Aid Spain', in so far as it can even be characterised as a single movement, had a strikingly diverse range of participants. Yet if we allow that the British Aid Spain movement was varied and heterogeneous, which it undoubtedly was, then this itself requires some explanation. Why, in other words, did Aid Spain look so different in different contexts? Part of the answer, once more, stems from the ways in which the Spanish Civil War was inevitably understood through reference to people's own lives. In existing accounts, this has been explored chiefly through references to national 'British' – occasionally more explicitly and accurately referred to as 'English' – character, history and perspectives.[32] However, the evidence explored here suggests instead – in line with Malcolm Petrie's recent argument – that the conflict could be understood not just through reference to Britishness or indeed Scottishness but through very local cultures, politics and struggles.[33] Moreover, the evidence explored here suggests that perhaps the Communist Party is more central than recent scholarship has allowed. Not in the sense that the CPGB was able to build the kind of embryonic 'Popular Fronts' envisaged by Jim Fyrth up and down the land – though its limited success in building pro-Republican coalitions in Scotland is explored – but rather that its role in shaping local political dynamics surrounding Aid Spain was often crucial, for better or worse. Perhaps particularly in Scotland, the CPGB was able to influence disproportionately the nature of pro-Republican activism, though not always in ways that they intended or welcomed.

One advantage of this approach is the ability to explore the connections between domestic activism and transnational mobilisation. The juncture between the two remains underappreciated, with existing studies across national contexts tending to adopt a neat division between those who volunteered to fight, and those who stayed home to raise money and awareness. Yet such neat distinctions do not reflect a more complex reality. Not only were many volunteers engaged in pro-Republican activism before and after their time in Spain, but a considerable proportion of fundraising in Britain was undertaken to support wounded volunteers and their dependants as well as the International Brigade medical services. From the perspective of the Communist Party itself, managing human resources between the front in Spain and activism at home was a not inconsiderable problem, particularly given the ongoing decimation of leading cadres in Spain. More conceptually, almost all volunteers framed their decision as being an expression of solidarity with the Spanish people. Yet given the scale and importance attached to domestic activism, there were clearly other ways to express solidarity. Volunteering, therefore, represents either an escalation or a divergence from what was possible at home – understanding volunteer motivation, in other words, requires an appreciation of what the other options were, and why, for a certain subset of pro-Republican activists, they were not sufficient.

Methodology and Sources

An overarching goal of this account is to construct a 'history from below' of Scottish involvement in the Spanish Civil War, exploring developments from the perspective of local and regional institutions, as well as those of ordinary volunteers and activists, in both Spain and Scotland. The needs of 'history from below' necessitate using varied methodological approaches to different sources and questions, and this book draws on fields as diverse as musicology, gender studies and social network analysis to explore aspects of the volunteering experience. As such, with the exception of several approaches that underpin the book as a whole, methods are discussed in context as necessary rather than here.

Many of recent innovations in Spanish Civil War historiography relate to the ongoing transnational turn. Whilst transnationalism is hardly a new methodological perspective, it has taken a surprisingly long time for historians of the conflict – as well as anti-fascism more broadly – to embrace transnationalism as an underlying methodology. Its applicability in this context is obvious: not only were International Brigade volunteers archetypical transnational actors but the intellectual and cultural frameworks in which they and other forms of solidarity operated were also inherently transnational.[34] Through the recent work of scholars such as Enrico Acciai, Helen Graham and Lisa Kirschenbaum, we have gained important new insight into participants' trajectories, tracing the place of the Spanish Civil War in lives shaped by exile, migration and resistance in the 1930s and 1940s. Ariel Mae Lambe, in contrast, traces the transnational basis of solidarity campaigns and anti-fascist networks between Cuba, Spain and the United States, offering perhaps the closest parallel to the methods and focus of the present study.

This account builds on these approaches in several ways. An inherent issue with biographical approaches to transnational participation in the

Spanish Civil War is that it becomes very difficult to generalise – that is, we gain detailed insight into the push and pull factors that affect specific individuals, but not necessarily in ways that help us understand the phenomenon more broadly. We can sketch out the connections between actors across borders – particularly as shaped by the structures of international communism – yet this in itself provides a functional explanation of how transnational participation was enabled, rather than what motivated it in the first place.[35] Instead, this account proposes what might be awkwardly termed a transnational national approach, focusing on the local nodes of transnational networks ahead of their wider international dimensions. In appreciating the fluidity of boundaries in both Scotland and Spain, it is intended that many of the methodological advantages of transnational history be preserved. Yet by exploring in depth a bounded, interconnected array of actors and organisations, it is possible to also borrow from the methods of social history, utilising quantitative as well as qualitative analysis, enabling an approach that is simultaneously cognisant of individual complexity yet able to offer insight into a wider picture. In doing so, the aim is to take seriously Michael Goebel's plea to go beyond simply demonstrating the existence of transnational networks, but tie them to concrete outcomes – in this case, what drove individuals to contribute their time, money and lives across borders in the name of the Spanish Republic.[36]

While a varied source base – including material from Spanish and Russian archives – has been consulted here, perhaps the single most important resource that has enabled a 'view from below' is oral testimony. No interviews were conducted as part of this project, but Scotland happens to have been well served when it comes to preserving the voices of participants. The work of Ian MacDougall in seeking out and interviewing Scottish International Brigaders and other activists has proved invaluable.[37] It is worth noting that the nature of these and other efforts usually fell in the 'recovery' mould of oral history, with the aim of preserving voices that might otherwise have been lost to history.[38] Interviewees were given free rein to discuss their stories as they saw fit, and were rarely pressed to discuss aspects of their service that did not reflect the image they wanted to convey. Shame, demoralisation and other negative emotions found correspondingly little place in their narratives. This could be personal – such as a failing marriage's role in deciding to volunteer in Spain – or collective, avoiding or downplaying the failures of comrades at home or in Spain.

As with any oral testimony, interviewees' narratives also need to be regarded as a product of a particular moment. Most interviews took place during the 1970s and 1980s, a period that saw the democratisation of

Spain – and thereby the vindication of the volunteers' stated aims – as well as heightened class and labour conflict in Britain.[39] Moreover, volunteers' testimony could not help but be affected by the mythology surrounding the International Brigades, especially as these grand narratives embody such a heroic, positive vision of their actions. In some cases, the recordings' public nature – notably those conducted at Loughborough University in 1976 – threw the collective shaping and maintenance of these narratives into sharp relief, with individuals drawing on, referring to and deferring to one another's testimony.[40] With interviewees given plenty of scope to fashion their testimony, these oral histories are often best understood as reflecting how the ex-volunteers came to view themselves.[41] However, these tendencies should not be regarded as deliberate distortion, or a sign that interviewees were not trustworthy or were unable to remember events accurately. Many evidenced accurate recollections of places, people and events, with errors tending towards minor confusion rather than fabrication.[42] Rather, their use required sensitivity towards emphasis, omission and language.

Finally, whilst the focus throughout is on exploring Scottish involvement in the Spanish Civil War in depth, this has been done with an eye to comparative history. This is perhaps most apparent within a British context, with England, Wales and Ireland providing logical points of comparison through which to establish continuities and divergences in Scottish experiences of the conflict. Particularly when it comes to the International Brigades, the work of Richard Baxell is invaluable in establishing the basis for quantitative comparisons, as are similar efforts in French and German contexts. More broadly, the aim here is to contribute to emerging wider discussions about the nature of transnational mobilisations. The Spanish Civil War, and the International Brigades in particular, form a distinctive chapter in the history of foreign war volunteering, a subject that has come in for increased scholarly and governmental scrutiny in recent years. Several scholars, most notably Nir Arielli, have made the case for viewing episodes such as Spain as part of a much longer history of such mobilisations.[43] In offering new explanations of how and why people were mobilised and recruited across borders in the 1930s, it is hoped that this account will be part of this broader conversation.

Structure

The remainder of the book is structured across seven chapters, charting a thematic journey from Scotland to Spain, and back again. Chapter 1 looks at the political and social context of Scotland in the 1930s, exploring the impact of the interwar slump, unemployment and changing political cultures, focusing in particular on responses to mass unemployment, and the state of the radical left by the mid-1930s. Building on this wider context, Chapters 2 and 3 link these observations with Scottish recruitment for the International Brigades, establishing the socio-economic backgrounds of the volunteers and exploring the ramifications, particularly with regards to their motives for going to Spain. In making the case for understanding volunteers' decisions as having a social as well as ideological basis, these chapters seek to link the disproportionate numbers of Scots in the British Battalion to the ways in which the radical left – especially the Communist Party – was constituted in Scotland during the 1930s.

Chapter 4 follows the consequences of these decisions to volunteer in Spain. Building on the observation that recruitment took place largely within tight-knit social-political networks, this chapter explores how these pre-existing networks and interconnections affected the lived experience of volunteering. Chapter 5 begins the return to Scotland, tracing the ways in which the volunteers were supported from Scotland after their departure, including through efforts to raise funds to support the dependants the volunteers had left behind. This was an ongoing effort that not only was vital in overcoming barriers to recruitment but also provides unique insight into the contours of pro-Republican activism in Scotland and Britain. Chapters 6 and 7 build on this theme, exploring how broader domestic solidarity movements were built and maintained in Scotland during the conflict. Chapter 6 focuses on the extent to which Spain acted as a unifying cause for the Scottish left, exploring the successes and failures of the 'Spanish Aid Committee' model in enabling effective co-operation across party lines. Finally, Chapter 7 examines the particular response of the labour movement to the Spanish Civil War, charting the evolving approaches of Scottish labour movement institutions towards building and leading Scottish efforts to support the Spanish Republic.

Notes

1. British studies include Tom Buchanan, *Britain and the Spanish Civil War* (Cambridge, 1997) and *The Impact of the Spanish Civil War on Britain* (Brighton, 2007); Brian Shelmerdine, *British Representations of the Spanish Civil War* (Manchester, 2006); Angela Jackson, *British Women and the Spanish Civil War* (London, 2002); Hugh Ford, *A Poet's War: British Poets and the Spanish Civil War* (Philadelphia, 1965). Studies explicitly focusing

on England, Wales or Ireland include Lewis Mates, *The Spanish Civil War and The British Left: Political Activism and the Popular Front* (London, 2007) and 'Durham and South Wales Miners in the Spanish Civil War', *Twentieth Century British History* 17:3 (2006), 373–95; Robert Stradling, *Wales and the Spanish Civil War: The Dragon's Dearest Cause?* (Cardiff, 2004) and *The Irish and the Spanish Civil War 1936–1939: Crusades in Conflict* (Manchester, 1999); Fearghal McGarry, *Irish Politics and the Spanish Civil War* (Cork, 1999); Hywel Francis, *Miners Against Fascism: Wales and the Spanish Civil War* (London, 1984).

2. Minor exceptions to this neglect do exist, though are limited to local case studies rather than Scotland as a whole. See Malcolm Petrie, 'Unity from Below? The Impact of the Spanish Civil War on Labour and the Left in Aberdeen and Dundee, 1936–1939', *Labour History Review*, 79, 3 (2015), 305–27; Fraser Raeburn, '"Fae nae hair te grey hair they answered the call": International Brigade Volunteers from the West Central Belt of Scotland in the Spanish Civil War, 19369', *Journal of Scottish Historical Studies*, 35:1 (2015), 92–114.

3. For theatre alone, see John Maley and Willy Maley, *From the Calton to Catalonia* (Glasgow, 1992); Robert Munro, *The Cry of Spain* (Unpublished script, 1986), MML, Box A-14, File E/1; Hector Macmillan, *A Greater Tomorrow* (Programme, 1997), MML, Box 21, File F/20; '549: Scots of the Spanish Civil War', Wonderfools [online], <http://www.wonderfools.org/549/>, accessed 24 January 2018.

4. By the mid-1990s, eleven dedicated memorials existed across Scotland. Colin Williams, Bill Alexander and John Gorman, *Memorials of the Spanish Civil War* (Stroud, 1996). According to the International Brigade Memorial Trust website, this number has since doubled. 'Memorials', International Brigade Memorial Trust [online], <http://www.international-brigades.org.uk/memorials>, accessed 2 August 2019.

5. *Weekend Scotsman*, 16 July 1983, clipping in John Dunlop Papers, File 5, Acc. 12087, NLS. See also MML Box 21, File F/9.

6. Daniel Gray, *Homage to Caledonia: Scotland and the Spanish Civil War* (Edinburgh, 2008). See also Mike Arnott, *Dundee and the Spanish Civil War* (Dundee, 2008); Mark Gillespie, *When the Gorbals Fought Franco* (Glasgow, 2014); George Scott, *Aberdeen Volunteers Fighting in the Spanish Civil War* (London, 2019); Chris Dolan, *An Anarchist's Story: The Life of Ethel MacDonald* (Edinburgh, 2009).

7. This is especially noteworthy in Malcolm Petrie's recent book, which barely mentions Spain, despite the author's own interest in the subject. Malcolm Petrie, *Popular Politics and Political Culture: Urban Scotland, 1918–1939* (Edinburgh, 2018). More broadly, see William Kenefick, *Red Scotland! The Rise and Decline of the Scottish Radical Left, c. 1872 to 1932* (Edinburgh, 2007); James Smyth, *Labour in Glasgow, 1896–1936* (East Linton, 2000). Alan McKinlay

and R. J. Morris (eds), *The ILP on the Clydeside, 1893–1932: From Foundation to Disintegration* (Manchester, 1991); Stuart Macintyre, *Little Moscows: Communism and Working-class Militancy in Inter-war Britain* (London, 1980).

8. Tom Buchanan, 'The Death of Bob Smillie, the Spanish Civil War and the Eclipse of the Independent Labour Party', *The Historical Journal* 40:2 (1997), 435–61; Christopher Hall, *'Not Just Orwell': The Independent Labour Party Volunteers and the Spanish Civil War* (Barcelona, 2009); Dolan, *An Anarchist's Story;* Gray, *Homage,* 155–76.

9. The most comprehensive account of this unit is Lina Palfreeman, *Aristocrats, Adventurers and Ambulances: British Medical Units in the Spanish Civil War* (Brighton, 2014). See also Jim Fyrth, *The Signal Was Spain: The Spanish Aid Movement in Britain, 1936–1939* (London, 1986), 181–91; Gray, *Homage,* 85–92.

10. Useful overviews of Scottish pro-Franco activity can be found in Ian Wood, 'Scotland and the Spanish Civil War', *Cencrastus* (Autumn 1984), 14–16; Tom Gallagher, *Glasgow: The Uneasy Peace: Religious Tension in Modern Scotland* (Manchester, 1987); Gray, *Homage,* 125–40. See also Gavin Bowd, *Fascist Scotland: Caledonia and the Far Right* (Edinburgh, 2013), 95–130.

11. Judith Keene, *Fighting for Franco: International Volunteers in Nationalist Spain, 1936–39* (London, 2001).

12. On the establishment and course of the Second Republic, see Gabriel Jackson, *The Spanish Republic and the Civil War, 1931–1939* (Princeton, 1965); Fernando del Rey Reguillo, *The Spanish Second Republic Revisited: From Democratic Hopes to Civil War (1931–1936)* (Brighton, 2012). For differing perspectives on the conflicts' causes, see Stanley Payne, *The Collapse of the Spanish Republic, 1933–1936* (New Haven, 2006); Paul Preston, *The Coming of the Spanish Civil War: Reform, Reaction and Revolution 1931–1936* (London, 1994).

13. There is a vast scholarly and popular literature on the conflict itself. Notable overviews include Stanley Payne, *The Spanish Civil War* (Cambridge, 2012); Paul Preston, *The Spanish Civil War* (London, 2006); Hugh Thomas, *The Spanish Civil War* (3rd ed., London, 2003); Burnett Bolloten, *The Spanish Civil War: Revolution and Counterrevolution* (Chapel Hill, 1991).

14. On the war's international context, see Michael Alpert, *A New International History of the Spanish Civil War* (Basingstoke, 2004). On the nature and conceptions of 'civil war' itself, see David Armitage, *Civil Wars: A History in Ideas* (New Haven, 2017).

15. Renton in Ian MacDougall, *Voices from the Spanish Civil War: Personal Recollections of Scottish Volunteers in Republican Spain 1936–39* (Edinburgh, 1986), 21.

16. Clarke in MacDougall, *Voices from the Spanish Civil War,* 66.

17. On British perceptions of Spain and the civil war, see Buchanan, *Impact,* 1–22.

18. British government perspectives are discussed in Enrique Moradiellos, 'The Origins of British Non-Intervention in the Spanish Civil War: Anglo-Spanish Relations in Early 1936', *European History Quarterly* 21 (1991), 339–64. For

the French, see David Pike, *France Divided: The French and the Spanish Civil War* (Brighton, 2011).

19. On these policies, see Douglas Little, *Malevolent Neutrality: The United States, Great Britain and the Origins of the Spanish Civil War* (Ithaca, 1985). On Soviet intervention, Daniel Kowalsky, *Stalin and the Spanish Civil War* (New York, 2004).

20. Michael Alpert, 'The Clash of Spanish Armies: Contrasting Ways of War in Spain, 1936–1939', *War in History* 6:3 (1999), 331–51.

21. Daniel Kowalsky, 'Operation X: Soviet Russia and the Spanish Civil War', *Bulletin of Spanish Studies* 91:1–2 (2014), 167–71.

22. Historical Commission Circular, [1937?], RGASPI, 545/2/164/179. These efforts resulted in a number of contemporary publications, such as Frank Ryan (ed.), *The Book of the XVth Brigade* (Madrid, 1938). William Rust, *Britons in Spain: The History of the British Battalion of the XVth International Brigade* (London, 1939). In the American context, see Edwin Rolfe, *The Lincoln Battalion* (New York, 1939).

23. Minutes of Historical Commission Meeting, 23 September 1937, RGASPI, 545/2/164/47.

24. For a historiographical overview, see Manuel Requena Gallego, 'Las Brigadas Internacionales: una aproximación historiográfica', *Ayer* 56 (2004), 16–18. Significant publications in a British context include Hamish Fraser, *The Truth about Spain* (Oxford, c.1950); Fred Copeman, *Reason in Revolt* (London, 1948); Stephen Spender, *World within World* (London, 1950).

25. Bill Alexander, *British Volunteers for Liberty: Spain, 1936–1939* (London, 1982). See also D. Corkhill and S. Rawnsley (eds), *The Road to Spain: Anti Fascists at War 1936–1939* (Dunfermline, 1987); MacDougall, *Voices from the Spanish Civil War*; Valentine Cunningham, *Spanish Front: Writers on the Civil War* (Oxford, 1986); Fyrth, *Signal*; Francis, *Miners*.

26. Robert Stradling, 'English-speaking Units of the International Brigades: War, Politics and Discipline', *Journal of Contemporary History* 45:4 (2010), 744–66, and *History and Legend: Writing the International Brigades* (Cardiff, 2003); James Hopkins, *Into the Heart of the Fire: The British in the Spanish Civil War* (Stanford, 1998). Richard Baxell has in turn balanced the narrative from the other side, writing several accounts which, while broadly celebratory, do a great deal to address and contextualise revisionist claims. Richard Baxell, *British Volunteers in the Spanish Civil War* (London, 2004), *Unlikely Warriors: The British in the Spanish Civil War* (London, 2012) and 'Myths of the International Brigades', *Bulletin of Spanish Studies* 91:1–2 (2014), 11–24.

27. For an overview, see George Esenwein, 'Freedom Fighters or Comintern Soldiers? Writing about the "Good Fight" during the Spanish Civil War', *Civil Wars* 12:1–2 (2010), 156–66. Explicitly anti-communist texts include Ronald Radosh, Mary Habeck and Grigory Sevostianov (eds), *Spain Betrayed: The Soviet*

Union in the Spanish Civil War (New Haven, 2001); R. Dan Richardson, *Comintern Army: The International Brigades and the Spanish Civil War* (Lexington, 1982); Cecil Eby, *Comrades and Commissars: The Lincoln Battalion in the Spanish Civil War* (University Park. PA, 2007).

28. For example Ariel Mae Lambe, *No Barrier Can Contain It: Cuban Antifascism and the Spanish Civil War* (Chapel Hill, 2019); Gerben Zaagsma, *Jewish Volunteers, the International Brigades and the Spanish Civil War* (London, 2017); Lisa Kirschenbaum, *International Communism and the Spanish Civil War* (Cambridge, 2015); Helen Graham, *The War and Its Shadow: Spain's Civil War in Europe's Long Twentieth Century* (Brighton, 2012).

29. Kirschenbaum, *International Communism*, 117–50.

30. Zaagsma, *Jewish Volunteers*, 46–50.

31. Fyrth, *Signal*. Fyrth's approach was subsequently critiqued in Tom Buchanan, 'Britain's Popular Front? Aid Spain and the British Labour Movement', *History Workshop Journal* 31 (1991), 60–72. Later scholarship has tended to follow Buchanan's position. See Mates, *Spanish Civil War*, 179–207; Emily Mason, *Democracy, Deeds and Dilemmas: Support for the Spanish Republic within British Civil Society, 1936–1939* (Eastbourne, 2017).

32. E.g. Shelmerdine, *Representations*, 3.

33. This point is made convincingly in Petrie, 'Unity from Below', 305–27.

34. Hugo García, 'Transnational History: a New Paradigm for Anti-Fascist Studies?', *Contemporary European History* 25:4 (2016), 563–72. See also Kasper Braskén, 'Making Anti-Fascism Transnational: the Origins of Communist and Socialist Articulations of Resistance in Europe, 1923–1924', *Contemporary European History* 25:4 (Nov. 2016), 573–96; Isabelle Richet, 'Marion Cave Rosselli and the Transnational Women's Anti-Fascist Networks', *Journal of Women's History* 24:3 (2012), 117–39; Dan Stone, 'Anti-Fascist Europe Comes to Britain: Theorising Fascism as a Contribution to Defeating It', in Nigel Copsey and Andrzej Olechnowicz (eds), *Varieties of Anti-Fascism: Britain in the Inter-War Period* (Basingstoke, 2010).

35. For example Nir Arielli, 'Getting There: Enlistment Considerations and the Recruitment Networks of the International Brigades during the Spanish Civil War' in Nir Arielli and Bruce Collins (eds), *Transnational Soldiers: Foreign Military Enlistment in the Modern Era* (Basingstoke, 2012), 219–30.

36. Michael Goebel, *Anti-Imperial Metropolis: Interwar Paris and the Seeds of Third World Nationalism* (Cambridge, 2015), 291.

37. Ian MacDougall, *Voices from the Spanish Civil War; Voices from the Hunger Marches* (Edinburgh, 1990); *Voices from War and Some Labour Struggles* (Edinburgh, 1995). Ian MacDougall was kind enough to allow access to the original unedited transcripts, but the light editing touch employed made it preferable to use the more accessible published versions.

38. For discussion of the predominance of 'reconstructive' approaches in Scotland, and MacDougall's work in particular, see Angela Bartie and Arthur McIvor, 'Oral History in Scotland', *Scottish Historical Review* 92 (2013), 113–26.

39. Lynn Abrams, *Oral History Theory* (London, 2010), 18. See also Ron Grele, *Envelopes of Sound: The Art of Oral History* (New York, 1991), 245.

40. A recording of a group session is in Tameside Local Studies Archive (TLS), Manchester Studies Series (MS), Tapes 228/A-B. Individual interviews sometimes referred back to narratives explored in this session, e.g. William Kelly, TLS, MS, Tape 238.

41. On 'official' narratives and individual testimony, see Josie McLennan, '"I Wanted to be a Little Lenin": Ideology and the German International Brigade Volunteers', *Journal of Contemporary History* 41:2 (2006), 289–90.

42. Given Spain's importance in many volunteers' lives, this is unsurprising. Abrams, *Oral History Theory*, 81.

43. Nir Arielli, *From Byron to bin Laden: A History of Foreign War Volunteers* (Cambridge, 2018). See also Enrico Acciai, 'Traditions of Armed Volunteering and Radical Politics in Southern Europe: A Biographical Approach to Garibaldinism', *European History Quarterly* 49:1 (2019), 50–72; David Malet, *Foreign Fighters: Transnational Identity in Civic Conflicts* (Oxford, 2013); Arielli and Collins (eds), *Transnational Soldiers*; Elizabeth Roberts, *'Freedom, Faction, Fame and Blood': British Soldiers of Conscience in Greece, Spain and Finland* (Brighton, 2010).

1

Scotland in the 1930s

There is a longstanding trend in Scottish history writing – reflected most starkly in the title of Christopher Harvie's *No Gods and Precious Few Heroes* – of representing twentieth-century Scottish history as a tale of retreat and retrenchment, a fundamentally pessimistic parable of social and economic decline.[1] A vibrant national tradition of innovation and excellence – albeit one safely cocooned in an overarching imperial identity through which these ambitions might be channelled – receded into a greyer, bureaucratic and painful process of de-industrialisation. This narrative, of course, obscures many nuances, and has been most fundamentally challenged by the rise of Scottish nationalism, and the attending need to seek explanations for its twenty-first century hegemony in twentieth-century history. Yet it is still rare to find any historical account of Scotland in the 1930s which is not fundamentally pessimistic. Scotland is hardly unique in this regard – both politically and economically, the decade is famed the world over for its catastrophes. Not least for those who lived through these years, it has been remembered as a time of hardship, magnified by failures of leadership, imagination and politics.

Yet this book is fundamentally about hope rather than despair. Those Scots who sought to support the Spanish Republic did so because they believed a better world was possible. For some, that ambition might have extended only to the alleviation of needless human suffering, a belief that their time and money could be well spent in mitigating the brutal effects of modern war on a civilian population. For others, the cause meant working for the defeat and curtailment of fascist expansion and aggression across Europe. However, for many the Spanish Republic was itself a beacon of hope, a reminder that the world itself could aspire to be better – that the forces of tradition, reaction and capitalism might be overcome, and a new society constructed in their place. Spain in this sense represented a myriad of often contradictory utopian projects, some mirrored on the ground in the diverse politics of the Spanish left, and some perhaps existing chiefly in the imagination of foreign observers. Understanding this sense of hope requires exploring the circumstances of interwar crisis and depression.

This short chapter cannot aspire to provide a general history of Scottish society and politics during the 1930s. Rather, the focus is on the nature and activities of the Scottish left in the years leading up to 1936. Perhaps even more so than elsewhere in Britain, the Scottish response to the Spanish Civil War was driven and shaped by left-wing organisations and activists, and therefore reflects the contours and faultlines which had developed over the course of the decade. In particular, the schism between Labour and the ILP, and the emergence of the Communist Party as a competitor to both, provides vital context for understanding the dynamics of domestic and transnational mobilisations on behalf of the Spanish Republic within Scotland. These dynamics, in turn, were inevitably shaped by the socio-economic context of interwar Scotland.

Economy and Society

By the time that Wall Street crashed in October 1929, Scotland had already been suffering from acute economic dislocation for almost a decade. Scotland's flagship heavy industries – buoyed to an unsustainable height by the material demands of fighting the First World War – faced a harsh postwar reality of reduced orders and heightened international competition. In Scotland, mass unemployment was worsened rather than created by the global recession of the early 1930s. Only with the threat of a second global conflict, and the attending need to urgently re-arm, did Scottish heavy industry see any lasting revitalisation.[2] For many who came of age in the interwar period – including some of those discussed in this book – the Second World War marked the first time that they were in stable employment. Whilst Scotland was hardly the only region of Britain to experience mass unemployment in the 1930s, the depth of the crisis in Scotland was particularly severe and long-lasting.

A few statistics bear repeating to illustrate the scale of the problems that Scottish society faced. There were approximately one hundred thousand left unemployed soon after the First World War, or approximately 10 per cent of the insured workforce.[3] Whilst some seasonal or temporary unemployment had hardly been unknown in earlier decades, this new phenomenon – which saw Scots without work for many months or even years – was a challenge that existing relief and insurance schemes were ill-equipped to deal with. The scale of the problem only deepened after 1929, with Scotland's export-orientated heavy industries particularly hard-hit by the sharp fall in international demand. Shipbuilding – long a barometer of Scottish industrial health – fell from launching 650,000 tons in 1919 to just 74,000 fourteen years later in 1933, and other key industries such as coalmining and iron- and steelmaking also faced severe contractions, not least due to falls in demand in shipbuilding.[4] Unemployment climbed as Scottish industry rusted, with over a quarter of the workforce idle by 1932, a figure that was considerably worse in industrial hubs such as Glasgow and other Central Belt towns such as Motherwell.[5] Incomes stagnated or dropped as a result, which in turn helped undermine any notion of diversification: establishing lucrative new industries producing new, profitable consumer goods in Scotland made little sense when local markets were relatively small and depressed.[6] As a result, existing gaps in affluence between Scotland and southern England only continued to widen during the interwar period, despite various inadequate schemes to encourage investment north of the border.

The impact of economic strife was apparent in migration figures, another visible source of anxiety. For the first time since detailed record-keeping began, the 1920s was the first decade in which the Scottish population decreased, with emigration to the United States and the Dominions exceeding natural population increase, and – despite the racially charged concerns of some churchmen – the exodus was no longer being matched by immigration from Ireland and elsewhere.[7] Yet even the return of many emigrants in the 1930s, after their new homes in Canada, Australia and the United States were also hit by economic downturn, only added to the worsening unemployment problems. This was far from the only deep structural issue facing interwar Scotland. Housing, a longstanding problem that had already ignited one of the most significant activist movements in British history in 1915, remained largely unsolved throughout the interwar period despite Lloyd George's optimistic postwar rhetoric.[8] Many working-class Scots continued to live in cramped and unsanitary conditions, with the scale of new building inadequate to address the problem despite a slow expansion of public-sector building, and many Scots continued to live in cramped, one- or two-roomed dwellings, often without basic amenities. Partly as a result of these inevitably unsanitary conditions, as well as poor nutrition, infant mortality remained stubbornly high in comparison with other British cities, not to mention elsewhere in Europe or North America. For a country that had learned to see itself in terms of industriousness, innovation and dynamism, stagnation and decay were not just a material problem but one which struck at a key pillar of Scottish identity.

The Scottish Left

Poor living conditions, economic malaise and the legacy of wartime industrial unrest led to significant shifts in Scottish politics after the end of the First World War. The Labour Party had been a marginal element in the pre-1914 political landscape, but emerged as a significant force over the course of the 1920s, winning the most Scottish seats of any party in 1922, 1923 and 1929.[9] Yet its dominance of Scottish politics was far from assured – the 1930s saw both acute internal divisions and a Conservative electoral resurgence. The disaffiliation of the ILP in 1932 was of particular significance. Not only did it mark the beginning of the end of an older radical tradition that had been particularly vibrant in Scotland, it also swept away most Labour Party structures north of the border. A new party organisation was gradually constructed, one less beholden to Scottish radical traditions, and the new emphasis on state planning and centralisation left correspondingly little space for Scottish distinctiveness, much less 'Home Rule', in any case.[10] Yet while Labour remained the largest of the left-wing parties in terms of representation, it was often far from hegemonic in a local sense during the 1930s, leaving space not only for varieties of local activism, causes and movements but also electoral opportunities for other leftist parties that rarely existed south of the border. Scottish leftist politics – as it was carried out on the street, in public life and to some extent at the ballot box – remained meaningfully diverse and dynamic for the rest of the decade.

Where exactly this distinctively Scottish political culture stemmed from, and what it actually meant in practice, is harder to pin down. Certainly, its influences can be traced from nineteenth-century Chartism, the rise of the labour movement and the industrial struggles during and after the First World War, and there was, as has been acknowledged in different ways by different authors, a distinctively Scottish brand of radical politics.[11] These politics, in so far as they can be generalised, drew on religion, temperance and respectability as much as Marx, on democratic localism as much as the state. These traditions were under considerable pressure by the 1930s: the internal reform of both the Labour Party and the labour movement acted to centralise control, strengthening the national leadership at the expense of institutions such as local Trades Councils (TCs).[12] The miners' defeat in the 1926 General Strike, and the disastrous effects of the disaffiliation of the ILP in 1932, seemed to spell the end of a distinctively Scottish road to a radical future. Further to the left, the Leninist democratic centralism of the new CPGB, built in homage to an imagined Bolshevik Party, seemingly left less space for a locally orientated revolutionary politics. London, if not Moscow, appeared to control the Party's agenda north of the border.

Yet this bleak picture – which may to some extent account for the reluctance of Scottish historians of the radical left to discuss the 1930s in much depth – disguises the extent to which local political organisation, leadership and cultures were still important.[13] Whilst the wartime and postwar trajectories of Scottish politics may suggest their own narrative, we should be wary of reading back the death of Scottish radical traditions to a single rupture in 1926 or 1932. Political cultures were undoubtedly not static – the expanding electorate, if nothing else, profoundly changed the nature of politics and campaigning, ushering in a new era of truly mass politics, complemented by the growing reach of print media, cinema and radio.[14] Yet when it came to organisation, activism and campaigning, older traditions and ways of doing things still mattered. So, while reactions to the war in Spain were profoundly shaped by new modes of representation, discourse and communication, the ways in which Scots sought to respond drew and expanded upon older models of activism. Thus, although from a post-1945 vantage point the unique features of Scottish labour politics appeared doomed to slowly fade away, this distinctiveness was far from dead in practical terms for the period in question here. The 1930s was the beginning, not the end, of Labour's efforts to build a centralised party machine in Scotland. The ILP clung on in Parliament and Glasgow municipal politics. Even newer forces, such as the Communist Party, were still compelled to play a local game: interwar communist successes, such as they were, stemmed from their co-opting rather than replacing older forms of popular politics. London, let alone Moscow, was in many ways a distant master.

In particular, the ILP's influence shaped the way in which the Communist Party operated in Scotland. Not only did many of their Scottish leaders have formative political experiences in the ILP during its heyday, the necessity of competing directly with the ILP during the 1930s also influenced its tactics and necessitated a degree of imitation. Throughout Scotland, the 'ILP's domination of labour politics until the party's disaffiliation from the Labour party in 1932' influenced how politics was lived and understood in a variety of ways.[15] This in turn reflected the divergent evolution of working-class politics in Scotland, which favoured structures that were more decentralised, democratic and local.[16] While it is important to distinguish between aspiration and reality – no political group was fully successful in building the kind of party they envisaged – the direction of their efforts were still important. According to Morris, the ILP attempted a different approach to socialism.

The experience of the Glasgow Labour movement was of thriving community politics. The ILP was a party at the centre of a network, harnessing the energies of everything from Socialist Sunday Schools and Clarion Clubs to the Co-op and Trades Council. Such experience brought a confidence in decentralised socialism which many trades union leaders and London intellectuals did not share. The difference between Attlee and Maxton was not a matter of left and further left but of democratic centralism versus diffused community authority.[17]

The ILP privileged local branches and community building over central-ised, powerful leadership, with 'the first loyalty of the individual ILP-er [being] to his or her own branch, not to the city or national organisation'.[18] It conceived of political parties as having purpose beyond political organ-isation, with a role in providing 'social, educational and cultural activi-ties'.[19] It was a strategy in which success depended on the Party's ability to sustain social networks alongside political belief – in other words, foster-ing the sort of interconnections that underpin the analysis presented here.

The ILP was a very different organisation from the CPGB, and it does not necessarily follow that the communists aped their approach to party-building. However, the CPGB did pursue similar strategies throughout Scotland. The language Stuart Macintyre uses when discussing Scottish 'Little Moscows', for instance, shows striking parallels to the description of the ILP presented by McKinlay, Smyth and Morris.

> The relationship of the Communists to the community was therefore ambiguous . . . the Party organised sport, musical events, evening socials and so on . . . It was also significant that Party members occupied an accepted place in the community, based on an extensive network of kin and friendship. The identity of the left was much broader than politics in the conventional sense.[20]

The phenomenon Macintyre observed was in fact not limited to rural set-tlements, but also existed in more diverse urban spaces. Neil Rafeek, for instance, noted similar trends in Glasgow – the Communist Party's ability not just to function as a political entity but to become the focus of a wider community.[21] Politics became entwined with everyday social and recre-ational activity in Party strongholds throughout Scotland, much as it had for the ILP before it. This reflected a wider reality that whilst communists were nominally subordinate to both national and international directives, in practice local traditions of organising and conceptions of radical politics retained much importance, not least due to continuities in membership across party lines.[22] Prominent activists such as Harry McShane, organiser of the Glasgow National Unemployed Workers' Movement (NUWM) and the Gorbals CPGB branch, had learned their trade in the ILP at its peak.[23] Even by the late 1930s, many younger activists had previously been ILP members. The Young Communist League (YCL) and NUWM organiser John Lochore, for instance, pointed to his time in the ILP youth wing as impressing him with the importance of social activity and being 'in the roots of the people'.[24]

The impact of older political traditions was compounded by the competitive nature of progressive politics in interwar Scotland. The ILP's disaffiliation from the Labour Party in 1932 had left a vacuum in Scottish leftist politics.[25] Overnight, the Labour Party lost its entire network of local representation – according to McKinlay and Smyth, 'in 1932 the Labour Party was little more than a shell organisation still dominated by the ILP'.[26] The new Labour Party secretary in Scotland, Arthur Woodburn, remarked that his task was to 'practically build from scratch'.[27] His efforts were alternately aided and hindered by the efforts of ILP defectors, notably Patrick Dollan, who founded the Scottish Socialist Party (SSP), theoretically as a new Labour affiliate but in practice often competing for resources and representation.[28] Especially in Glasgow, the ILP managed to survive disaffiliation from the Labour Party, retaining multiple Parliamentary and local government representatives throughout the 1930s, with its influence in Glasgow municipal politics actually peaking in 1935–6.[29] This allowed considerable space for other progressive parties to operate. Again, Glasgow provided the richest opportunities during the 1930s, with Labour, the SSP, the ILP, communists and anarchists all striving to expound effectively their vision of socialist progression – quite often in a literal sense, with rival speakers attempting to outdo each other on street corners in terms of both rhetoric and volume.[30] To succeed, communists needed to challenge other parties' strengths – particularly the ILP's entrenched presence in many of Glasgow's poorest districts.[31] This involved not just enunciating a rival political message, but fostering rival communities.

Importantly, these very local tendencies tended to complement rather than complicate the dominant trajectory of international communism. As has been noted by Brigitte Studer, interwar communism's transnational networks operated down to a 'local' or 'microsocial' level, with even relatively isolated branches or members still meaningfully connected to wider exchanges of communist ideas, representations and experiences.[32] Yet these processes often reinforced any existing tendency towards the localisation of communist life. Thanks not least to the stringent obligations required of members, as well as the proliferation of cultural, social and leisure activities tied to the Party, becoming a communist was far from a tokenistic commitment. A growing body of research into British communism has acknowledged and examined the ways in which belonging to the CPGB formed a unique way of life, entirely distinctive from most other modes of political affiliation.[33] This was far from universal – individual experiences reflected local Party organisation, culture and leadership. Yet it is this very lack of a universal communist experience that points the way forward to understanding what made Scottish responses to the Spanish Civil War distinctive. In Scotland, where communist politics encountered a strong pre-existing – and for most adherents highly familiar – tradition of grassroots politics and activism, the ground proved relatively fertile for fostering a communal approach to politics, resulting in the emergence of a communist social sphere united not just by politics but by ties of friendship, kinship and shared experiences. This, as explored in later chapters, was to have particular consequences when it came to Scottish responses to the war in Spain.

Unemployment

Prior to the outbreak of the Spanish Civil War, few political campaigns in Scotland run by the CPGB could be said to have linked local communities with national and transnational politics in a particularly sustained fashion. While Scots were certainly not ignorant of wider political issues, they rarely provided much scope for sustained mobilisation or activism in a local setting. Scottish opposition to fascism, for instance, was generally not a local concern in the same way that it proved in London's East End, or even in regional English cities such as Manchester.[34] The particularly English brand of nationalism espoused by Britain's leading fascist movement, the British Union of Fascists (BUF), found few adherents in Scotland. With a partial exception in Aberdeen, where a concerted BUF effort was countered by a well-organised and dynamic anti-fascist movement, anti-fascism was not a basis for local political organisation.[35]

The sole communist campaign that was consistently able to link local communities and activism with a wider movement was that against unemployment. The CPGB certainly did not invent activism and organisation among the unemployed, but the Party was able to channel localised resentment and anger into regional and national campaigns more effectively and consistently than other groups. Aside from the relative neglect of the unemployed by the labour movement itself – for whom the focus on the workplace as the main site of organisation implicitly excluded those who were out of work – the CPGB was well-placed to address an issue grounded in local perspectives and concerns. Everyday anti-unemployment activism – from resisting the imposition of the Means Test, protesting evictions and street meetings – was grounded in local community solidarity, of the sort that communist activists were experienced in and adept at fostering.[36] This, as Malcolm Petrie has argued, was a continuation of older traditions of public politics, a tradition largely abandoned by Labour over the course of the 1920s, but which remained a central feature of communist organisation and tactics into the 1930s.[37]

Yet the crucial – and most visible – success of interwar unemployment activism was the linkage of local activism with a national movement. Campaigns against unemployment – particularly through the NUWM – exerted a profound influence on the Communist Party's organisation in Scotland. Such was the eventual dominance of unemployed members, Party leaders worried that many local branches were being run 'by an unemployed comrade who is generally not the most capable', compared to those who were 'employed and unable to give the necessary attention to the work'.[38] While this trend was encouraged by other factors – notably that victimisation in the workplace and official labour movement discouraged open membership – years of relatively successful work with the chronically unemployed had deeply shaped Party demographics, with over half of its Scottish members unemployed in October 1936.[39] By offering a path to actively resist unemployment, and the deeply unpopular measures associated with government responses such as the Means Test, the Communist Party was able to effectively tap into community anger, which often manifested itself in collective action to thwart unwelcome government intrusion.

By offering a holistic critique of the system failing many Scottish communities, and dynamic forms of protest through the NUWM, the Communist Party was able to translate localised anger into a wider mobilisation that transcended the boundaries of local politics through national and regional campaigns. The NUWM's tactics stretched conceptual frontiers of political activism. Although much of its activity was local, their most famous undertakings were the Hunger Marches, which saw groups of unemployed marchers converge from across the country on a single destination. Such marches made activism mobile, altering the participants' perceptions of their ability to effect change outwith their immediate surroundings. It was also activism on the offensive. Rather than defending against government intrusions locally, appealing Means Test verdicts or complaining about conditions, marchers took the fight to where it could achieve the most.

By 1937, however, the NUWM was slowly dying out. The improving economic situation undermined its purpose, and the CPGB itself was doubtful regarding its continued future.[40] However, the movement had helped to bring in a new generation of activists who were intensely motivated and frustrated, and often had no stable employment, family or even fixed abode limiting their mobility.[41] The structure of the NUWM itself helped provide a natural bridge to wider participation in communist politics and social activity. Although Party members were a minority, they tended to be in charge.[42] The Glasgow NUWM activist Tom Fern, for example, recalled that out of 'about 200 members' of his branch, 'a dozen' at most were communists – but 'they were the driving force'.[43] Michael Clarke of Greenock was forceful in his recollection of this process: 'I think – I don't think, I *know* – that the NUWM was a recruitin' ground for the Party.'[44] The result was an influx of relatively young individuals to the Communist Party, who sought hope beyond the capitalist status quo and had few fixed ties keeping them at home. These characteristics, as shall be seen in the next chapter, lent themselves to certain forms of mobilisations after the outbreak of the Spanish Civil War.

Conclusions

From the perspective of the Communist Party, the outbreak of the war in Spain was exceptionally well timed. It came as its ongoing campaigns against unemployment started to lose urgency and impetus, and as its priorities shifted towards co-operation and integration with the mainstream British labour movement. Formal affiliation of the Communist Party to the Labour Party was to be debated at Labour's annual conference in Edinburgh in October 1936. Spain offered tangible evidence, it seemed, of the benefits of co-operation and unity between progressive forces, with the Spanish Popular Front offering a model by which electoral success – and resistance to fascism and militarism – might be realised. The urgency of the Republican cause also lent itself to practical co-operation across party lines, with frantic initial activity to organise demonstrations, petitions and fundraising often paying little heed to formal affiliation. The CPGB was outspoken – particularly ahead of the October conference – on the desirability of centralised, official channels for fundraising, diverting the funds that Party branches and affiliates raised almost exclusively to the Trades Union Congress (TUC)-affiliated International Solidarity Fund (ISF). Though its hopes at Edinburgh were dashed, the quest for affiliation continued, and

pro-Republican activism offered an obvious vehicle through which communist desires for unity might be realised, at least on a local basis. Though
historians disagree – vehemently, on occasion – as to how successful the
CPGB was in using the Spanish Civil War to build ties with Labour and
the labour movement, there is no doubt that this was seen as key a goal of
its activism on behalf of the Republic.[45]

The CPGB was far from the only political organisation in Scotland to
take notice of the war in Spain. Spain was a rallying point for all leftist
organisations in Scotland, from the Glasgow-based anarchist Guy Aldred
to the ILP, SSP and Labour itself. Most elements of progressive civil
society – such as the trades union movement, Co-operators and Fabian
Society – were soon actively involved in raising money and awareness. Sir
Daniel Stevenson, the Chancellor of Glasgow University, established the
first distinctively 'Scottish' response to the conflict, sponsoring a Scottish
Ambulance Unit to work in and around Madrid. They were soon joined
by other Scots seeking to make their mark on the conflict. Among the
first was Annie Murray, who arrived in Spain in September as part of
a British medical team sent by the London-based Spanish Medical Aid
Committee. Murray was to spend longer in Spain than any other Scot,
returning to Britain only in spring 1939. During her time there, she was
joined by numerous others. Past and present British MPs flocked to Spain
on fact-finding and political missions, including Scots such as Jennie Lee,
John McGovern, John McNair and the Duchess of Atholl. Political activists such as the ILP's David Murray and the Glaswegian anarchist Ethel
MacDonald acted as both observers of, and participants in, the sometimes
tense internal politics of Republican Spain. However, of all the early
Scots to make the journey to Spain, the Glaswegian Phil Gillan stands
out. He left Britain in secret on 19 September 1936, not as a journalist,
activist or observer, but as one of the first Britons to take up arms for the
Republic. Gillan was in Spain for just a few months: he was soon seriously wounded in action, and returned home in February 1937. By the
time he left, however, he had been joined by dozens more of his compa-
triots, who flocked to Spain over the winter of 1936–7 to join what were
becoming known around the world as the International Brigades.

Notes

1. Christopher Harvie, *No Gods and Precious Few Heroes: Twentieth Century
   Scotland* (Edinburgh, 1998). A close runner-up is Ewen Cameron, *Impaled
   upon a Thistle: Scotland since 1880* (Edinburgh, 2010).

2. Peter Payne, 'The Economy' in Tom Devine (ed.), *Scotland in the 20th Century* (Edinburgh, 1996), 19.
3. Neil Buxton, 'Economic Growth in Scotland between the Wars: the Role of Production Structure and Rationalization', *The Economic History Review* 33:4 (1980), 541.
4. William Knox, *Industrial Nation: Work, Culture and Society in Scotland, 1800–Present* (Edinburgh, 1999), 189.
5. Buxton, 'Economic Growth', 541.
6. Knox, *Industrial Nation*, 190.
7. Cameron, *Impaled*, 125–6.
8. Cameron, *Impaled*, 128–31.
9. Cameron, *Impaled*, 151.
10. Iain Hutchinson, *Scottish Politics in the Twentieth Century* (Basingstoke, 2001), 65–9; William Knox and Alan McKinlay, 'The Re-making of Scottish Labour in the 1930s', *Twentieth Century British History* 6:2 (1995), 175–81.
11. A great deal of literature details the broader distinctiveness of Scottish radical and socialist political cultures. Fraser, for example, traces a 'distinctively Scottish radical thread'. W. Hamish Fraser, *Scottish Popular Politics: From Radicalism to Labour* (Edinburgh, 2000), X. Similarly, Knox traces Scottish distinctiveness back to Calvinism and the Enlightenment, pointing to their continued influence in interwar Scotland, Knox, *Industrial Nation*, 20–6, 232–48. Michael Fry points to Scottish socialism as more 'idealistic' and 'intellectual' than in England, pointing to egalitarianism, universal education and Presbyterianism. Michael Fry, *Patronage and Principle: A Political History of Modern Scotland* (Aberdeen, 1987), 149.
12. Tom Buchanan, *The Spanish Civil War and the British Labour Movement* (Cambridge, 1991), 8–11.
13. Studies explicitly discounting much of the 1930s include Kenefick, *Red Scotland*; Smyth, *Labour in Glasgow*; McKinlay and Morris (eds), *ILP on the Clydeside*. Even accounts which implicitly deal with the second half of the decade tend to focus elsewhere, e.g. Petrie, *Popular Politics*; Macintyre, *Little Moscows*.
14. Petrie, *Popular Politics*, 5–6.
15. Annmarie Hughes, *Gender and Political Identities in Scotland, 1919–1939* (Edinburgh, 2010), 38–9.
16. This is one of William Kenefick's contentions, see *Rebellious and Contrary: The Glasgow Dockers, 1853–1932* (East Linton, 2000), 7–9; *Red Scotland!*, 2. It is echoed in R. J. Morris, 'The ILP, 1893–1932' in Alan McKinlay and R. Morris (eds), *The ILP on Clydeside 1893–1932: From Foundation to Disintegration* (Manchester, 1991), 14–15.
17. Morris, 'The ILP, 1893–1932', 14.
18. Alan McKinlay and James Smyth, 'The End of "the agitator workman": 1926–1932' in Alan McKinlay and R. Morris (eds.), *The ILP on Clydeside 1893–1932: From Foundation to Disintegration* (Manchester, 1991), 183. This

was reflected to some extent throughout the Scottish labour movement. Kenefick, *Red Scotland!*, 2.

19. McKinlay and Smyth, 'End of "the agitator workman"', 199. See also Knox, although he places emphasis on the moralism which underpinned these efforts, and on local agency as a continuance of Scottish radical tradition. William Knox, 'The Red Clydesiders' in Terry Brotherstone (ed.), *Covenant, Charter, and Party: Traditions of Revolt and Protest in Modern Scottish History* (Aberdeen, 1989), 93–4, 100.

20. Macintyre, *Little Moscows*, 107.

21. Neil Rafeek, *Communist Women in Scotland: Red Clydeside from the Russian Revolution to the End of the Soviet Union* (London, 2008), 25–41. This is echoed in the observation that only Glasgow and London were able to 'sustain a network of [Communist Party] social and cultural institutions', Kevin Morgan, Gidon Cohen and Andrew Flinn, *Communists and British Society, 1920-1991* (London, 2007), 7–8.

22. Rafeek, *Communist Women*, 41. See also Petrie, *Popular Politics*, 15–43.

23. Harry McShane and J. Smith (eds), *No Mean Fighter* (London, 1976), 25–6; also McShane in MacDougall, *Voices from the Hunger Marches*, 16–28. Many older communists had similar connections. Tom Murray, for instance, was an ILP member until 1931. 'Biographical Notes – MURRAY, Thomas', 17 April 1938, RGASPI 545/6/176/121.

24. Lochore in MacDougall, *Voices from the Hunger Marches*, 316.

25. On these developments, with particular regard to Scotland, Gidon Cohen, 'The Independent Labour Party, Disaffiliation, Revolution and Standing Orders', *History* 86:282 (2001), 200–21.

26. McKinlay and Smyth, 'End of "the agitator workman"', 199.

27. Arthur Woodburn, *Some Recollections* [unpublished autobiography], NLS, Acc. 7656, Box 4, File 3, 68.

28. Ian Donnachie, 'Scottish Labour in the Depression: the 1930s' in Ian Donnachie, Christopher Harvie and Ian Wood (eds), *Forward!: Labour Politics in Scotland, 1888-1988* (Edinburgh, 1989), 60; Knox and McKinlay, 'Re-making of Scottish Labour', 178–80.

29. Smyth, *Labour in Glasgow*, 192–3.

30. This atmosphere pervades memories of this period, see the 'vociferous groups on the pavements' in Ralph Glasser, *Growing up in the Gorbals* (London, 1997), 39; or Garry McCartney's testimony in MacDougall, *Voices from the Spanish Civil War*, 241.

31. The attention paid to the ILP by communist leadership in Scotland (and London) shows this clearly. For example Central Committee Meeting, 5 January 1936, RGASPI, 495/14/185/51. The CPGB also monitored the ILP newspaper and spied on its major conferences, 'The ILP Conference', 27 April 1937, RGASPI, 495/14/253/81-85; 'Review of the New Leader', 3 February 1937, RGASPI, 495/14/244/68.

32. Brigitte Studer, *The Transnational World of the Cominternians* (London, 2015).
33. For this period, see in particular Morgan, Cohen, and Flinn, *Communists and British Society*; Matthew Worley, *Class against Class: The Communist Party in Britain between the Wars* (London 2002); Thomas Linehan, *Communism in Britain: 1920–39: From the Cradle to the Grave* (Manchester, 2007).
34. Stephen Cullen, 'The Fasces and the Saltire: the Failure of the British Union of Fascists in Scotland, 1932–1940', *Scottish Historical Review* 87:2 (2008), 306–31.
35. On anti-fascism in Aberdeen, see Bob Cooney, *Proud Journey* (London, 2015), 8–27.
36. Hughes, *Gender and Political Identities*, 193–8.
37. Malcolm Petrie, 'Public Politics and Traditions of Popular Protest: Demonstrations of the Unemployed in Dundee and Edinburgh, c.1921–1939', *Contemporary British History* 27:4 (2013), 490–513.
38. 'Scottish District of the CPGB', RGASPI, 495/14/190/48–51.
39. 'Information Material Concerning Party Organisation and Cadres', 17 December 1936, RGASPI, 495/14/215/29–32.
40. By August 1937, it was considered to be 'largely bad' and even an 'obstacle' to organisation. Central Committee (CC) Meeting, 6 August 1937, RGASPI, 495/14/235/44.
41. The Means Test was calculated on the basis of household income, so claiming benefits often meant leaving home. John Stevenson and Chris Cook, *The Slump: Britain in the Great Depression* (Harlow, 2010), 79–81.
42. Although the totality of CPGB 'control' of the NUWM is debatable, the close organisational links are undeniable. Alan Campbell and John McIlroy, 'The National Unemployed Workers' Movement and the Communist Party of Great Britain Revisited', *Labour History Review* 73:1 (2008), 61–88.
43. Fern in MacDougall, *Voices from the Hunger Marches*, 138, see also 282, 335.
44. Clarke in MacDougall, *Voices from the Hunger Marches*, 164.
45. For the origins of this debate, see Buchanan, 'Britain's Popular Front', 60–72; Jim Fyrth, 'The Aid Spain Movement in Britain 1936–1939', *History Workshop Journal* 35 (1993), 153–64.

2

The Volunteers

All told, approximately thirty-five thousand volunteers journeyed to Spain between 1936 and 1938 to help defend the Republic. Though only ever a minority of the Republic's soldiers, these foreign volunteers became a defining feature of the conflict, not just to observers at the time but also to subsequent generations who read Orwell and Hemingway, saw the photographs of Capa or Taro or, in many cases, heard the stories passed down through their families, friends and communities. It is not difficult to see why. As part of a global effort to support the Republican cause, the volunteers were uniquely powerful symbols of solidarity, contributing not just their money and voices but their very lives for the Spanish people, an act of generosity that resonated in Spain and far beyond. It is remarkable enough that any one person sought to realise their seemingly abstract and distant connection to the unfolding struggle in Spain; it is astounding that this same decision was made by tens of thousands of volunteers from across the world.

The overwhelming majority of these volunteers sought to join what became known as the International Brigades.[1] These units – among them a small handful of Scots such as Phil Gillan – first saw action in the desperate defence of Madrid in November 1936, after General Franco's Army of Africa had fought its way across southern Spain before being stopped on the capital's outskirts. In early 1937 – by which time a British Battalion had been formed as part of the XV International Brigade – they fought in a series of defensive efforts to protect Madrid's lines of communication, with several International Brigades playing important roles in defensive victories at Jarama and Guadalajara. These battles would mark the high point of the International Brigades' direct contribution to the Republican war effort, with foreign volunteers thereafter making up a progressively smaller proportion of both the Republican Army and the

International Brigades themselves. For the British, exhausted after months of frontline service, July 1937 saw further substantial losses in a failed offensive north of Madrid at Brunete. The British then moved to Aragon, fighting at Belchite and Teruel, both costly Republican victories that were reversed in early 1938. In March 1938, the British Battalion again suffered catastrophic losses during Franco's Aragon offensive, which saw Republican territory split in two, with the International Brigades in Catalonia. The British Battalion's last major actions took place here during the final Republican offensive across the River Ebro. This, as with other Republican offensives, was only a temporary, costly success. Most Scots, along with the other British volunteers, were finally withdrawn from the line at the end of September 1938, and from Spain altogether two months later.

The tale of the British Battalion's exploits in Spain has been told several times, and their battles will not be recounted in detail here.[2] Yet despite the continued popular resonance of their story in Scotland, historical accounts of the Scottish International Brigade volunteers have remained strangely absent. While comparable contingents – from Wales, Ireland, Australia or Canada, for instance – have been the subject of detailed scholarly investigation since the 1980s or earlier, the historical record in Scotland has been shaped almost entirely by celebratory accounts created as a by-product of a thriving commemorative culture. Such accounts have succeeded in highlighting a Scottish place within the overall narrative of British and international participation in the conflict, but have also been guilty at times of advancing an uncritical picture of Scottish exceptionalism. In particular, the number of Scots in Spain has been the subject of dubious mythmaking, particularly surrounding the claim that Scotland, per capita, sent more volunteers to Spain than any other nation.[3]

This assertion can be refuted swiftly by anyone with access to a calculator and historical population figures. It is undoubtedly true, however, that within a British context, Scotland did see a particularly effective mobilisation on behalf of Spain, with Scots making up the largest regional contingent within the British Battalion. Yet the question of why this was the case has received next to no attention, even in a purely British context. At first glance, any objection to this historical oversight appears parochial – why has so little attention been paid to 'our' contingent? – yet the absence of answers points to a deeper issue in the broader literature on the mobilisation of volunteers for Spain. History writing has been dominated in recent decades by a strict divide between 'national' and 'transnational' studies. Both approaches have limitations when it comes to the important question of volunteer motivation. National studies, concerned with a central, bounded narrative, have often proved ill-equipped to appreciate local nuance and embrace comparative perspectives. Transnational studies, on the other hand, have tended to focus on individual lives, tracing the paths of exile and migration that led people to Spain, offering a richer explanation of individual decisions but less insight into any sort of collective impetuses.

This account seeks to refocus this debate towards what is perhaps the key outstanding question regarding transnational mobilisation and the Spanish Civil War: just why did so *many* people choose to fight? In answering why Scots were relatively more willing to enlist in the International Brigades than those from elsewhere in Britain, this study aims to identify factors that enabled large-scale transnational recruitment for Spain more broadly. Whilst it is argued that Scotland was distinctive, the factors identified here were not uniquely Scottish, but rather reflect the extent to which certain modes of political organisation and culture found fertile soil in many Scottish contexts. In other words, the reasons that Scotland proved an effective recruiting ground for the International Brigades offer insight into the broader question of why certain places across the world saw particularly concentrated recruitment. Indeed, existing studies of other notable clusters, such as New York or Vancouver, make some similar observations, though do not quite join the dots in the same way.[4]

This issue is addressed in this and the subsequent chapter. This particular chapter concentrates on the Scots in a collective sense, identifying the areas in which their lives bore similarities, intersected with each other and diverged. Richard Baxell's work on British volunteers provides a crucial point of reference, as it rests on a detailed examination of demographic factors across Britain.[5] Whilst Baxell's figures are improved upon here, thanks to the smaller sample under consideration and availability of new sources, the goal is to go beyond marginal improvements in accuracy and instead redefine the way the International Brigades are collectively perceived in Scotland and elsewhere. Rather than a disparate group of individuals who were thrown together once in Spain, the International Brigade volunteers should instead be seen as a relatively cohesive group even before they left home. In the Scottish case, the volunteers clustered along the intersection of class, geography and politics, defined most of all by formal and informal connections to the Communist Party. While there were inevitable exceptions, the bulk of Scots who fought in Spain can be understood as coming from this milieu.

To support this claim, this study utilises a database measuring key biographical variables across the volunteering contingent, including ages, affiliations, occupations and points of origin, as well as other information relating to their service in Spain, drawing on archival material relating to the International Brigades held in Britain and abroad. While detail is uneven across the entire sample of volunteers, it proved possible to measure each variable for a substantial majority of volunteers.[6] Using this database, this chapter explores the commonalities and differences among the Scottish volunteers. It begins by establishing the number of Scottish volunteers, as well as their age and occupation. The focus then moves to the geographic distribution of volunteers, and lastly to their political affiliations. Taken together, the data show that clusters of volunteers can be located along the intersections between community, locality and politics. Rather than a tiny minority of the Scottish population or even the Scottish working class, the recruitment of the International Brigade volunteers took place within this relatively well-defined and small social-political sphere.

Numbers

Despite the limited historiography dealing with the Scottish volunteers, estimates of their numbers have varied considerably in existing British and Scottish accounts. Tom Buchanan gave the figure as 437, while Ian MacDougall estimated 'about 500'.[7] Baxell counted 549, which has settled as the generally agreed-upon total.[8] This variation in figures reflects methodological problems that have plagued many accounts of the International Brigades. Earlier imprecision reflected uneven access to sources, yet even more recent attempts are still undermined by the inherent difficulty of defining origins precisely.[9] Complex and overlapping local and national identities, muddled further by migration, make this a non-trivial task. In an attempt to resolve this longstanding issue, Antonio Celada and Daniel Pastor Garcia sought to establish a single- or dual-national label for each English-speaking volunteer.[10] Rather than resolving the question, however, their work provides further evidence of the difficulty in enumerating the volunteers. Errors led to significant distortion in their figures, with approximately one fifth of Scottish entries found to contain false information. Typical of such errors or inconsistencies is the entry for Robert Beggs, correctly listed as Glaswegian but classified as English, or George Shaw, who was listed as a dual national (Scotland and United States) for which there is no supporting evidence.[11]

The approach used here aims to address these limitations. By ensuring that all entries were confirmed by at least two independent sources, and applying a residential rather than ethnic definition of 'Scottish', this account considers that 520 Scottish volunteers left Britain with the intention of joining the International Brigades. This includes a small handful whose services were subsequently rejected, either en route in Paris or on arrival in Spain, generally for reasons of health, age or wavering dedication to the cause, or some combination thereof. By relaxing either the definition of 'Scottish' or the requirement for independent verification, dozens more might conceivably be included. It could certainly be argued that some of those excluded might have seen themselves as Scottish. However, as my argument rests on analysing specific socio-political cultures and networks rather than the innate power of being 'Scottish', their inclusion here would serve little purpose beyond inflating the headline number. With confirmed Scots alone making up at least 22 per cent of the British contingent – over double their share of Britain's population – even a strict definition suffices to substantiate the overrepresentation of Scots in the International Brigades.

Age

Although volunteers were supposed to be over 21 and less than 40 years old, and ideally between 25 and 35, in practice there was considerable flexibility. Any attempt to enforce this rule was undermined by individuals' willingness to lie about their age, often aided and abetted by their peers. Steve Fullarton, eighteen when he volunteered in April 1938, recalled discussing this with local Party organiser George Campbell.

> He says, 'you better say you're 19' 'OK, I'll be 19 if they ask.' They did ask. They told me . . . 'You'll be going down to London now and they'll see you in London and you better tell them ye're 20 because 19 sounds a bit young' 'Aye OK I'll be 20.' Well, when I went to London my age increased from 20 to 21: 'You better say you're 21.' And when I got to Paris that was me 21.[12]

Judging by Fullarton's enlistment paperwork, by the time he reached Spain he had had several more such conversations, eventually giving his age as 23.[13] Similarly, the oldest Scot, Francis Casey, was 53 years old when he joined the British Battalion in December 1936, but admitted to being only 42. The youngest, 16-year-old Robert McGuire, claimed to be 21 when enlisting.[14]

Table 2.1 Volunteers' ages in Scottish, British, French and American contingents (%)

Age	Scottish	British, inc. Scots	French	American
Under 21	5.3	4.2	2.6	} 38.0
21–25	26.3	32.2	24.8	
26–30	26.3	23.6	32.6	26.0
31–35	21.1	20.4	21.9	} 36.0
36–40	12.9	12.3	13.7	
Over 40	8.0	7.3	4.4	

This widespread practice of creative imprecision with ages hinders meaningful comparisons across groups (Table 2.1).[15] Baxell identified several cases of volunteers lying about their age, but a systematic attempt to correct such 'errors' appears to have been impossible at the time.[16] Thanks to new source material, this account was able to catch many more creative age-related claims, although this makes comparisons more difficult. As such, while the variation between groups could conceivably be meaningful – for example, higher proportions of older volunteers might point to a drop in acceptance standards – methodological inconsistency makes such arguments difficult to substantiate.

As indicated in Table 2.2, Scottish volunteers grew steadily younger as the conflict lengthened. Prior to May 1937, fewer than 30 per cent of volunteers in any given period were under 25, compared to at least 31.5 per cent from May onwards, including nearly 60 per cent in November and December 1937. This change likely reflects shifting attitudes on the part of recruiters. Despite the optimistic claim by one British commander that 'there were men of over fifty who did as well as those half their years', older volunteers often struggled to cope with strenuous demands of military service, with many relegated to rear duties.[17] Concerns about the suitability of new recruits were raised as early as February 1937.[18] By mid-1937, with the number of volunteers unfit for frontline service rapidly outstripping the number of useful jobs for them, preventing overage recruits became a higher priority.[19] The concern was also financial; the Communist Party had promised to support volunteers' dependants while they were in Spain, and subsidising the presence of volunteers who were unable to contribute meaningfully to the war effort was proving a substantial burden, particularly as repatriation was heavily restricted. For these reasons, it is unsurprising that younger recruits became preferred.

Table 2.2 Age of Scottish volunteers arriving between December 1936 and April 1938 (%)

Age	Dec 1936	Jan 1937	Feb 1937	Mar–Apr 1937	May–Jun 1937	Jul–Aug 1937	Sep–Oct 1937	Nov–Dec 1937	Jan–Feb 1938	Mar–Apr 1938
Under 21	4.6	6.4	0	0	0	7.1	2.9	9.4	7.4	9.1
21–25	20.2	22.2	13.6	21.1	37.5	32.1	28.6	50.0	31.5	27.3
26–30	23.9	19.2	22.7	52.6	33.3	35.7	25.7	18.8	25.9	29.5
31–35	21.1	26.3	22.7	10.5	29.2	0	20.0	18.8	18.5	27.3
36–40	14.7	14.1	22.7	10.5	0	21.4	11.4	3.1	14.8	6.8
Over 40	15.6	11.1	18.2	5.3	0	3.6	11.4	0	1.9	0

Occupation

Details of prior employment are available for 417 Scottish International Brigaders, allowing for a relatively complete picture. Few had had prestigious or well-remunerated careers, and even those with traditionally middle-class professions were hardly models of bourgeois respectability. The lone accountant, for instance, was still a trainee when he volunteered, while one chemist had recently been fired due to his communist sympathies.[20] A teacher was actually working as a 'salesman' when he volunteered, suggesting teaching was going poorly, while the three journalists tended to have worked for the Communist Party newspaper, the *Daily Worker*.[21] Beyond these quasi-professionals, few were non-manual workers: eleven clerical workers of various descriptions, two music hall performers and two nurses. The rest – 95 per cent of those for whom information is available – worked with their hands.

It is difficult, however, to locate any particular occupational cluster beyond the dominance of manual labour. No industry stands out as having supplied especially disproportionate numbers of volunteers, especially when placed within a British context (Table 2.3).[22] Patterns of trades union membership reflect this trend. 170 Scots were known to be trades union members, compared to Baxell's figure of approximately five hundred for Britain as a whole, although this high proportion is again likely due to the broader source base consulted here. A few divergences emerge between the samples. Mining unions were the second-largest grouping in Scotland; in England they did not make the top ten. There were fewer Scottish members of the National Union of Seamen, while Boilermakers and Railwaymen were better represented. However, the similarities are more striking than the differences.

Table 2.3 Proportion of Scottish and British volunteers in occupational sectors (%)

Occupational sector	Scotland	Britain, including Scotland
Manufacturing and construction	37.6	30
Transport	20.6	22
Trades	11.5	20
Mining	16.5	9
Publishing	1.8	6
Professionals	1.2	6
Local government	0.2	1
Arts and crafts	0.9	1
Miscellaneous	9.7	4

For these reasons, the only firm conclusion is that Scots had more traditionally 'working class' occupations than the British overall, with Scots three times less likely to work in publishing, local government or as a professional than the British average, which was not high to begin with.[23] Beyond this, only the disproportionate number of miners stands out, though this distinctiveness is overshadowed by the Welsh contingent. According to Hywel Francis and Robert Stradling, between 99 and 110 Welsh miners served in Spain, representing two-thirds of the Welsh contingent, compared to 55 Scottish miners comprising a sixth of the Scots.[24] This, along with Scotland's more dispersed coalfields, contrasts with the exceptional mobilisation along regional-occupational lines seen in Wales. However, Scots and Welsh together made up three-quarters of all miners who volunteered. Clearly, English miners were considerably less willing to go to Spain than their Welsh and Scottish comrades, pointing to substantial differences in coalfield political cultures across the three nations.[25]

Unemployment

It is unclear how many individuals were actually employed in the occupations they claimed when they departed Scotland. Many appear to have listed either a customary trade or a previous position instead of admitting to being unemployed. Although it is generally held that between an eighth and a quarter of all British volunteers were unemployed, the Scottish figure is likely much higher.[26] This is most clearly demonstrated by the demographics of Scottish

Communist Party membership – which, as discussed further below, was the main source of recruits. Scotland had a higher proportion – 'over 50%' – of unemployed members than any other CPGB district in October 1936.[27] This figure improved only slowly, with 45 per cent of Scottish communists still unemployed by November 1937.[28] Even by June 1938, the figure was 43 per cent.[29] Compared to other major districts such as London, where just 185 from 4806 members were unemployed by April 1937, or Lancashire where the figure was 16 per cent in November 1937, this points to the Scottish contingent containing a much higher proportion of unemployed volunteers than the British average.[30]

Studies of British International Brigade volunteers have generally been content to note an apparent connection with unemployment activism without considering the precise ways that it actually shaped recruitment patterns.[31] While some few volunteers may have seen Spain as an 'escape' from the ennui of unemployment, as the decision has occasionally been portrayed, it is entirely unsatisfactory as a collective explanation, if only because such a tiny proportion of unemployed workers went to Spain.[32] Yet there were certainly indirect ways that mass unemployment influenced the Communist Party's capacity to recruit for the International Brigades. As discussed in the previous chapter, unemployment provided the CPGB with space in which to build a vibrant political movement.[33] The relative dynamism and scale of unemployment activism not only influenced the CPGB's ability to expand and attract recruits but also qualitatively shaped the way the Party operated, effectively linking local activism with national mobilisation.

The Hunger Marches in particular affected the CPGB's organisational capabilities, both real and perceived. The complex logistics of marshalling hundreds of marchers over a trek that lasted up to six weeks helped develop important skills for many Party cadres who later took on military or political responsibilities in Spain.[34] Moreover, the success of the Hunger Marches helped develop faith in the Party itself. In their being able to clothe, feed, shelter and protect their charges adequately, faith in the tactics and capabilities of communist leadership was reinforced among their followers. Among the most active NUWM members – those most likely to be drawn into the political orbit of the Communist Party itself, given the evident strength of their conviction as well as the opportunities for propagandising that a six-week march afforded – the Communist Party had developed strong foundations for a successful recruitment campaign for Spain. In the last large march, not coincidentally just as mass recruitment for the International Brigades got underway in November-December 1936, over five hundred Scots marched on London.[35] Their minds, however, were already consumed not by the prospect of continued unemployment, but by 'complete discussions about Spain all the time' – including the news that Scotland's first volunteer, Phil Gillan of Glasgow, was involved in the fighting around Madrid.[36] Several of these Hunger Marchers had already decided that they would follow his example.

Class

As indicated by their occupations, Scottish volunteers were overwhelmingly of working-class origins. Whilst it is possible to list some Scots who did not fit this mould – such as David Mackenzie, a medical student – these examples are exceptions. Most estimates place the proportion of working-class volunteers in the British battalion as being between 80 and 90 per cent, but given the overwhelming preponderance of working-class volunteers among the Scottish and Welsh contingents, this suggests that most middle- or upper-class volunteers were English.[37] By comparison, the American contingent contained a somewhat higher proportion of professionals, intellectuals and students.[38]

These class differences between the British national groups are reflected in the pattern of arrivals. Many middle-class volunteers arrived in the early months of the war. These tended to be those for whom going to Spain was a choice made independently, for very personal reasons. For them, the cause and opportunity were enough, and further enabling factors unnecessary. Yet making such a decision required the means to see it through. There may have been working-class Scots with similar ambitions – George Drever, for instance, claimed to have tried to volunteer to fight in Abyssinia in 1935, an indication that he was perhaps looking for somewhere to fight rather than swept up by specific enthusiasm for Spain.[39] However, without money to pay fares, a passport or knowledge of international travel, most working-class volunteers were unable to reach Spain before a route was established through cooperation between the Comintern and British and French Communist Parties.[40] The difference this made to recruitment in Scotland in particular is stark. Of the British volunteers trickling into Spain from August to November 1936, just seven per cent were Scots. However, once a route was established, the next three months saw Scots make up 42 per cent of British arrivals. Class was inextricably bound up with the mechanics of mobilisation.

Disparities in social composition among the different national groups in the English-speaking XV International Brigade had ramifications beyond recruitment patterns. Leadership representation came to reflect the varying proportions of middle- or upper-class volunteers in each national group.

Americans came to dominate the higher ranks, to the chagrin of the other nationalities – an internal report written in 1938 acknowledged the failure to promote Canadian and Latin American officers, and the British too were forced to contend for adequate representation at Brigade level.[41] Among the British, however, a similar process was under way, with English volunteers coming to dominate the higher ranks over time. That is not to say that Scots were completely passed over. Jock Cunningham and Harry Fry, for instance, were two of the Battalion's most celebrated officers. Moreover, Scots such as George Aitken and Bob Cooney also exercised significant authority as Political Commissars, a distinctive feature of the Republican Army with broad responsibility for volunteers' welfare, morale and political development. However, the disproportionate number of Scottish volunteers was not matched by a disproportionate presence in leadership roles. This reflects Michael Petrou's observations regarding the chiefly working-class Canadian contingent, which was often provided with middle-class American officers.[42]

There are several reasons why rank and social background became connected in Spain. Middle- or upper-class volunteers were more likely to have participated in Officer Training Corps schemes at school or university, training which assumed relative importance given the scarcity of volunteers with significant military experience.[43] Above all, few working-class Scots could speak a language other than English, a prized ability in the multinational environment of the International Brigades.[44] One document from January 1938 listed all British volunteers able to speak other languages; just four out of 76 were Scottish.[45] Finally, the nature of the training available for officer candidates could make it difficult for working-class volunteers to excel. Owing in part to the chronic shortage of materiel, officer training was heavy on theory and short on practice, favouring those used to formal education and with higher degrees of literacy and numeracy. In one graduating class of officer candidates in late 1937 for which evaluations are available, most Scots were posted to units as non-commissioned officers, with only the well-educated, middle-class volunteer John Dunlop noted to have any immediate potential for higher rank.[46] Fewer and fewer Scots even had the chance at acquiring higher rank as time went by: the next graduating class contained just two Scots out of 54 English-speaking candidates, both classed as 'not recommended for promotion'.[47]

Religion and Marital Status

Enumerating the Scottish volunteers' religious and marital backgrounds presents similar challenges with regards to source material. Richard Baxell found fewer than one hundred British volunteers for whom a denominational background could be established – 80 Catholics and 'a very small number' of

Protestants – and it is difficult to improve on this picture directly for the Scots.[48] One important difference is the relative absence of Jewish volunteers, with Alec Marcovitch and Charles Hyman the only volunteers confirmed to be Scottish Jews.[49] This is in stark contrast to estimates for Britain as a whole, which range up to 20 per cent of all volunteers.[50] This in turn likely reflects differing contexts of anti-fascist mobilisation. While countering BUF attacks on Jewish communities was an important focus for anti-fascist activism in places like Manchester and London, these incursions were generally absent in Scotland.[51] This meant that while Scottish Jews were hardly pro-fascist, these communities were less politically mobilised, and volunteering for Spain was not an obvious extension of earlier anti-fascist campaigns.[52]

By reputation, Irish Catholics were prominent in the Scottish Communist Party, particularly in Glasgow. One ILP member, David Murray, referred to Scottish 'CPers' as 'a pack of Irish not very ex-Papists'.[53] Less pejoratively, Chris Smith recalled that 75 per cent of the Scottish Communist Party were Catholic, although this likely reflected his immediate circles in and around Glasgow rather than the Party throughout Scotland.[54] Such remarks, along with the number of common Irish names such as 'Kelly' or 'Kennedy', indicate that many volunteers likely had a Catholic background. Several such volunteers were listed as being born in Ireland in various sources, or can be traced in the census as having at least one Irish parent.[55] However, direct references to individuals' religion, past or present, are too rare to establish any sort of proportionality – those such as James Cassidy who were specifically referred to as being Catholic were rare exceptions.[56]

Similarly, observations about marital status were too infrequent to establish a full picture. Despite recruiters' stated preference for single men without dependants, this was often ignored in practice.[57] Would-be volunteers could also deceive recruiters by initially claiming to have no dependants, only to ask for financial support later, as suggested in one missive written by Peter Kerrigan.

> Here is another dependants claim, and, as usual, from Scotland. L. Inglis 75 Florence Street Glasgow C5. Wife and two children. The argument or excuse put up by these lads is that they understood they would be rejected if they had dependants.[58]

Kerrigan's words hint at a possibility that Scots were more likely to have dependants. However, there is little concrete evidence suggesting that this was the case, and Kerrigan's gripe could just as well reflect that the Scottish recruiters – faced with a sudden rush of volunteers in the months immediately prior – could afford to be stricter about accepting volunteers with dependants, encouraging some would-be volunteers to lie.

Perhaps surprisingly, the best data on volunteers' religious beliefs and marital status is not found in International Brigade records. Rather, the information comes from the medical publications of the Francoist psychiatrist Antonio Vallejo Nágera, who ran a series of investigations into groups of captured International Brigade volunteers. Despite the caution with which Vallejo Nágera's own pseudoscientific views must be treated, many observations made about basic attributes such as age, occupation and class do correspond to other sources, suggesting that the material was not fabricated out of hand.[59] Other information, such as the religious background and marital status of the volunteers, goes well beyond what is available in other sources, and these results are summarised in Table 2.4.[60]

Table 2.4 Religious and marital backgrounds of British prisoners

Religion	Total	%	Marital status	Total	%
Catholic	12	29.3	Widowed with children	1	2.4
Retain their beliefs and practise	2	4.6	Married with children	6	14.6
Retain their beliefs and don't practise	5	12.1	Married without children	2	4.6
Converted to Protestantism	1	2.4	Single, cohabiting	1	2.4
Converted to Catholicism and practise	1	2.4	Single, sexual activity outwith prostitution.	24	58.2
Lost their beliefs	3	7.3	Single, abstinent	6	14.6
Protestant	17	41.4			
Retain their beliefs and practise	12	29.2			
Retain their beliefs and don't practise	4	9.7			
Converted to Catholicism	1	2.4			
Atheist	12	29.3			
No family religion	3	7.3			
Protestant family religion	9	21.9			
Total	41			41	

Whilst these figures cover all of Britain and cannot be broken down by region, their detail and internal consistency provide a useful overview of the volunteers' personal lives. Two-thirds did not have children, and fewer than a quarter had ever been married. Only a minority claimed any Catholic heritage, although hidden regional variation likely obscures a greater Catholic presence among volunteers from cities such as Glasgow and Liverpool. It is possible that reconciling active Catholicism with socialism or anti-fascism was considerably more difficult than for Protestants. Although Protestants often professed to retain their religion, the author made it clear in the commentary that they believed that 'an overwhelming majority are religiously indifferent and many of them atheists'.[61] However, such judgements need to be treated sceptically, especially as Vallejo Nágera's key thesis was that 'irreligiosity' was a major cause of Marxist tendencies.[62]

Origins

Thus far, whilst a demographic analysis has identified trends and offered a basis for comparison with other nationalities, it has done relatively little to narrow the scope of the enquiry. No precise commonalities have emerged across the categories examined. However, the geographical distribution of volunteers' origins offers considerably more scope for such clustering to emerge. Baxell's breakdown of where volunteers came from shows notable concentrations in the industrial regions where the Communist Party had made the most significant inroads, namely Wales, North-West England, Scotland and the South-East, with particular urban concentrations in Liverpool, Manchester, Glasgow and London.[63] However, whilst a regional analysis is helpful, it remains a very broad measure of where volunteers came from. The approximately 370 volunteers from North-West England, for example, came from a relatively large population even once age, class and occupation are taken into account.[64]

A more detailed breakdown of Scottish volunteer origins in Table 2.5 reveals that the Scottish volunteers came from very specific places. The distribution among Scotland's major urban centres reflects the nature of their economies, with heavily industrialised Glasgow and Dundee home to nearly half of the Scottish volunteers, with proportionally smaller numbers coming from Edinburgh and Aberdeen. Other Clydeside industrial towns are similarly prominent, albeit on a smaller scale. The Scottish coalfields are also well represented, with clusters among mining communities in Fife, Lanarkshire and to a lesser extent East and West Lothian. These patterns correspond to the volunteers' occupational data, concentrated in locales with economies dominated by industry, transportation and manual labour.

Table 2.5 Scottish volunteers' point of origin

Location	Total	Location	Total
		Lanarkshire	
Major cities		Airdrie	10
Aberdeen	23	Bellshill	8
Dundee	57	Blantyre	5
Edinburgh	48	Cambuslang	7
Glasgow	199	Wishaw	5
Total major cities	327	Other	21
		Total Lanarkshire	56
Dunbartonshire		*Fife*	
Clydebank	11	Cowdenbeath	5
Vale of Leven	15	Kirkcaldy	13
Other	4	Methil/Buckhaven	7
Total Dunbartonshire	30	Other	12
		Total Fife	37
Renfrewshire		*Other*	
Greenock	17	Ayrshire	8
Paisley	8	Lothians	9
Other	5	Misc/unknown	23
Total Renfrewshire	30	Total Other	40
		Total Scotland	520

Another way of looking at this picture is that it reflects not only the volunteers' socio-economic backgrounds but also that they lived in close proximity to one another. 438, or just over 84 per cent, came from places that saw at least five individuals go to Spain. In other words, most Scots who chose to go to Spain lived and worked around others who made the same decision. In fact, many among the other sixteen per cent still lived in close proximity to other volunteers. In Fife and Lanarkshire, the two areas with the highest proportion outside these clusters, the sample is fractured by the prominence of volunteers from smaller villages – typically mining villages – in close proximity to each other or to neighbouring towns.

Furthermore, even for the smallest clusters such as Prestonpans in East Lothian, there is evidence that volunteers knew each other.[65] In very few cases was the choice made in complete isolation from other volunteers.

Glasgow is the most notable single cluster, providing the point of origin for almost two-fifths of the Scottish contingent. However, Glasgow's status as Scotland's largest city at the time means that this is to some extent expected, and does relatively little to narrow down exactly who the volunteers were. Yet the Glaswegian volunteers also came from very specific places within the city (Table 2.6). Discounting the 28 volunteers for whom Glasgow is the best approximation available, the proportion that came from a neighbourhood with at least five volunteers – just under 85 per cent – is almost identical to the same measure applied to the whole of Scotland. Over 60 per cent came from the six densest suburban clusters alone. As was the case with the previous table, this likely underestimates the Glaswegian volunteers' close proximity to each another – Glaswegians' high mobility within the city meant that individuals could develop connections outwith their place of residence or work. The specific hubs of volunteering are also significant. These areas were among the most deprived in Glasgow,

Table 2.6 Point of origin of Glaswegian volunteers

Location (within Glasgow)	Total	% (of known total)
Anderston	5	2.9
Bridgeton	16	9.4
Central	9	5.3
Dennistoun	5	2.9
Gorbals	23	13.5
Govan	14	8.2
Maryhill	16	9.4
Possilpark	9	5.3
Shettleston	11	6.4
Springburn	19	11.1
Townhead	18	10.5
Other known districts	26	15.2
Total known	171	100.0
Unknown	28	–
Total	199	–

often home to recent immigrants, most frequently from Ireland. The structural downturn in heavy industry and the reduced demand for manual and industrial labour had hit these areas the hardest, resulting in extremely high unemployment rates in the years prior to the Spanish Civil War. Low-skilled populations, structural unemployment and, in some cases, Irish Catholicism were the same ingredients that underpinned successful communist campaigning and recruitment in interwar Scotland more broadly.[66]

That immediate geographical proximity was such a universal commonality for Scottish volunteers suggests this physical closeness could also have been accompanied by direct personal ties between individuals. However, even with the relatively complete picture available of who the volunteers were in a demographic sense, solid connections among volunteers are still generally absent in the data examined so far. There are some exceptions – Robert Milton and George Gowans, for instance, were the same age and belonged to the same trade union branch in Ayrshire.[67] The two volunteers from Peterhead, George Eddie and James Buchan, were both seamen in their mid- to late thirties.[68] At least nine Dundonians had some connection to the textile trade, through either stated occupation or union membership. Many mining areas showed connections in terms of occupation and union membership, notably in Bellshill, Bathgate, Prestonpans and several places throughout Fife. However, these specific intersections of occupation and geography remain very much the exception rather than the rule. If there were direct connections between individual volunteers from the same place, these connections were not typically fostered in the workplace or in the official labour movement.

Politics

This picture changes substantially once the volunteers' political affiliation is explored. It was an open secret that the CPGB was the driving force behind recruitment for the International Brigades in Britain, and volunteers could not help but be aware that the Party continued to exert control and influence over the British contingent during their service.[69] Most estimates claim that Communist Party members made up over 60 per cent of the International Brigades.[70] However, efforts were made to recruit from other parties, especially the Labour Party, for which Baxell counted some 110 members in Spain out of a sample of 1489 volunteers.[71]

At first glance, the Scottish contingent conforms to wider observations regarding the political composition of the International Brigades (Table 2.7).[72] Taking the CPGB and YCL together, some 56 per cent of

Table 2.7 Political affiliations of Scottish volunteers prior to enlistment

Political affiliation	Number in Spain (from 520)
CPGB	238
Young Communist League (YCL)	54
Labour Party	20
Independent Labour Party (ILP)	1
NUWM	105
Left Book Club (LBC)	1
Other	5
No affiliation found	177

Scots were Party members – slightly under the estimate for Britain as a whole. On initial appearances, the number of Labour Party members is also roughly in proportion with the British total. However, in Scotland this diversity proved somewhat illusory. Although twenty volunteers indicated some attachment to the Labour Party or local affiliate, at least eight of these were also members of the Communist Party or a front organisation such as the NUWM. The CPGB had long fostered influence within the Labour Party, with many communists believing that 'even if you agree with the Communist Party and its basic aims that you can render better service to the Party by remaining in the Labour Party'.[73] By 1939, there were some fifteen hundred of these 'concealed' CPGB members.[74] It is difficult to avoid concluding that many – perhaps even most – Labour Party members in Spain held similar dual allegiances, and were far from disconnected from the local communist milieu.

The lack of ILP members – despite Glasgow representing their major stronghold at the time – also speaks to the extent that the volunteers' political beliefs were perhaps more homogenous than has previously been allowed.[75] The absence of Left Book Club (LBC) members is also telling. While the LBC had substantial membership in Scotland – and was noted to be growing quickly in Glasgow by 1937 – it primarily catered for a middle-class readership rather than the working-class communities from which volunteers came.[76] However, as LBC membership was never a matter of particular administrative interest in Spain, this figure may be under-reported. Finally, very much in the 'Other' category, Robert Grierson of Dumfries had actually once belonged to the BUF, an affiliation that naturally excited considerable suspicion in Spain. However, even the most zealous Stalinists were forced to conclude that he was 'mostly harmless', before his death in March 1938 rendered him no political threat whatsoever.[77]

When individuals joined the Communist Party was also important. While such detailed biographical information is not available for the majority of Party members, it is available for those who joined the Spanish Communist Party (PCE). Applicants filled out a *'Biografia de Militantes'*, detailing their personal, social and political histories. Some 47 Scottish Party members, and three active non-members, completed these declarations. Of these, 60 per cent had joined the Party prior to the adoption of the Popular Front line, even though at most 40 per cent of the Party's members in 1938 had joined before this point.[78] This disproportionate favouring of longstanding members is unsurprising, as such individuals were more experienced and had had more opportunity to earn trust and favour. This also reflects a generational effect: whilst the CPGB, like other communist parties, had significantly expanded after the abandonment of the controversial 'Class Against Class' line in 1934, those who had stuck by the Party during this phase represented a tough, loyal elite, at least in their own minds.[79]

These biographies also give a qualitative insight into the Scottish contingent more broadly. Membership of the PCE is a useful proxy for understanding the spectrum of political loyalties in Spain. Admittance to the Spanish Party was an honour reserved for those who had a good record in Spain and had continued to demonstrate their political dedication.[80] It was a voluntary act of commitment to the Party – those who had started to harbour doubts or had lost interest in politics in Spain were unlikely either to apply or to be accepted – making this group the best approximation of a 'Party faithful' among the Scots. Given that almost all applications dated from April 1938 or later, this group made up a quarter of the approximately 220 Scots who served in the British Battalion in this period. Over a similar period, approximately one-sixth of British volunteers were classified as 'bad' by Party leaders, indicating that between a core of committed activists and somewhat smaller group of disaffected individuals, a majority were not doctrinaire communists but did retain some attachment to the Party or its principles throughout their service.

To understand this middle ground, which covered a spectrum of political attachment or attraction to communism, it is necessary to appreciate membership numbers as just one facet of the CPGB's presence in Scotland. The period from 1935 onwards was generally characterised by expansion, thanks to the aforementioned Popular Front policy and the impetus sparked by the rise of fascism in Europe, including the Spanish

Civil War itself.[81] During the main period of recruitment for the International Brigades from December 1936 to May 1938, Party membership in Scotland grew from eighteen hundred to nearly three thousand.[82] However, this expansion masked a great deal of fluidity in individual and regional experiences before and during the conflict.[83] Many drifted in and out of the party during the 1930s. One particularly common cause was being unable to afford membership dues during periods of unemployment – even by 1939, 14 per cent of Scotland's members were known to be in arrears with their dues, still 'a definite improvement' over previous years.[84] Disagreement about politics, personality clashes or migration could also act to interrupt membership. Some, such as the Glaswegian William Hunter, had previously been expelled from the Party, or, like George McDermott, had let their membership lapse. At least 25 Scots – almost 10 per cent of the CPGB total – fell into these categories. Given the lack of detailed knowledge regarding many volunteers' personal histories, the actual number is likely higher. For these and other individuals, their relationship to the CPGB was liminal – integrated into its orbit, but not with full or permanent membership of the Party itself.[85]

These ambiguities mean that there are numerous examples within Scotland and Britain where membership figures do not accurately reflect actual Party influence or a district's potential recruitment base for Spain. By May 1937, for instance, London had double Scotland's membership, yet saw significantly fewer of these members volunteer for Spain.[86] The pattern was similarly variable within Scotland. In Glasgow, membership was noted to be 'far from commensurate with Party's influence and prestige'.[87] The CPGB's only MP at the time was elected in West Fife, and thousands of Fife miners had been members of the Party-controlled United Mineworkers of Scotland.[88] Yet in September 1936, the Fife District of the Communist Party had just 232 members. This was partly due to the blacklisting of CPGB members by the official mining union and pit owners, meaning that most Fife communists faced unemployment.[89] Similarly, the Vale of Leven had only 47 Party members in July 1937, yet was singled out by Stuart Macintyre as being an archetypical 'Little Moscow', where the CPGB enjoyed unusual local social and political clout.[90] Clearly, the Party could count on influence beyond the relatively limited circles implied by its membership figures in these locales. Opposite examples can also be given: Kilmarnock had one of the largest concentrations of Party members in western Scotland, with 72 members in July 1937, higher than comparable nearby towns such as Greenock (34), Paisley (38) or Clydebank

(62).[91] Yet unlike in these other towns, no International Brigade volunteers were recruited from Kilmarnock, indicating limitations when it came to mobilising this membership base. Such examples indicate the need to appreciate communist strength in terms of social and political influence as well as membership – and, just as importantly, how effectively this influence could be translated into mobilisation, especially as the call to arms reached beyond the inner core of the Party faithful.

The qualitative variation in Communist Party influence is reflected in the absence of significant clustering along union membership lines noted above. This is unlikely to be a matter of poor record-keeping. The Party had every motive to collect this information, as it was seen as useful leverage when negotiating with the official labour movement.[92] More likely, this reflected structural factors pertaining to how the Communist Party operated within the labour movement. Many unions operated some form of anti-communist discrimination. Although these measures' actual effectiveness tended to vary, and did not altogether prevent communist penetration, they did tend to preclude the sort of community-building that could take place around the Party branch system.[93] In Glasgow, it was noted that the Party had failed to 'draw active Trade Unionists into Branch meetings and Branch life' and despite many individual successes in achieving positions of influence in local trade unions, there were 'active and influential Trade Union comrades' who over 'a period of years, have failed to recruit a single new member'.[94] So, whilst the Communist Party clearly had significant influence in the Glasgow trade union movement – it claimed to 'have 60 delegates and a majority on the [Trade Council Executive Committee]' – it was not a sphere for active Party-building.[95] Whilst the labour movement remained a key theatre of activity for the Party, success was achieved through the placement and promotion of key individuals, not creating and sustaining communities that could provide a solid basis for recruitment for either the International Brigades or the Party itself.

Even without considering broader definitions of 'influence', the number of Scottish CPGB members who volunteered for Spain represents a considerable proportion of the Party's strength. On the basis of membership figures from September 1937 adjusted only for gender, nearly 15 per cent of Scottish communists fought in Spain, including nearly 20 per cent of the Dundee membership, 18 per cent in Glasgow and over a quarter in Greenock.[96] These are likely slight overestimates, as the total likely includes some volunteers who joined the Communist Party after September 1937. Yet even using the membership figures from mid-1938–3070, including approximately five hundred women – over 10 per cent of male Scottish communists fought in Spain, even before accounting for age or fitness.[97] Whilst a minority, it was nonetheless a remarkable mobilisation of such a small organisation.

Conclusions

The Scottish volunteers' demographic profile shows that volunteers shared important commonalities in terms of class, locality and political beliefs, while remaining disparate in terms of occupation, age and status within the official labour movement. The particular concentration of recruitment within the ranks of the CPGB strongly suggests that the volunteers likely had pre-existing relationships with one another. The comparatively large proportion of Scottish communists that went to Spain indicates that it must have been near impossible that these decisions were made in isolation – if a significant fraction of a given branch went to Spain, it seems wildly unlikely that each member did so without knowledge of or discussion with the others. This in turn has important implications – it meant that going to Spain was not an abstract prospect, but a decision being made or considered by their friends, families and colleagues. This, as shall be explored in the next chapter, suggests that we need to revise our understanding of volunteer motivations as having collective as well as individual dimensions.

The centrality of CPGB membership, networks and influence in framing these connections indicates the need for a nuanced appreciation of the Communist Party's strength, defined not simply by membership figures but by their tactics, influence and ability to attract and develop those who were particularly predisposed towards volunteering. This points to the necessity of understanding communist 'influence' as having qualitative differences in different places. The Party could develop intellectual influence through initiatives such as the LBC, or organisational influence through infiltrating the labour movement and winning over key figures, but these were not spaces that greatly facilitated the mobilisation of volunteers. Rather, mobilisation – for Spain or other direct, sustained activism – required influence to be built around a community. The connections between volunteers indicate the ways and places in which the communists were successful in developing this sort of influence, with their success in Scotland being based on locality rather than industry or the labour movement.

Instead of a rigid differentiation between 'communists' and 'non-communists', such an explanation posits that the vast majority of volunteers were part of a broader social-political web, the core of which was made up of Party members but the influence of which spread considerably further. The 177 volunteers for whom no formal political affiliation could be discerned should, therefore, be regarded not as neutral, or disassociated from the communist political sphere, but rather as having potentially different forms of involvement or connection. The next chapter explores the basis for Communist Party influence in Scotland in greater depth, and the importance of integration into such networks for non-communists. It suffices to note here that successful recruitment for the International Brigades in Scotland was achieved not just through a relatively strong membership base, but also the influence the Party had been able to build by leveraging broader political and community identities. This in turn implies that the Scottish contribution to the International Brigades was not a product of the broader left as it has sometimes been portrayed in Scotland or elsewhere – rather, it was almost exclusively a Communist Party enterprise.[98] This should not be seen as resurrecting older narratives of the communist-led 'Good Fight' in Spain – rather, it indicates the CPGB's failure to establish the International Brigades as an embodiment of the hoped-for united front.

This lack of diversity has broader significance for studies of transnational foreign fighters in other contexts. Such fighters are most often seen as scattered individuals, with potential recruits vastly outnumbering the number of individuals who actually decide to volunteer. This is an outcome of treating recruitment as a process that takes place among a much larger general population. As seen here, however, the Scottish International Brigade volunteers should not be seen as a tiny minority of the Scottish population, or even of Scots who supported the Spanish Republic. Rather, they need to be appreciated as a intensive mobilisation of a very specific, comparatively small community. By more carefully appreciating who makes up the bulk of volunteers and searching for connections between them, it may be possible to re-evaluate the recruitment of foreign fighters in other conflicts as a concentrated mobilisation of smaller groupings rather than necessarily diffuse, sporadic or entirely self-driven individuals.

Notes

1. The best overview of the International Brigades remains Remi Skoutelsky, *Novedad en el frente: las Brigadas Internacionales en la guerra civil* (Madrid, 2006). Other significant accounts include Vincent Brome, *The International Brigades: Spain 1936–1939* (London, 1965); Verle Johnston, *Legions of Babel: The International Brigades in the Spanish Civil War* (University Park, PA,

1967); Jacques Delperrie de Bayac, *Les Brigades Internationales* (Paris, 1968); Andreu Castells, *Las Brigadas Internacionales de la Guerra de España* (Esplugues de Llobregat, 1974); Michael Jackson, *Fallen Sparrows: The International Brigades in the Spanish Civil War* (Philadelphia, 1994).

2. Baxell, *British Volunteers* and *Unlikely Warriors*; Ben Hughes, *They Shall Not Pass!: The British Battalion at Jarama* (Oxford, 2011); Hopkins, *Heart of the Fire*; Alexander, *British Volunteers*.

3. The source of this claim appears to be a misreading of Daniel Gray's book, and Gray himself has challenged it on several occasions. Nevertheless, it persists. Gray, *Homage*, 19.

4. For example. J. Byrne, 'From Brooklyn to Belchite' in Peter Carroll (ed.), *Facing Fascism: New York and the Spanish Civil War* (New York, 2007), 72–82; Michael Petrou, *Renegades: Canadians in the Spanish Civil War* (Vancouver, 2008), 25–7.

5. Baxell, *British Volunteers*, 8–24. Other useful points of statistical comparison are Rémi Skoutelsky, 'L'engagement des volontaires français en Espagne républicaine', *Le Mouvement Social* 181 (1997), 7–29; Michael Uhl, *Mythos Spanien: Das Erbe der Internationalen Brigaden in der* DDR (Bonn 2004), 53–65; Petrou, *Renegades*, 10–25.

6. Owing to this fragmentary source base, it was not considered appropriate to embark on complex statistical analyses. Another approach was taken by Ariel Mae Lambe, by sampling a single source base – Comintern personnel files – and comparing it with the 1931 Cuban census. Whilst nominally allowing for more complex statistical analyses, this was not considered to offer sufficient analytical insight to justify the limitations in scope, nor were the Comintern files considered to be internally consistent samples. Ariel Mae Lambe, *Cuban Antifascism and the Spanish Civil War: Transnational Activism, Networks, and Solidarity in the 1930s* (PhD Thesis: Columbia University, 2014), 73–158.

7. Buchanan, *Britain and the Spanish Civil War*, 126; MacDougall, *Voices from the Spanish Civil War*, 3.

8. Baxell, *British Volunteers*, 159n. See also Gray, *Homage*, 1.

9. Baxell, *British Volunteers*, 159n–160n.

10. Antonio Celada and Daniel Pastor Garcia, *Los brigadistas de habla inglesa y la Guerra Civil Española* (Madrid, 2002).

11. George Shaw himself made it clear that aside from service during the First World War, he had never previously lived outside Glasgow. See 'Autobiography of George Shaw', 25 April 1937, RGASPI, 545/6/199/26.

12. Fullarton in MacDougall, *Voices from the Spanish Civil War*, 290.

13. '7.4.38–14.4.38', RGASPI, 545/6/91/169.

14. 'Arrivals during and before Dec 1936' and 'Arrived prior to 10.1.37' RGASPI, 545/6/91/57, 82; 'MCGUIRE, Robert' and 'CASEY Francis', TNA, KV 5/119, 127.

15. For the British figures, see Baxell, *British Volunteers*, 16. The American data come from a 1937 roster, which is problematic in light of changing age patterns

over time. Peter Carroll, *The Odyssey of the Abraham Lincoln Brigade: Americans in the Spanish Civil War* (Stanford, 1994), 15–16. French data is from Skoutelsky, 'L'engagement des volontaires français', 11.

16. Baxell, *British Volunteers*, 16–18.
17. Tom Wintringham, *English Captain* (London, 1939), 115. The increasingly weary attitude towards older volunteers was evident in Matthew Murphy's rejection in February 1938: '43 years old. He would not be sent to the line because of his age, and there is no room for him in the rear. Sent home', 'MURPHY, Matthew', RGASPI, 545/6/176/33.
18. For example, Kerrigan to Pollitt, 6 February 1937, MML, Box C, File 10.
19. Paynter to Pollitt, 9 June 1937, MML, Box C, File 13; 'Observations', 22 December 1937, RGASPI, 545/6/87/39–40.
20. Dunlop and Drever in MacDougall, *Voices from the Spanish Civil War*, 117, 277–8.
21. 'BURNS, Timothy', TNA KV 5/118; 'Transport of 2-4-37', RGASPI, 545/6/91/100. For journalists, see for example 'John Paterson: Signed statement', January 28 1937, RGASPI, 545/6/183/79–81.
22. British figures from Baxell, *British Volunteers*, 22.
23. Some of this difference can be explained by differences in sector size between Scotland and the rest of Britain, A. K. Cairncross, *The Scottish Economy* (Cambridge, 1954), 41. However, the number of Scottish volunteers working in non-manual categories was still small compared to Scotland as a whole. Census of Scotland, 1931. Vol. III Occupations and industries (1934), xiv.
24. Francis, *Miners*, 95; Stradling, *Wales*, 104.
25. Mates discusses these differences in the context of South Wales and Durham. Mates, 'Durham and South Wales', 375–86.
26. Baxell, *British Volunteers*, 23–4, 30. See also Wintringham, *English Captain*, 330; K. Watkins, *Britain Divided: The Effect of the Spanish Civil War on British Political Opinion* (London, 1963), 283–99.
27. 'Information Material Concerning Party Organisation and Cadres', 17 December 1936, RGASPI, 495/14/215/29–32. See also Knox, *Industrial Nation*, 189–95.
28. 'Report on some main tactical, organisational and cadre problems confronting the CPGB', December 1937, RGASPI, 495/20/91/35.
29. 'Report on Scottish District', 3 June 1938, RGASPI, 495/14/260/56.
30. 'Membership Report', April 1937, RGASPI, 495/14/239/197; 'Report on some main tactical, organisational and cadre problems', December 1937, RGASPI.
31. Baxell, *British Volunteers*, 42–3; Mates, *Spanish Civil War*, 210; Gray, *Homage*, 25–6.
32. For example, Roberts, *'Freedom, Faction, Fame and Blood'*, 202.
33. Whilst Knox is justified in characterising the unemployed as 'fatalistic rather than radical', this overlooks the impact that even a small minority of the vast number of unemployed could have on what was a very small communist movement. Knox, *Industrial Nation*, 13.

34. Donald Renton, for instance, was secretary and organiser of the Edinburgh NUWM, leading its contingent in the 1936 Hunger March. He was made Company Commissar on arrival in Spain. Renton in MacDougall, *Voices from the Spanish Civil War*, 20–1; 'RENTON, Donald', TNA, KV 5/130.

35. MacDougall, *Voices from the Hunger Marches*, 6.

36. Lochore in MacDougall, *Voices from the Hunger Marches*, 320.

37. Baxell, *British Volunteers*, 22; Hopkins, *Heart of the Fire*, 155.

38. A survey of 1225 American volunteers in Spain showed at least 290 coming from these backgrounds. 'Professions', RGASPI, 545/3/455/148–52.

39. Drever in MacDougall, *Voices from the Spanish Civil War*, 277.

40. Baxell, *British Volunteers*, 48–9.

41. 'Report on the political development of the XVth International Brigade' and 'Report on the work of the North Americans the XV Brigade', 1938, RGASPI, 545/6/21/21–2,61–2.

42. Petrou, *Renegades*, 110–11.

43. Baxell, *British Volunteers*, 13. Only two Scots had OTC experience: John Ross of Edinburgh, an insurance clerk, and John Dunlop, a trainee accountant. Ross died soon after arriving in Spain, so it is unknown how this experience was regarded. Dunlop was selected for officer training in Spain and finished the conflict as a sergeant, although his training results indicated he '[could] become company commander'. 'List of arrivals', RGASPI, 545/6/91/139; Dunlop in MacDougall, *Voices from the Spanish Civil War*, 118; 'Escuela Officiales: Dunlop, John', RGASPI, 545/6/126/77.

44. Jorge Marco and Maria Thomas, '"Mucho malo for fascisti": Languages and Transnational Soldiers in the Spanish Civil War', *War & Society* 38:2 (2019), 139–61.

45. 'Liste de camarades anglais parlant plusieurs langues', 16 January 1938, RGASPI, 545/6/89/12–13.

46. 'The Anglo-American Section of the Officer's Training School', 16 November 1937, RGASPI, 545/2/263/144.

47. 'Recommendations for promotion of graduates of the Officer's Training School', 16 January 1938, RGASPI, 545/2/264/20.

48. Baxell, *British Volunteers*, 18.

49. This claim was made by Marcovitch, whose ties to both the Communist Party and the Gorbals Jewish community put him in a position to know. There are several other volunteers, such as David Grossart or Martin Messer, whose names may have had Jewish origins but whose background remains unclear. Alec Marcovitch, TLS, MS, Tape 182.

50. Baxell, *British Volunteers*, 18, 159n. A lower estimate is found in Watkins, *Britain Divided*, 168. Bill Alexander gave the figure as 180–200, based on 'Jewish sounding names', Alexander, *British Volunteers*, 33.

51. On 'Blackshirts' in Glasgow, James Maley, IWMSA, Tape 11947/1. For comparisons, Elaine Smith, 'But What Did They Do? Contemporary Jewish

Responses to Cable Street' and Neil Barrett, 'The Threat of the British Union of Fascists in Manchester' in Tony Kushner and Nadia Valman (eds.), *Remembering Cable Street: Fascism and Anti-Fascism in British Society* (London, 2000), 48–54, 56–70.

52. Little research touches on Jewish involvement in the CPGB in Scotland. Jason Heppell notes significant Party activity in 'Jewish areas' of Glasgow, but does not explore concrete connections, which is problematic as these areas, such as the Gorbals, were never exclusively Jewish enclaves. Jason Heppell, 'A Rebel, not a Rabbi: Jewish Membership of the Communist Party of Great Britain', *Twentieth Century British History* 15:1 (2004), 34.

53. Murray to Dott, 4 August 1937, NLS, David Murray Papers, Box 2, File 6.

54. Chris Smith, IWMSA, Tape 12290/2.

55. For example, William McDade, born in 'Ireland' but living and politically active in Dundee prior to Spain. Arnott, *Dundee*, 13. Several others can have their Irish heritage traced in the 1911 census, e.g. Robert Ball in 1911 Census of Scotland, Registration District Anderston, Enumeration District 22, Page 17, Household 109, Lines 2–11.

56. Cassidy's Catholicism was the theme of a brief eulogy in the *Daily Worker*, 25 March 1937, 3.

57. See Burns in MacDougall, *Voices from the Hunger Marches*, 157.

58. Kerrigan to Pollitt, 6 February 1937, MML, Box C, File 10.

59. [Antonio Vallejo Nágera], 'Psiquisismo del Fanatismo Marxista: Internacionales ingleses', *Semana Médica Española* (*SME*) 27 (September 1939), 308–12. On the wider context of these experiments, see Michael Richards, 'Morality and Biology in the Spanish Civil War: Psychiatrists, Revolution and Women Prisoners in Málaga', *Contemporary European History* 10:3 (2001), 395–421.

60. 'Psiquisismo del Fanatismo Marxista: Internacionales ingleses', 310–11.

61. 'Psiquisismo del Fanatismo Marxista: Internacionales ingleses', 310.

62. 'Psiquisismo del Fanatismo Marxista: Internacionales ingleses', 310–12. See also [Antonio Vallejo Nágera], 'Psiquisismo del Fanatismo Marxista: Investigaciones biopsiquicas en prisoneros internacionales [North American]', *SME* 22 (January 1939), 108–12; [Antonio Vallejo Nágera], 'Psiquisismo del Fanatismo Marxista: Investigaciones biopsiquicas en prisoneros internacionales [Portuguese]', *SME* 34 (1939), 522–4.

63. Baxell, *British Volunteers*, 19.

64. Baxell, *British Volunteers*, 19.

65. Watters in MacDougall, *Voices from the Spanish Civil War*, 34.

66. Chris Cook, *The Age of Alignment: Electoral Politics in Britain* (London, 1975), 82–7; Smyth, *Labour in Glasgow*, 30–1; Hughes, *Gender and Political Identities*, 70–2.

67. *Glasgow Herald*, 6 May 1938, 14.

68. See 'EDDIE George' and 'BUCHAN James' in TNA KV 5/118,121.

69. Baxell, *British Volunteers*, 14.

70. For example, Thomas, *Spanish Civil War*, 455; Baxell, *British Volunteers*, 14–15.
71. Baxell, *British Volunteers*, 15.
72. These affiliations were not mutually exclusive. Some had simultaneous membership of different groups.
73. CC Meeting, 24 June 1939, RGASPI, 495/14/265/142
74. CC Meeting, 24 June 1939, RGASPI.
75. Gray claimed that a fifth of volunteers were Labour or ILP members, and that up to 100 Scottish ILP members fought in Spain. The basis for the first claim is unknown but is unsupported by the findings here. The second appears to be based on reports of 100 ILP fighters being recruited to join the small contingent fighting with the POUM. There is no evidence that this group departed Britain. Gray, *Homage*, 35, 142; *Glasgow Herald*, 12 January 1937, 9.
76. 'Left Book Club', CPGB Scottish District Congress, 4–5 September 1937, RGASPI, 495/14/263/9.
77. Whether or not this evaluation was heavily cut down by unsympathetic editors is sadly unclear in the archive. 'GRIERSON, Robert' in RGASPI, 545/6/143/1–4.
78. 'From the 17th to the 18th Congress of the Communist Party of the Soviet Union', 3 November 1939, RGASPI, 495/14/265/207.
79. In a Spanish context, see Tim Rees, 'Living Up to Lenin: Leadership Culture and the Spanish Communist Party, 1920–1939', *History* 97:326 (2012), 230–55. On Britain, Worley, *Class against Class*.
80. Baxell, *Unlikely Warriors*, 351.
81. Andrew Thorpe, 'The Membership of the Communist Party of Great Britain, 1920–1945', *The Historical Journal* 43:3 (2000), 793–5.
82. For December 1936 figures, see 'Report on basic measures for the growth of the CPGB', 3 December 1936, RGASPI, 495/14/215/21. For 1939, see 'Party membership', January 1940, RGASPI, 495/14/265/24. Total membership was 11,500 and 16,000 in December 1936 and May 1938 respectively.
83. Variation and retention difficulties are discussed in Thorpe, 'Membership of the Communist Party', 795–9.
84. 'Party membership', January 1940. Whilst there was a degree of pragmatic flexibility, the Party did occasionally crack down on those who failed to pay their dues. For example, Vale of Leven circular, January [1936?], RGASPI, 495/14/194/48; CC Meeting 3–4 December 1937, RGASPI, 495/14/259/86.
85. On the variable nature of membership and its meanings, see Morgan, Cohen and Flinn, *Communists and British Society*, 13–18.
86. XIV Party Congress, 28 June 1937, RGASPI, 495/14/227/4; Baxell, *British Volunteers*, 19, 160n.
87. 'Party Growth in Glasgow', Scottish District Congress, 4–5 September 1937, RGASPI.
88. Worley, *Class against Class*, 163–5.

89. Noreen Branson, *History of the Communist Party of Great Britain, 1927–1941* (London, 1985), 183; Alan Campbell, *The Scottish Miners, 1874–1939, Volume Two* (Aldershot, 2000), 387–8; 'Fife District', September [1936?], RGASPI, 494/14/190/56.

90. Macintyre, *Little Moscows*, 79–107.

91. 'Scottish Report', Scottish District Congress, 4–5 September 1937, RGASPI, 495/14/263/6.

92. For example, Brailsford to Citrine, 22 February 1937, *Trabajadores Collection*, University of Warwick (TC), 292/946/34/192i-193xii.

93. Buchanan, *British Labour Movement*, 12, 34–5.

94. 'Party Growth in Glasgow', Scottish District Congress 4–5 September 1937, RGASPI, 495/14/263/19.

95. 'Report on Scottish District', 3 June 1938, RGASPI, 495/14/260/59.

96. 'Scottish Report', Scottish District Congress 4–5 September 1937, RGASPI, 495/14/263/6.

97. 'Report on Scottish District', 3 June 1938, RGASPI, 495/14/260/56.

98. The view of the International Brigades as embodying an ideologically diverse united front remains a live trope in both popular and scholarly writing, e.g. Paul Corthorn, 'Cold War Politics and the Contested Legacy of the Spanish Civil War, *European History Quarterly* 44:4 (2014), 691–2. See also Gray, *Homage*, 35; Baxell, *British Volunteers*, 15.

3

Thinking and Acting

The specific decision to fight in the Spanish Civil War has long fascinated historians, and with good reason. The foreign volunteers' motives appear distinct from the usual pressures to take up arms – the International Brigades were not defending their homes and families, they did not stand to gain financially nor did they owe Republican Spain any personal loyalty. Eighty years later, it seems almost completely irrational, harkening back to a noble, almost chivalric ideal of risking one's life for the sake of purely held beliefs. It is these beliefs, therefore, which have dominated scholarly discussion of their decisions to volunteer.[1] Even accounts that suggest other, less flattering motivations, such as adventure, profit or unemployment, still acknowledge the importance of political belief.[2] This is understandable – more than anything else, the volunteers were defined by their collective belief in the need to combat the rise of European fascism, and choosing to act on this belief offers a seemingly straightforward explanation of why they went to Spain.

Yet as much as anti-fascism was a unifying cause for the majority of International Brigaders, this explanation of their motives has limitations. For one, it leaves aside the important question of what they were fighting for – opposing fascism is one thing, but anti-fascism was not a singular, unitary ideology, and adherents did not agree on the best way to oppose fascism, let alone what sort of society should be built instead. As Tom Buchanan has noted, 'it is easier to define what the volunteers were fighting against than what they were fighting for', reflecting in turn a growing historical consensus that, instead of a monolithic movement, there were 'multiple meanings of anti-fascism as a concept'.[3] Whilst opposing fascism in the late 1930s was an understandable, laudable goal in itself, it is hard to accept the conclusion that this was all there was to it. Fighting in Spain was not a fundamentally conservative act – preserving the status quo seems too small an ambition to be the basis of such a radical decision.

This observation is at the heart of a new wave of scholarship that seeks to understand volunteers' decisions on a much more personal basis. These approaches have been pioneered by historians such as Nir Arielli, Enrico Acciai and Helen Graham, who seek to portray the decision as the function of complex personal motivations and contexts, of which ideology is but one facet.[4] These contributions have been fruitful, not least by opening up discussion on neglected dimensions such as recruitment networks, but also in providing a better sense of the particular draw of Spain in the context of the late 1930s, and how it could have such a profound appeal to so many.[5] Ideology has not been entirely displaced in importance, but rather placed within the context of individuals' life trajectories.

Yet this turn to transnational biography, and towards appreciating the nuances of personal motivation, does not resolve all the problems of earlier approaches. In particular, by focusing on the intricacies of individual decisions, it becomes very difficult to talk about questions of scale – that is, not just why did people volunteer, but why did so many? This was an implicit issue with earlier scholarship as well, but from the other direction – far more than 520 Scots opposed fascism by 1936, so why did only a specific minority go to Spain? More broadly, strong ideological principles were hardly unique to the late 1930s, so why was the Spanish Civil War so especially attractive for foreign fighters in a way that conflicts before or since have not been? In other words, to understand volunteers' motivations, we need to balance acknowledging the myriad and diverse sets of individual beliefs and circumstances with trying to advance some kind of collective explanation of the broader phenomenon.

This task can be achieved only by revisiting a fundamental assumption about who the International Brigade volunteers were and what they believed. Building on the observations of the previous chapter, an answer begins to suggest itself: that rather than being representatives of Scotland as a whole, or even Scottish anti-fascists, the Scottish International Brigade volunteers were in fact a relatively homogeneous grouping who were recruited from very limited socio-political circles.[6] The answer then is that the specific decision to join the International Brigades was for the most part attractive and practical only to a very particular, limited audience – and recruitment was highly successful within this sphere. Yet equally, these particular circles were objectively small in Scotland – the answer to why there were not more than 520 volunteers is that the call to arms struggled to reach beyond its core audience. Volunteering, in this view, did not taper off as the conflict went on because sympathies receded – the growing success of Scottish Aid Spain movements in 1938 explored in later chapters indicates the opposite – but rather because the pool of potential recruits was largely exhausted by mid-1937.

Aside from addressing the crucial question of scale, at least in the Scottish context, this argument has some profound implications for understanding the decision to volunteer itself. Namely, if recruitment was this concentrated in a particular socio-political sphere, then individualised explanations of volunteering cannot be sufficient, because their decisions cannot have been isolated. Going to Spain, in other words, was a prospect to be considered not introspectively, but alongside friends, family and colleagues. The Scots who volunteered did so among those who were responding to the Spanish Civil War in similar ways, and indeed were often pondering the same choice of whether to go to Spain. Recruitment for the International Brigades, in other words, had an important yet hitherto neglected social context. Not only does this enable collective analysis of the decision to volunteer, it also offers an explanation of why Scotland proved so effective a recruiting ground for the International Brigades compared to elsewhere in Britain.

This chapter also reflects a tension between the competing perspectives of transnationalism and localism. The recruitment model proposed here – in contrast to the work of scholars such as Helen Graham – is local as well as transnational, pointing to volunteers' immediate social contexts as being key to explaining their decisions. In Scotland, this means understanding local communities, but this clearly not need be true in all contexts – exiles and migrants were more than capable of constructing and maintaining their own forms of community. Yet even in Scotland, locality does not suffice to explain the phenomenon – even those who had never previously left home were participants in a transnational exchange of ideas, cultures and values.[7] Their reaction to the Spanish Civil War was inevitably shaped by this intellectual context – in particular, in their desire to emulate an imagined, idealised Bolshevik activist, a mythical figure cultivated by the CPGB and Communist International alike.

Anti-fascism

International Brigade volunteers' ideological views have already received substantial historical attention, with most scholarship agreeing that the volunteers desired to oppose fascism at home and abroad. In a British context, Richard Baxell has demonstrated that the vast majority of volunteers were anti-fascists, and describes the various ways that they had become anti-fascists over the 1920s and 1930s.[8] Yet the 'anti-fascist' label serves to conceal a great deal of ambiguity. Communist Party opposition to fascism cannot be seen as inherently conservative – communism hardly embraced pluralistic parliamentary democracy as either the means or the end of its struggle.[9] Yet even within the Communist Party, shifts in doctrine – notably towards the 'Popular Front' – meant that different generations of Party members might have different ideas about what fighting under an anti-fascist banner actually meant.[10] Moreover, this formulation allows little space for positive intent in going to Spain, with Baxell forced to conclude that the variety of volunteers' beliefs beyond hating fascism makes further analysis impossible.[11]

However, there are indications that Spain was attractive not just as a place to oppose fascism but also where volunteers could potentially realise their own vision of a socialist and democratic society. Fearghal McGarry used revolutionary statements made prior to the Spanish Civil War to complicate communist assertions that they were merely defending democracy in Spain.[12] Whilst suggestive, such evidence does not necessarily prove that volunteers left with revolutionary intent, as it remains plausible that their understanding had genuinely changed along with the context. Although oral histories avoid these problems, their use in this context has other issues. Most Scottish volunteers' testimony follows the 'recovery' mould of oral history, in which the primary goal is to preserve voices that might otherwise escape the historical record rather than engage critically and actively with the narrative being told.[13] Respondents were given free rein to tell their stories as they wished, and so tended to emphasise narratives that portrayed their service in the most favourable light possible. As such, it is unsurprising that the motivations that resonated best in a postwar climate – such as the defence of democracy and the prevention of the Second World War – are most common.[14] When volunteers were questioned more closely, such as Garry McCartney being asked whether he thought volunteers expected to stay in Spain after a Republican victory, responses soon veered into different territory.

> I'm quite sure that a number of people possibly had that in mind, you know, because those people who did not have family ties for example, would no doubt have these ideas in mind in some respects and why not? After all they were fighting for a cause and if successful, they would want to share in the joys of reconstructing what had been destroyed.[15]

Moreover, testimony naturally avoids topics that were either painful or shameful. In one case, Eddie Brown's testimony does not mention his wife once, although his friends considered that their deteriorating relationship 'may to a certain extent have accounted for his decision to go to Spain'. Any pre-existing difficulties were compounded when his wife eloped to London after falling pregnant with a fellow Perth communist during his absence in Spain.[16] Clearly, his silence reflected not its irrelevance but rather an understandable desire to avoid a painful issue.

Even aside from questions of emphasis and focus, the meanings of volunteers' ideological touchstones have shifted over time. In particular, a contemporary audience brings its own assumptions about 'democracy' that do not necessarily translate to this era. This is taken up by Tom Buchanan, who questioned 'what kind of democracy anti-fascists were seeking to defend' and 'what type of democracy they were trying to create'.[17] According to Buchanan, for Party leaders and theorists the Soviet Union represented 'true democracy', meaning that 'defence of democracy' entailed substantial and necessary changes to liberal parliamentary systems.[18] A similar thread can be detected in oral testimony. Many linked their politicisation to their experiences of British capitalism during the interwar slump. For David Anderson, it was experiencing unemployment that convinced him 'that there was something wrong with the system'; for George Watters, the reaction of the police and government to the miners' strike of 1921 did the same.[19] Hugh Sloan was more explicit in questioning whether France and Britain 'had been truly democratic governments'. For Sloan, the Soviet Union and by extension the Spanish Republic represented an ideal truer to his own vision of democracy, precisely because they opposed capitalism.[20] Similar perspectives are evident in contemporary sources. In one survey, Party members were asked to identify their formative political influences. By far the most common responses were explicit or implicit critiques of British capitalism: working conditions, strikes, unemployment and social problems.[21] Yet these surveys were rarely a space in which volunteers explicitly tied their beliefs to their motivations in coming to Spain, and in oral testimony such discussion is secondary to more appealing narratives about preserving democracy and peace. Neither provides straightforward insight into what the volunteers were fighting for.

There is however a neglected source base that sheds some light on the volunteers' collective beliefs and intentions in Spain – their music. Although there has been longstanding interest in volunteers' literary output, their more lyrical compositions have rarely received much attention.[22] Yet particularly in an age before mass visual media, the collective performance of and participation in singing served an important role in establishing and re-affirming group identity, alongside many other purposes.[23] Songs are by their very nature performative, allowing the collective expression and celebration of identity, reinforcing communal understandings in a natural and often enjoyable manner.[24] Volunteers' own compositions were often dense with meaning, with amateur songwriters crafting their own lyrics to existing tunes. Moreover, by choosing whether to participate and help make a song popular, or by subverting a song's intended meaning through parody or appropriation, singing offered a degree of individual and group agency in determining the volunteers' collective self-image.[25] In this way, songs offer untapped insight into how the volunteers perceived the purpose of their fight in Spain, and the deeper meanings of their collective anti-fascism.

Moreover, songs and singing were essential to the experience of serving in the International Brigades.[26] Many written records dealing with their music have survived, including several songbooks published by the International Brigades during the conflict.[27] The act of publication itself indicates the degree of significance attached to these songs. The importance of songbooks could transcend the Brigades themselves: one such songbook was the subject of an official request from the German Condor Legion, who asked Nationalist spies to secure them a copy in Madrid.[28] Interestingly, their contact claimed that copies were not for sale, having been printed only for internal distribution in the International Brigades.[29] If true, this is further indication of the songbooks' importance specifically for the volunteers themselves, an act of inward self-definition rather than externally directed propaganda. Even unpublished songs were treated with some respect: many were written down and found their way into trench newspapers, others were specifically collected by the International Brigade administrators and preserved in their archives.[30]

The obsession with songs was not merely an administrative peculiarity. Omnipresent singing litters volunteers' recollections of Spain – 'any time you went on the march, you didn't go without singing'.[31] Singing helped overcome language and national differences, a perennial concern in the International Brigades.[32] For many volunteers, their first efforts at communication came on their arrival to Spain at the old fortress of Figueras, where each group used songs to proclaim its national and political identities.[33] This pattern repeated whenever different linguistic groups came together, such as Burns Night in January 1937, featuring 'Scottish, Irish and French songs' alongside 'two Dutchmen yodelling and playing concertinas'.[34] One song in particular lent itself to overcoming these linguistic barriers: *The Internationale*. The communist anthem had official lyrics in many different languages, but used the same tune the world over, allowing everyone to sing their own version together. When John Dunlop crossed the frontier, he remembered each nationality singing their own songs until

> At last, somebody started up singing *The Internationale*, which of course we all knew, and we joined in. I find it extremely difficult to explain the feelings that swept through me when this singing of *The Internationale* started up. Here we were, all young men from really all the nations in Europe, and some from outside Europe as well, joining in this one song in their own language.[35]

The Internationale soon became the defining song of the International Brigades, with their official songbook giving it pride of place, publishing the lyrics in eleven different languages.[36] Yet the political implications were not lost on singers and audiences alike. Dunlop recalled the reaction of some Spanish anarchists in their ranks to its ubiquity.

> They said, 'Why do we have to sing *The Internationale?* After all *The Internationale* is not a Spanish song. It is not the Anarchist song. It is the international Communist song . . .' The short simple answer to that was, 'Well, we're in the International Brigade and it happens to be one of the songs of the International Brigade . . . Apart from that we consider that it's the song of the international working class all over the world.' But I don't think they were very well convinced about that.[37]

In this light, the International Brigades' adoption of *The Internationale* was one of the many practical and cultural expressions tying the volunteers to both communism and the Soviet Union.[38] It was a useful shibboleth for the anti-fascist fighters, allowing each national group to understand itself as fighting the same struggle, using a common signifier of political intent that transcended language. Yet while *The Internationale* presents a positive vision of the dissolution of differences and uniting to achieve common goals, it is still about revolutionary societal change. If *The Internationale* represented what the International Brigades were fighting for, it is clear that International Brigade volunteers did not expect postwar Spain to resemble British parliamentary democracy.

The Internationale was not alone in promoting a particular vision of democratic Spain. Other published songs included *Comrades, March Shoulder to Shoulder* ('Militant, strong and defiant / Workers will conquer the world /

And the red banner in triumph / Will be forever unfurled'), *Red-Front* ('In the face of our class enemy / We ask no quarter, they shall not turn us back / We're standing ready for the final attack / On our enemy the bourgeoisie') and many others with similar themes.[39] However, aside from *The Internationale* it is unclear whether these songs, many of which predated the Spanish struggle, found especial resonance among rank-and-file volunteers. Better evidence comes from the songs that the volunteers wrote for themselves. The archives of trench newspapers are filled with poetry and songs written by volunteers attempting to express the emotions engendered by their service in Spain. Not all were overtly political. The most famous, *There's a Valley in Spain Called Jarama*, written by the Glaswegian volunteer Alex McDade in mid-1937, draws instead on pride in loss and adversity, though the original version contained satirical elements that were quietly dropped from the 'official' lyrics.[40] Perhaps in part because it avoids overt political statements, it was widely adopted by the English-speaking volunteers, and has had a long life as a folk song commemorating the British and North American volunteers to this day.[41]

However, many other songs composed by the volunteers did draw on political themes. *No Pasaran* linked their struggle to the Russian Revolution ('Twenty long years into history have passed / Since red revolt was victorious last') and projected the Soviet Union as the model for Spain and the world ('Great beacon lights that in Russia were bright').[42] Another, *Ours Alone*, makes it clear that postwar Spain was being envisaged in very specific ways:

> Let victory, when it comes, be ours alone
> And jealously this triumph we shall hold
> Lest others try to snatch it from our grasp
>
> This war-torn Spain is ours to gain and keep
> That on that day when shall reign supreme
> We bend our backs to build our land anew
> And those who toil shall own the things they make.[43]

Similar themes are evoked by another work simply titled *International Brigade*, which depicted the volunteers, including 'Scots from Glasgow slums', uniting to 'hammer the world into shape'.[44] These are typical of a genre of volunteers' compositions that went well beyond the official line that this war was in defence of the status quo. It was natural, perhaps inevitable, that the volunteers envisaged the society they fought for, and that this society best resembled an idealised Soviet model.

This is not to say that volunteers' claims to be defending democracy were cynical. Rather, their belief that the Soviet Union represented a genuinely democratic model should be taken at face value. The communist critique of capitalism was rarely so powerful as during the interwar slump, while the Soviet Union retained mystique and moral standing as the world's first socialist state. That the volunteers believed in this ideal and fought for it should not be taken as evidence that they were 'dupes of Moscow' or fighting to establish a similar dictatorship to those later seen in Eastern Europe.[45] That the Soviet Union failed to live up to its ideals does not invalidate the desire of individuals to fight for them, just as the failures of British democracy in the 1930s and before does not invalidate the choice to fight in 1939. Yet equally, it is important to contextualise the assertions of volunteers like Garry McCartney who claimed that they went to Spain to fight only for 'the freedom of a people to put a cross on a ballot paper', not to 'usher in socialism or communism'.[46] The vision of democracy they fought for was often considerably more complex than this.

Instead, the ideological attraction of fighting in Spain should be understood in terms of both oppositional and positive factors. In resisting a 'fascist' takeover, Spain's struggle took on a mythic allure for activists more used to defeats and setbacks. Importantly, the nature of anti-fascism itself facilitated understanding Spain as a flashpoint in a worldwide conflict. Communism and anti-fascism were inherently internationalist, encouraging adherents to view their struggles as interconnected with those taking place elsewhere. For Scottish volunteers, it was easy to understand Spain within their own frame of reference: just as confronting the BUF at home reflected a wider international struggle, so too was Spain already part of the same fight before they left. For volunteers such as John Lochore, this way of thinking was second nature.

> I made a speech at a mass unemployed meeting . . . I got quite a severe telling off afterwards . . . [as] it was purely a demonstration against the [Unemployment Assistance Board] and here I was talking about recruiting for the International column in Spain. The two issues, for me, were connected.[47]

In the few parts of Scotland that saw active fascist campaigns, this connection was even more apparent.[48] According to the anti-BUF activist John Londragan, the fight, 'whether it be here in Aberdeen against the British Union of Fascists' or 'against Hitler and Mussolini in Spain, was exactly the same fight to me, no difference at all'.[49] For volunteers like Lochore and Londragan, there was no need to distinguish between the cause at home and the fight in Spain. This seamless integration mattered – the more that the decision to go to Spain appeared as a natural extension of individuals' activism, the prospect was less likely to seem impractical or unappealing.

Yet no matter how far volunteers could reconcile volunteering with their previous activism, going to Spain still represented an escalation of those activities. This too was a vital part of the appeal: Spain was a place where individuals might make a positive difference in a way that seemed impossible elsewhere. Unlike in Britain and Scotland, here the enemy was out in the open, not hiding behind institutions, law and tradition, and thus could be dealt with decisively. Moreover, only in Spain did the struggle against fascism appear to be delicately poised – not only was there the prospect of victory, but it also seemed plausible that their personal interventions might tip the balance. Nir Arielli has described the decision to volunteer as a 'search for meaning', yet 'search for agency' appears more apt in this case. The positive stakes at hand also mattered. For those whose anti-fascism was based on socialist beliefs, as for most volunteers, radical change appeared not just possible but already under way, and the chance to realise these aspirations beyond anything possible at home was a key part of Spain's attraction. This could be especially true for those whose work in Britain was stagnating. Some CPGB branches seen by the Party as 'weak' saw especially high rates of volunteering. Greenock and Rutherglen, both singled out as branches in decline, saw a third and half of male members volunteer respectively.[50] Such patterns echo Fearghal McGarry's observation that Irish communists' poor progress at home encouraged them to go to Spain, where their efforts might bear more immediate fruit.[51] Only in Spain did victory – both against fascism and for the society they dreamed of – seem possible.

It is in this context that the aspirational songs of the International Brigade need to be understood. It is the expression of the hopeful, positive vision of Spain that was an important part of the conflict's attraction. This should not be seen as the culmination of a Soviet plot to export communism. Rather, Party leaders worried that articulating such desires could provoke division and controversy, and actually worked to dilute and restrict volunteers' spontaneous efforts to envisage a new Spain. Lochore, despite being chastised for subverting the leadership's pragmatic approach at home, evidently learned this lesson eventually.

There was still quite a lot of confusion in our ranks as to the role of the Brigade and the nature of the struggle taking place. Confusion arose from the failure to recognise the difference between a Socialist Red Army establishing workers' power and a Republican Army fighting against fascism.[52]

While, judging from later testimony, many volunteers accepted this line by the time they left Spain, their initial 'confusion' is still important. Spain was attractive not just as a place to confront fascism but as a space in which a new society seemed possible – a sentiment that many International Brigade volunteers continued to express throughout their time in Spain. Whilst the International Brigades were not intended as a Stalinist plot to overthrow the Republic and turn Spain into a Soviet satellite, and the aims of Soviet intervention were considerably more modest, it does not follow that the volunteers themselves shared such a clinical view of their role.[53] Rather, as their self-expression through song often indicated, their emotional investment in being part of positive change should be appreciated as an essential aspect of their motivation to enlist.

Networks, Party and Community

It was no coincidence that the Communist Party, in Scotland and across the world, could call on so many people who saw Spain as an opportunity for action. Interwar communist movements actively inculcated such values, and sought out – and were sought out by in turn – those who were eager to take action as the vanguard of the proletariat. It has been observed across contexts that volunteers in Spain, and other contexts, often had a limited theoretical grasp of the ideology they were nominally fighting for. This was at times especially true of the Scottish and British volunteers, particularly those from working-class backgrounds – the Dundonian David Menzies, for instance, was noted to share 'the usual British characteristic of indifference to theory'.[54] Steve Fullarton provided a pithy label: his political beliefs were 'more instinctive than theoretical or dogmatic'.[55] Volunteers such as Fullarton may have had little time for the finer points of Marxist theory and other 'Party bullshit', but this should not lead us to dismiss the sincerity and depth of their 'instinctive' political beliefs.[56]

Above all, theory was not necessary to grasp communist values and ideals. Rather, these beliefs were developed through socialisation and action – learned as part of their upbringing, through experiences of solidarity on picket lines and through the constant, ceaseless activism and proselytising that was an integral part of the interwar communist lifestyle. Representations and discussions of communist ideals guided not only their political response to events both close and far from home but also who adherents should strive to become. Here, they were participants in an international discussion of what it meant to be a true Bolshevik, a discussion led from the headquarters of the Comintern in Moscow, but hardly a monolithic, one-way imposition. Attributes such as political and personal discipline, loyalty, industriousness and decisiveness were highly valued traits in those who hoped to lead the revolution some day.

Perhaps above all, the ideal Bolshevik was willing to sacrifice for a common cause. In the words of the Glasgow-Irish volunteer Sydney Quinn, having preached the need to confront fascism in the years prior to Spain, now 'you've got to put your life where your mouth was'.[57] Maintaining a communist identity in this context also became bound up with more local identities, perhaps most pervasively a masculine, 'hard man' self-image rooted in Scottish working-class identity, which required standing by one's friends, particularly in a fight.[58] The gendered nature of the call to arms is reflected by the absence of Scotswomen in the International Brigades. Only one, Annie Murray, joined the International Brigades themselves, serving as a nurse in the British medical section. Although many Scotswomen shared Murray's sense of solidarity with the Spanish Republic, there was not the same expectation that women's sympathies were best expressed by participating in the struggle directly, though many women did find other avenues to contribute to the cause in Scotland and Spain, as discussed in later chapters.

These influences were not, of course, purely local. Prospective volunteers were frequently already participants in a transnational exchange of ideas on what it meant to be a communist, anti-fascist or revolutionary. Aside from formal methods of transmission such as lectures and required reading material, actual and prospective communists were part of a cultural space in which collective values were reinforced through both socialisation and action. First- and second-hand knowledge of the Soviet Union and the idealised new 'Bolshevik man' filtered down from the likes of Peter Kerrigan and Bob Cooney, both graduates of the International Lenin School in Moscow, whilst representations in communist publications, films, activism and mass events all served to help foster a transnational 'sense of identity and shared belonging'.[59] Crucially, this was an inherently communal process, which relied on adherents being active participants in political discussion and action rather than passive recipients of knowledge. Yet existing discussion of the International Brigaders' motivations is still rooted in the assumption that the impetus for their choice must have come from within, neglecting the inherently communal nature of interwar radical politics.

This focus on internalised, introspective ideological belief stems in part from International Brigades' status as 'volunteers'. This usage is omnipresent in both primary and secondary sources, not least because they consistently used the word to describe themselves. Yet though enlistment required a voluntary act, this does not mean that the impetus for making the decision came entirely from within. Creating the social expectation of military service has always been a powerful tool in attracting voluntary recruits. If a society collectively accepts the necessity of fighting, it creates an implicit or explicit expectation that members will help defend the community and its perceived vital interests in this moment of crisis. Such pressure is compounded by success – the choices of friends, family and colleagues acting as a powerful impetus to follow suit. Notably, Britain relied on impetus created by communal appreciations of patriotism and empire to sustain voluntary recruitment in conflicts such as the Boer War and the First World War.[60] Although service on such terms did require a voluntary act, the social context of the decision led to significant external influences. This is not to suggest that they were compelled or 'conscripted' to enlist.[61] The CPGB's limitations lend credence to this – it could in no way emulate the power of a nation state in requiring military service. In Scotland, certainly, no individuals were forced to join the International Brigades.[62] Yet whilst the Communist Party was not able to compel enlistment, it could foster similar social pressure to enlist in certain spaces throughout Scotland.

The Party's ability to do this rested on the extent – suggested in the previous chapter – that prospective volunteers came from the same social circles. While we know little about the pre-Spain lives of many individuals, where relevant evidence does exist, it almost always shows that they already knew one or more other volunteers before leaving for Spain.[63] Hugh Sloan, who was especially forthcoming about his personal relationships, shows how a Communist Party member of middling standing developed connections with future volunteers. From his home in Methil, Sloan knew several local activists who also went to Spain, including his foster-brother George Smith, and fellow CPGB member Malcolm Sneddon.[64] Sloan had also spent time in Dundee in 1933, where he 'acquainted [him]self' with local CPGB members such as Arthur Nicoll, a future political commissar in Spain. These new connections led to his appointment as the Dundee YCL secretary, in which capacity he recruited several future volunteers to the Party, including William McGuire and John Kennedy. His involvement in the NUWM from 1930 also brought him into contact with Hunger Marchers such as Fraser Crombie and Tommy

Bloomfield of Kirkcaldy and Jock Tadden of Dundee.[65] He even met the Scottish District Leader and future CPGB representative in Spain, Peter Kerrigan, when both attended the Fife miners' gala and discovered a mutual appreciation for ocean swimming.[66] In all, Sloan mentioned pre-existing relationships with nine other volunteers over the course of a single interview, including Hunger Marchers, Party members and local colleagues, friends and family.

Whilst Sloan's geographic range of contacts was unusual, it was hardly exceptional – many volunteers had similar histories of activism or internal migration in the 1930s.[67] Even volunteers with less involvement in political activism still often knew each other. Steve Fullarton, who 'wasn't a member of any party at all', convinced his friend William Gauntlett to join him, and knew two neighbours who had gone to Spain.[68] Brothers volunteering together were also relatively common, such as Daniel and George Gillan of Dundee and James and John Miller of Alexandria.[69] Family, local and Party loyalties were often intertwined: Donald Renton and Bill Cranston of Portobello were brothers-in-law as well as members of the same CPGB branch.[70] Whilst Jimmy Maley was the first volunteer in his own circles, he noted that 'quite a few' later 'followed [his] example'.[71] John Dunlop even noted that background checks for aspiring recruits were unnecessary as most 'were already known to each other from their home towns'.[72] Of all the Scottish volunteers, George Murray summarised the resulting atmosphere most succinctly.

> I was active in left-wing politics and of course when the Spanish War started all my mates were of like opinion more or less. A lot of them were going to Spain, you know, and I decided to go too. It was one of the things you did at that particular time.[73]

This situation was hardly spontaneous, but rather reflected the longstanding use of social and personal connections for Party-building purposes. As Thomas Linehan has noted, communism and family and social ties often became intimately intertwined as a result, with certain kinship groups emerging as 'Party families', of which the Murrays, with three siblings in Spain including George quoted above, were a prime example.[74] The process of recruitment described in contemporary sources is often deeply intimate, the product of individual and group relationships, social activity and earnest proselytising. This was a constant, tireless process: a letter from another of the Murray clan, Lily, to her sister Margaret updated her on several such cases.

Ida we are getting more and more into our way of thinking and I think we will soon have her 'one of the fold'. They have had her to YCL meetings and J. Moir has also had his sister, who is progressing favourably![75]

Thanks to such efforts, political spaces connected to the Party emerged in youth and sporting groups such as Clarion Cycling Clubs. Jimmy Crichton recalled that the Musselburgh Clarion Cycling Club branch he helped found underwent a factional split when it started organising Aid Spain activities, with the Catholic and apolitical members leaving and setting up a new club. In Crichton's eyes, political activity was an integral part of the club's purpose and he was more willing to see it split than compromise.[76] This is also reflected in Chris Smith's recollections of his hiking group – it was never 'just hiking', rather 'you always made a point of holding a meeting somewhere, doing something, selling the YCL paper'.[77] While it officially 'wasn't a YCL club', Mary Johnstone remembered her 'Vikings' cycling club as being dominated by the YCL, who 'used to sit and have a lot of political discussions' during outings.[78] Some, such as Marion Henry, attended the local Socialist Sunday School, where communists developed a presence from 1930 onwards.[79] Similarly, John Lochore recalled that the Socialist Sunday School, along with members of his hiking club, proved a ready source of recruits for the Youth contingent of the 1936 Hunger March, in turn a source of recruits for Spain.[80] Mary Johnstone also remembered that

> We were all Esperantists. That was outside the YCL. But on the other hand you could say a lot of them were political. Some of the teachers were also Party members. It was the Esperanto Society that actually ran the classes.[81]

Few of these spaces were absolutely dominated by the Party, as testimony and indeed the momentous split of the Musselburgh Clarion Cycling Club make clear. This was part of their utility – they offered an avenue to expand Party membership and influence. Desperate to increase its numbers, the Party seized on these methods as being the most effective way to recruit and retain members. In a circular directed to Fife branches in March 1936, explicit instructions were given on how to achieve the district quota of 113 new members. The onus was placed on exploiting the personal connections of existing members, as well as the latent sympathies of individuals already under some communist influence, calling for

The mining fractions in East and West Fife and the Rail and Textile fractions in Kirkcaldy to arrange special meetings for the purpose of discussing the Party and its importance to the workers in those industries. *Sympathisers and contacts to be invited with the objective of recruiting them to the Party.*

Specially prepared recruiting meetings organised by branches in each Area. Each branch member to be responsible for bringing *along TU, Co-operative or labour Party contacts; members of Study classes etc, Youth from sport organisations* [original emphasis].[82]

The circular went on to highlight the importance of engaging socially with new recruits:

We draw attention to the importance of *Social activity* by our Branches, which the Secretariat and Area Committees will do everything to encourage. *Also* the *Educational Classes* and *Open branch meetings* on important local issues in the Area, pit and factory [original emphasis].

Social activities have a two-fold value; not only is the work of the Party lightened and its contacts widened, but a source of income is created for assisting in carrying on the general Party activities.[83]

By using such tactics, the Communist Party did more than foster a new generation of revolutionary cadres: it created groups of friends. Yet while the importance of such social and familial interconnections in understanding the recruitment process for Spain has been acknowledged in some individual cases, historians have tended to treat these as isolated examples.[84] Yet the evidence among the Scots, at least, suggests that this was much more the norm than the exception. In other words, most individual decisions to enlist cannot be regarded as isolated or internalised.

This simple observation alters any understanding of the choice to fight in Spain. Volunteering became in part a group decision, based on a collective rather than an individual understanding of the conflict's meaning. Most fundamentally, this meant that group members were subject to external pressure from their peers, not only in developing their understanding of the conflict and its stakes but in determining what their response should be. Once it was collectively decided that volunteering was the most appropriate response to the war in Spain, the pressure to follow through and commit to this course of action was considerable, and any individual defying this decision risked losing respect or standing in both social and political terms. This need not be framed negatively – a collective decision to act together might strengthen existing bonds of friendship and comradeship, representing a highly positive emotional experience that could sweep up the undecided or uncommitted. Yet either way, once made in a social context, the decision to volunteer needed to be followed through – someone who decided to volunteer in isolation might abandon the project while disappointing only themselves, but, for most volunteers, abandoning the decision meant disappointing their friends, an altogether different prospect. In this sense, volunteering was a way in which to demonstrate commitment not only to a Bolshevik ideal but also to a group identity, making the decision to enlist as much about maintaining social standing and reputation as fulfilling a personalised political imperative. The communal nature of volunteering, in other words, should be seen as a vital factor in converting latent sympathy into direct action. Whilst many thousands of Scots felt acute sympathy and solidarity for the Spanish Republic, a much smaller number faced these kind of immediate social and political expectations.

For those in the right circles, however, it is not difficult to imagine how, in the charged political atmosphere of the time, these pressures might multiply and accumulate, as more and more individuals chose to go to Spain. As recruitment for the International Brigades reached its zenith over the winter of 1936–7, volunteering for Spain almost became the norm rather than the exception in some circles. The centrality of this particular period for Scottish recruitment is hard to overstate. It represents the point at which a trickle of isolated individuals turned into a critical mass, with groups of friends and acquaintances volunteering together becoming common. Nearly half of all Scottish volunteers left between December 1936 and February 1937. In contrast, recruitment in England, Wales and Ireland was more evenly spread, with just over a quarter arriving in these three months.[85] This points to a recruitment rush particular to Scotland, with decisions to volunteer cascading throughout tight-knit communities, and collective enthusiasm outweighing any doubts. In such an atmosphere, choosing not to go to Spain could become a decision needing considerable justification and soul-searching rather than the other way around.

These pressures are particularly apparent among those who considered volunteering but did not. As for those who refused to serve in more conventional conflicts, the lionisation of the International Brigades has left little space for those who subscribed to the same beliefs but chose not to fight.[86] Recounting their choice not to go to Spain decades later still evoked defensive or regretful responses from those who were part of the same social-political circles as the volunteers. Several such perspectives are found in Ian MacDougall's various oral history projects, as well as one published autobiography and, distinctively, in Sorley Maclean's poetry.[87] They tend to fall into two categories. Some, such as Tommy Kerr and John Carroll, were on the periphery of Party circles. Kerr was still in the process of joining the Communist Party when he considered volunteering.

> Aboot joinin' the International Brigade maself, well, the funny thing, ye know, ah kind o' regret it tae some extent. But there was only one time ever there wis an approach, and it wis a casual meetin', because ah hadnae been in nae party at the time . . . ah used tae go intae the pub tae meet, ken, some o' the pals, and I met Fred Douglas either when ah wis comin' oot or gaun in and the question wis raised aboot recruits for the International Brigade. But it never went nae further. Oh, well, ah never volunteered.[88]

Similarly, Carroll recalled that volunteering 'widna ha' took much, you know. if there had been a boy there that said, "Right, get on wi' it," we might ha' been on it'. Carroll was also not a Party member at the time although, like Kerr, he was part of the same social sphere.[89] Without the impetus that might have come from an immediate friend making the same decision, or the prospect being a more active subject of debate and discussion in their immediate circles, sympathy never translated into action.

Other accounts come from those more fully integrated into this social-political sphere, with each decision made in the context of close friends enlisting. Their responses make it clear that they sought to defer their own agency – maintaining their identity as dedicated anti-fascists required that they demonstrate a thwarted desire to go to Spain. That is not to say that the various reasons given were illegitimate, yet it is also clear that, even decades later, they wanted to avoid being perceived as having shirked their duty. James Allison of Kirkcaldy was the most open about this in admitting he was not 'an awfy brave man'. Yet when two friends decided to volunteer, and looked to Allison to join them, he still seized on other reasons to avoid joining them, claiming that 'I wid like tae go but I know if I was oot there I widnae eat and they would need tae send me hame'.[90]

Most claimed to have wanted to volunteer, or taken active steps to do so, but were thwarted by a higher power. Jack Caplan and Guy Bolton blamed the official British ban on volunteers in early 1937 – in Bolton's case, on the very day he departed for Spain from Lesmahagow with two friends.[91] When Jimmy Crichton attempted to enlist, the local organiser refused to let him before he finished his apprenticeship, while Thomas Davidson was rejected as he was newly married.[92] William McVicar, having enlisted in the RAF prior to the outbreak of the Spanish Civil War, claimed to have been convinced by his friend Michael Clarke to go to Spain. This put him in a difficult position: going would have risked prosecution for desertion. He still went to pains to point out that the ultimate decision was not his, but rather his peers', who decided that 'they couldn't guarantee that [he] could get out of the country before the RAF would start lookin' for [him]'.[93] Others deferred to the needs of their families. John Brown, whose friend attempted to convince him to volunteer, was uncomfortable leaving his mother alone, especially since his father had died in the Great War.[94] John Lennox had already volunteered when his then-girlfriend threatened to dump him if he actually went. However, in light of their subsequent long and happy marriage, Lennox cheerfully admitted that he did not fully regret missing out.[95]

An unsympathetic reading of these narratives might suggest that these individuals were seizing pretexts to avoid following through on a daunting decision. The British ban on volunteers in January 1937, for instance, was poorly enforced and many others subsequently made it to Spain despite it.[96] However, such readings are speculative, and there are no specific grounds to question the sincerity of the testimony. What is telling is that they all felt it necessary to provide justification in the first place. For those deeply involved in the communist movement, for whom the vital nature of the Spanish Civil War and the International Brigades was deeply impressed and whose friends were making the decision to fight, not going was not simply a matter of casual refusal. To maintain their social and political standing, not to mention their own self-image, they needed a concrete justification for staying.

These accounts also help confirm that participation in communist politics was linked to belonging to the requisite social circles, and this in turn meant that, for those embedded in the movement, the choice to fight in Spain was partly a product of group dynamics. While ideology is clearly not irrelevant, the presence of others in the decision-making process meant that rather, than being a passing consideration, as it was for Kerr and Carroll, it was impossible to avoid making an active decision so long as volunteering was continually being discussed and acted upon by one's peers. This in turn helps explain why Spain saw so such a large volunteering phenomenon. Unlike many other instances, where foreign fighters generally enlisted alone for their own reasons, the concentration of recruitment within such specific social-political circles meant that, instead of recruiting isolated individuals, the International Brigades recruited in clusters, multiplying their numbers considerably.

Even though little about the recruitment process is well documented, what we do know tends to support this interpretation. Most public discussions of the British volunteers were notably vague, skirting potential illegalities by avoiding specifics and merely expressing that it was desirable for British volunteers to go to Spain.[97] Due to this legal ambiguity, there could be no 'official' recruitment campaign, and little was committed to paper regarding how the CPGB went about it.[98] Instead, the Party relied primarily on word of mouth, with public praise and discussion of early volunteers supplemented by the private efforts to spread the word on how prospective volunteers might actually get to Spain.[99] Over time, local Party officials – such as Fred Douglas in Edinburgh or George Middleton in Glasgow – became known in certain circles as the person handling local applications.

In practical terms this meant that the call for volunteers, particularly in the crucial early months, was transmitted through the Communist Party's existing networks and contacts, with the Party utilising its hierarchy of local and regional officials to sound out and vet potential recruits. The Glasgow communist James Smellie, for instance, who had a change of heart upon reaching Paris, told police on his return that he had been asked to consider volunteering by a local CPGB organiser named Joseph Gerrard, who then took Smellie to be interviewed by George Middleton.[100] The intimate – Gerrard was well-known to Smellie, who recruited him to the Party in 1934 – and hierarchical nature of this process suggests another way of looking at the connections discussed here: they reflect not just the extent of pre-existing acquaintance among the volunteers but also how concrete knowledge of how to volunteer was spread across Scotland. In this respect, the conclusion that the Scottish International Brigade contingent was largely drawn from Communist Party social-political spheres is unsurprising, because these were the spaces in which Party officials could effectively and conveniently transmit a private call for volunteers.

Scale

This model of recruitment – based on understanding prospective volunteers' immediate social context alongside the specific political attraction of the Spanish Civil War – suggests some new answers to the question of why the International Brigades attracted so many volunteers. Above all, it suggests that the most successful recruitment took place in spaces where communist activism took on the characteristics of a community as much as a traditional political movement. That such communities were relatively common reflected not only the particular predilections of Scottish radical-ism but also the wider transnational cultures of interwar communism, which encouraged local movements to develop along certain lines. While the intersection between transnational communism and pre-existing local political cultures naturally led to differing outcomes, it is precisely these differences that can perhaps account for variations in recruitment for the International Brigades across contexts. Importantly, this explanation sug-gests not only why recruitment for the International Brigades was as suc-cessful as it was but also why it was not even more successful. Interwar communism was, in some spaces, able to foster small, tightly knit commu-nities of outcasts or exiles, but the transition towards mass politics in some contexts led to the dilution, rather than expansion, of these community bonds. A small, tight-knit vanguard was more readily mobilised than a larger, more diverse and less intimately interconnected movement.

As has already been noted, Scots made up the largest regional group-ing in the British Battalion, with more than twice as many volunteers as the better-known Welsh or Irish contingents. It is clear at this point that the explanation for this must lie with the Communist Party, the organisa-tion that provided the primary social and political context for the volun-teers' networks and beliefs. Yet, as discussed in the previous chapter, the relationship is more complex than the simple arithmetic of membership, reflecting the reality that communist influence was constructed differently in different spaces during the 1930s. Scottish universities proved less fer-tile ground than Oxbridge for incubating middle-class Marxists, and the Party's Scottish literary connections peaked with their soon-regretted recruitment of Hugh MacDiarmid.[101] While trades unionism provided slightly better prospects, there is no comparison to the influence built in the South Wales Miners Federation by the 1930s, where trades union-ism, communism and local communities became intimately intertwined. Yet the Scottish district was consistently more successful in developing community-based activism, based around strong local branches, leaders and causes. In other words, the members were particularly successful in laying the groundwork for the kind of collective, communal response to the Spanish Civil War that proved vital in mobilising their followers to fight in Spain.

Although it is tempting to fall back on narratives of exceptionalism to explain the CPGB's relative success in building political communities across Scotland, and assume it was a product of innate Scottish progres-siveness, this is hardly a satisfactory basis for historical analysis. Quite aside from anything else, the objectively small size of the CPGB and

Scottish International Brigade contingent compared to the population as a whole makes any link with an innate Scottish 'character' impossible to sustain. A more convincing answer lies in the wider political cultures of the Scottish left discussed in Chapter 1, which predated the Communist Party yet continued to influence its development during the interwar period. In particular, the lingering influence of the ILP's decentralised, community-driven approach to branch politics could not help but shape Communist Party strategies. Not only had many CPGB activists had their formative political experiences as part of the ILP in its heyday, but, for much of the 1930s, the ILP represented the communists' main rivals on the left. To overcome the entrenched ILP community presence in many local districts across Scotland, particularly in key Glasgow constituencies, a degree of imitation was necessary. This tendency was reinforced by the centrality of unemployment campaigns for Scottish communism in the 1920s and 1930s, campaigns which were necessarily grounded in local communities rather than the workplace. Whilst neither the ILP nor CPGB ever fully succeeded in building the kind of community-centred politics they envisaged, their greater progress in a Scottish context helps account for the relative success in recruiting for the International Brigades compared to elsewhere in Britain.[102]

Importantly for their recruitment efforts for the International Brigades, communism was also particularly attractive to those keenest for direct action. It was this same attraction that enabled the NUWM's campaigns – for those who wanted to challenge the system, it was the communists whose rhetoric was most satisfactory, as was their track record of revolutionary success overseas.[103] This is reflected in the recollections of activists from the time. When Tom Fern became interested in socialist politics, he carefully considered which party to join, and made up his mind after coming 'to the conclusion that the Communist Party was the party that was putting up the greatest fight on behalf of the working class'.[104] This yearning to do, not just observe or protest, is one that shaped many International Brigade volunteers' political choices before Spain, and doubtless played some role in their decision to intervene personally.

However, it is important to avoid overgeneralising political cultures across Scotland, particularly given Glasgow's exceptional status as 'the politically most advanced city in Britain' in the eyes of the Communist Party.[105] As William Kenefick notes, the focus on the politics in the west of Scotland 'marginalis[es] and often ignor[es] events taking place elsewhere in Scotland', but it does not necessarily follow that these events were fuelled by precisely the same political cultures by virtue of their happening in the same country.[106] Malcolm Petrie, for instance, has shown that Dundee's political climate on the eve of the Spanish Civil War was shaped by the relative absence of ILP influence, and the early polarisation of politics between Labour and communism.[107] However, the evidence discussed here does still indicate that Scottish recruitment for the International Brigades was underpinned by the way in which the Communist Party had gone about organising itself across Scotland in the years beforehand. These methods, in turn, owed as much to the context of Scottish radical traditions as they did to the communists' particular brand of political activism.

It is of course possible that Scotland was unique in seeing mobilisation for Spain occur along the communal, micro-social lines described here. Yet this appears unlikely. For one, Scottish communism did not develop in isolation. The promotion of a particular mode of communist activism found fertile ground in various Scottish contexts, but did not originate there. These political cultures were inherently transnational in nature, and interwar communism is distinguished by the extent that its political cultures were formally and informally communicated, developed and co-ordinated across borders, not least through Comintern's efforts. It appears more likely that indigenous Scottish political cultures happened to lend themselves particular well to this vision of a communist way of life, rather than Scotland developing an entirely unique version of communist organisation. This explanation raises another interesting possibility – if recruitment really was so intense among specific Scottish networks, then it follows that these networks would likely continue to exist and function after being transplanted to Spain. The next chapter takes up this question, and examines how pre-existing networks and connections between Scottish volunteers continued to operate in the International Brigades, shaping a distinctive Scottish experience of service in the British Battalion.

Moreover, while the possibility has not been explored directly, plenty of evidence suggests that similar forces were at work elsewhere. The other major British hub of volunteering, London, was also a place in which the CPGB enjoyed considerable, sustained success in grassroots activism and mobilisation prior to Spain.[108] The clusters of volunteers in North American cities such as New York and Vancouver also hint at similar patterns of recruitment in particular physical and cultural spaces.[109] The differential success in mobilising the French Communist Party (PCF) observed by Rémi Skoutelsky provide another point of reference. Although the PCF was far more successful than the CPGB – it had three hundred thousand members and won 15 per cent of the vote in 1936 – there was a marked generational shift, with 90 per cent of these members joining since 1933. Yet almost half of French International Brigade volunteers had joined the PCF before 1933.[110] The recruitment of thousands of volunteers among a mere thirty thousand pre-Popular Front communists is indicative of differences in how communists organised and lived across different contexts, with some types of membership or association simply less conducive to mobilisation. In France, the new mass party could not sustain recruitment as well as the tight-knit, well-established networks of the pre-Popular Front PCF.

If we allow that Scotland is not an isolated case, these findings suggest an answer to the question of why Spain saw such exceptional levels of foreign fighter mobilisation. Much of this answer lies within the particular involvement and nature of the Comintern. This impact was, on one level, eminently practical: without assistance in making the journey, many working-class volunteers would have been unable to reach Spain. This shift is indicated by the arrival patterns of the British volunteers, with the early months seeing small numbers of more mobile, well-resourced volunteers, few of whom were Scots. These first volunteers resembled, in fact, the contingents of foreign fighters in conflicts such as the Greek War of Independence – small numbers of often privileged, independent and eclectic individuals, whose heterogeneity makes for difficult analysis of motive.[111] Yet after November 1936, when Comintern networks had smoothed the path to Spain, there was a rush of more cohesively working-class volunteers, a disproportionate number of whom now came from Scotland.

Comintern's impact on volunteering was not merely a matter of practicalities. After November 1936, volunteers grew not only more numerous but more socially and politically cohesive. This is explained by the recruitment model proposed here: rather than accepting disparate, self-motivated volunteers, recruitment became concentrated within very specific sociopolitical spheres, grounded in existing networks and communities shaped by shared political values and experiences. That these spheres existed across so many national contexts was in no small part an outcome of the Comintern's efforts since its founding, and the inspirational role that the Bolshevik Revolution – and its idealised revolutionaries – was able to play in the decades after 1917. Crucially as well, their worldview was already grounded in internationalist assumptions. Interwar communists were readily able to understand the value of defending the 'Spanish people', both in terms of an imagined shared kinship in terms of class solidarity but also as fellow participants in the same fight. Whether volunteers had been Scots marching against unemployment, or German or Italian exiles from fascist repression, the continuities between past struggles and the Spanish Civil War were instinctively apparent.

Yet as much as the Comintern had done to shape a transnational movement that was ideally suited to being mobilised for such purposes, it would be a mistake to divorce this question from local contexts and agency. Local political cultures, leadership and institutions all shaped the way in which the Spanish Civil War was perceived and responded to. Above all, in the spaces where recruitment for the International Brigades was most successful, these responses were inherently communal. Not only did this inevitably shape the way that the conflict and its stakes were understood, the collective nature of the decision to volunteer was a powerful way to convert widespread sympathy into specific action. While historians need to understand the wider transnational cultures and networks, as well as the particular circumstances faced by individuals, community has been neglected as the key factor that binds these perspectives together.

Notes

1. Baxell, *British Volunteers*, 25–46; Hopkins, *Heart of the Fire*, 42–57. For Scotland, see Gray, *Homage*, 23–36.
2. Buchanan, *Britain and the Spanish Civil War*, 127; Thomas, *Spanish Civil War*, 454–5; Roberts, 'Freedom, Faction, Fame and Blood', 202.
3. Buchanan, *Britain and the Spanish Civil War*, 127–8. García, 'Transnational History', 571.
4. Nir Arielli, 'Induced to Volunteer? The Predicament of Jewish Communists in Palestine and the Spanish Civil War', *Journal of Contemporary History* 46:4 (2011), 854–70; Acciai, 'Traditions of Armed Volunteering', 50–72; Graham, *War and Its Shadow*, 75–8. This approach has proved influential in newer literature, see Zaagsma, *Jewish Volunteers*, 19–20; Tom Buchanan, 'Ideology, Idealism, and Adventure: Narratives of the British Volunteers in the International Brigades', *Labour History Review* 81:2 (2016), 123–40.
5. Arielli, 'Getting There', 219–30.
6. This reality has been hinted at in existing scholarship, though the implications for recruitment have not previously been explored. For example Mates, *Spanish Civil War*, 59–60; Petrou, *Renegades*, 24–5.
7. Studer, *Transnational World*. See also Kirschenbaum, *International Communism*.
8. Baxell, *British Volunteers*, 25–46. For further analysis, see McLennan, '"Little Lenin"', 287–304.
9. Revolutionary political intent has been mooted in other contexts, e.g. Amirah Inglis, *Australians in the Spanish Civil War* (Sydney, 1987), 116–17; McGarry,

Irish Politics, 60-1. However, even revisionist British accounts avoid such questions. For example Stradling, 'English-speaking Units', 744–66.

10. Baxell differentiates between 'doctrinaire' communists and those who saw communists as fascism's most effective opponents. Baxell, 'Myths', 14.

11. Baxell, *British Volunteers*, 30; Buchanan, *Britain and the Spanish Civil War*, 127–8.

12. McGarry, *Irish Politics*, 61.

13. Bartie and McIvor, 'Oral History in Scotland', 113–26.

14. For example McCusker, McCartney and Murray in MacDougall, *Voices from the Spanish Civil War*, 45, 260, 324.

15. Garry McCartney, TLS, MS, Tape 168.

16. Lily Murray to 'Tom and Jen', n.d., NLS, TMP, Box 1 File 5.

17. Tom Buchanan, 'Anti-Fascism and Democracy in the 1930s', *European History Quarterly* 32:1 (2002), 40. See also Zaagsma, *Jewish Volunteers*, 65. For broader discussion of the evolving relationship between anti-fascism and democracy in the period, see Michael Seidman, *Transatlantic Antifascisms: From the Spanish Civil War to the End of World War II* (Cambridge, 2017), esp. 9–51.

18. Buchanan, 'Anti-Fascism and Democracy', 53.

19. Watters and Anderson in MacDougall, *Voices from the Spanish Civil War*, 33, 89.

20. Sloan in MacDougall, *Voices from the Spanish Civil War*, 238–9.

21. For example 'Biografa de Militantes' of William Moses, RGASPI, 545/6/204/98; Frank Webster, RGASPI, 545/6/213/7; James Cunningham, RGASPI, 545/6/121/39.

22. In Valentine Cunningham's classic anthologies of civil war writing, for instance, poetry and prose dominate, with songs almost absent. Valentine Cunningham, *The Penguin Book of Spanish Civil War Verse* (London, 1980) and *Spanish Front*.

23. On the First World War, see Grahame Seal, '"We're Here Because We're Here": Trench Culture of the Great War', *Folklore* 124:2 (2013), 178–97. For the American Civil War, see Christian McWhirter, *Battle Hymns: The Power and Popularity of Music in the Civil War* (Chapel Hill, 2012).

24. McLennan, '"Little Lenin"', 301–2.

25. For example Dunlop in MacDougall, *Voices from the Spanish Civil War*, 146.

26. On uses and meanings of such songs, see Joaquina Labajo, 'La práctica de una memoria sostenible: el repertorio de las canciones internacionales de la Guerra Civil Española', *Arbor* 187:751 (2011), 847–56.

27. A collection is found in RGASPI, 545/2/409–13.

28. Oficina de la Legion Condor to SIM Jefatura, 20 September 1937, AGMA, C.2914,11, d.1.

29. SIFNE to SIM Jefatura, 25 October 1937, AGMA, C.2914,11, d.5.

30. For example 'Notes, poems, song lyrics, slogans and drawings by 15th Brigade volunteers', RGASPI, 545/3/473.

31. Anderson in MacDougall, *Voices from the Spanish Civil War*, 97.
32. Kirschenbaum, *International Communism*, 95–8.
33. Lochore in MacDougall, *Voices from War and Some Labour Struggles* (Edinburgh, 1995), 114. The British used *It's a Long Way to Tipperary* to similar effect. Fausto Villar Esteban, *Un valencianito en la Brigada Lincoln* (Unpublished manuscript, 1988), Labadie Collection, University of Michigan, 49–50.
34. Lochore in MacDougall, *Voices from War,* 119–20.
35. Dunlop in MacDougall, *Voices from the Spanish Civil War*, 125.
36. 'Canciones de guerra', 1937, RGASPI, 545/2/409/58–9.
37. Dunlop in MacDougall, *Voices from the Spanish Civil War*, 148.
38. The popularity of Soviet culture in Spain is discussed in Kirschenbaum, *International Communism*, 120–5.
39. 'Comrades, March Shoulder to Shoulder' and 'Red Front' in 'Canciones de guerra', RGASPI 545/2/409/10,18–19.
40. For example, 'For 'tis there that we wasted our manhood / And most of our old age as well' became 'It is there that we gave of our manhood / And most of our brave comrades fell'. Cunningham, *Spanish Civil War Verse*, 75–7.
41. Artists such as Billy Bragg and Woody Guthrie have performed famous versions. 'Billy Bragg and Maxine Peake in CD Tribute', *IBMT* [International Brigade Memorial Trust] *Newsletter* 32 (2012), 1. It is still commonly performed at commemorations, for example 'Music, Words and Wreaths in Jubilee Gardens to Remember the Volunteers', *IBMT Newsletter* 30 (2011), 4.
42. 'No Pasaran', RGASPI, 545/3/473/26.
43. This composition was 'rejected', presumably for publication in the Brigade newspaper, likely because it explicitly contradicted the official line. 'Ours Alone', RGASPI, 545/3/473/41.
44. 'International Brigade', RGASPI, 545/3/473/54.
45. In a British context Robert Stradling is most cynical about the Comintern's role, although selective quoting is required for his argument to resemble 'Stalin-controlled dupes betrayed by the Communists', as characterised by Baxell. Stradling, 'English-speaking Units', 752–3; Baxell, 'Myths', 14. Elsewhere, particularly in America, critical work comes closer, e.g. Radosh, Habeck and Sevostianov, *Spain Betrayed*, 103–4, 231–5.
46. McCartney in MacDougall, *Voices from the Spanish Civil War*, 260.
47. Lochore in MacDougall, *Voices from the Hunger Marches*, 320.
48. Cullen, 'Fasces and the Saltire', 306–31.
49. Londragan in MacDougall, *Voices from the Spanish Civil War*, 171.
50. 'Scottish Report', July 1937, RGASPI, 495/14/263/6; 'Lanarkshire', November 1936, RGASPI, 495/14/239/6.
51. McGarry, *Irish Politics*, 63–4.
52. Lochore in MacDougall, *Voices from War*, 118–19.
53. On Soviet aims, see Kowalsky, *Stalin and the Spanish Civil War*, 446–9.
54. 'Menzies, Dave', RGASPI, 545/6/172/52.

55. Fullarton in MacDougall, *Voices from the Spanish Civil War*, 303.
56. For discussion of such attitudes, see Baxell, *British Volunteers*, 144. A comparison might be made with contemporary press reports of Islamist volunteers' apparent lack of knowledge of Islam, e.g. 'UK Imams Condemn Isis in Online Video', *BBC News*, 11 July 2014. Accessed 14 August 2019: <http://www.bbc.co.uk/news/uk-28270296>.
57. Sydney Quinn, TLS, MS, Tape 202.
58. The 'hard man' archetype has a long history, particularly in a Glaswegian-industrial context. Hughes, *Gender and Political Identities*, 3–4; Ronnie Johnston and Arthur McIvor, 'Dangerous Work, Hard Men and Broken Bodies: Masculinity in the Clydeside Heavy Industries, c.1930–1970s', *Labour History Review* 69:2 (2004), 135–51; Hilary Young, 'Hard Man, New Man: Re/Composing Masculinities in Glasgow, c. 1950–2000', *Oral History* 35:1 (2007), 71–2. This was hardly unique to Scotland; see Lisa Kirschenbaum, 'The Man Question: How Bolshevik Masculinity Shaped International Communism', *Socialist History*, 52 (2017), 76–84.
59. Studer, *Transnational World*, 8. On Britain in particular, see Linehan, *Communism in Britain*, 160–79; Morgan, Cohen and Flinn, *Communists and British Society*, 217–29.
60. On community identity and recruitment in the Boer War, see Brad Beaven, 'The Provincial Press, Civic Ceremony and the Citizen-Soldier during the Boer War, 1899–1902: a Study of Local Patriotism', *Journal of Imperial and Commonwealth History* 37:2 (2009), 207–28; Stephen Miller, 'In Support of the "Imperial Mission"? Volunteering for the South African War, 1899–1902', *Journal of Military History* 69:3 (2005), 703–4. On the First World War, see Alexander Watson, 'Voluntary Enlistment in the Great War: a European Phenomenon?' in Christine Krüger and Sonja Levsen (eds), *War Volunteering in Modern Times: From the French Revolution to the Second World War* (Basingstoke, 2011), 167–72; Edward Spiers, 'Voluntary Recruiting in Yorkshire, 1914–15', *Northern History* 52:2 (2015), 300, 312–13. More generally, Peter Simkins, *Kitchener's Army: The Raising of the New Armies, 1914–16* (Manchester, 1988).
61. Francis and Mates refer to 'inner-party conscription' among Welsh miners. Francis, *Miners*, 159; Mates, 'Durham and South Wales', 380. In Palestine, Nir Arielli argues that the volunteers were induced to go not by the Communist Party but by British authorities: Arielli, 'Induced to Volunteer?', 854–70.
62. Several senior Party figures were asked to go to Spain by the CPGB, e.g. Cooney, *Proud Journey*, 28–9. Tom Murray's file reveals that 'Party District and Central (British) Committees decided that he should volunteer for I. Brigade as a special effort to break through lethargy of official labour leadership'. Murray himself was more equivocal: 'His personal view is that . . . in view of his growing influence and opportunities within the Labour Party, he would probably be of more value by continuing in his present sphere. Nevertheless, he feels that . . . the

Party ought to take final responsibility for a decision.' 'Biographical Notes – MURRAY, Thomas', 17 April 1938, RGASPI, 545/6/176/121; Untitled note, 3 February 1938, NLS, Tom Murray Papers (TMP), Box 1, File 7.

63. For further discussion, see Fraser Raeburn, 'Politics, Networks and Community: Recruitment for the International Brigades Reassessed', *Journal of Contemporary History* (available online ahead of print: https://doi.org/10.1177/0022009419865005).

64. Sloan in MacDougall, *Voices from the Spanish Civil War*, 233, 236.

65. Sloan in MacDougall, *Voices from the Hunger Marches*, 277–82.

66. Sloan in MacDougall, *Voices from the Spanish Civil War*, 227.

67. Eddie Brown, like others, was driven 'further afield – Dundee, Perth, Glasgow, Edinburgh, then down to London, picking up work wherever [he] could'. Brown in MacDougall, *Voices from the Spanish Civil War*, 107.

68. Fullarton in MacDougall, *Voices from the Spanish Civil War*, 289.

69. Arnott, *Dundee*, 12; *Lanarkshire Catholic Herald*, 24 April 1937, 2.

70. Cranston in MacDougall, *Voices from the Hunger Marches*, 185–6.

71. James Maley, IWMSA, Tape 11947/1.

72. 'Dunlop to Kiernan' n.d., NLS, John Dunlop Papers, Acc. 12087, File 3.

73. George Murray in MacDougall, *Voices from the Spanish Civil War*, 101.

74. Linehan, *Communism in Britain*, 67–86.

75. Lily to Margaret Murray, 6 March 1937, NLS, TMP, Box 1, File 5.

76. Crichton in MacDougall, *Voices from Work and Home: Personal Recollections of Working Life and Labour Struggles in the Twentieth Century* (Edinburgh, 2000), 429.

77. Chris Smith, IWMSA, Tape 12290/2.

78. Johnstone in MacDougall, *Voices from the Hunger Marches*, 243.

79. Henry in MacDougall, *Voices from the Hunger Marches*, 49–50. On Socialist Sunday Schools, see Jessica Gerrard, '"Little Soldiers" for Socialism: Childhood and Socialist Politics in the British Socialist Sunday School Movement', *International Review of Social History* 58:1 (2013), 71–96.

80. Lochore in MacDougall, *Voices from the Hunger Marches*, 320–1.

81. Johnstone in MacDougall, *Voices from the Hunger Marches*, 243.

82. 'Fife District Plan', March 1936, RGASPI, 495/14/194/38–9.

83. 'Fife District Plan', March 1936, RGASPI.

84. See, for example, discussion of Nan Green in Paul Preston, *Doves of War: Four Women of Spain* (London, 2002), 149–51.

85. This is extrapolating from Baxell's study, which provided an arrival date for 1500 British volunteers. Baxell, *British Volunteers*, 17.

86. Similar points are raised in Cynthia Eller, 'Oral History as Moral Discourse: Conscientious Objectors and the Second World War', *Oral History Review* 18:1 (1990), 45–8.

87. Jack Caplan, *Memories of the Gorbals* (Edinburgh, 1991), 55–6.

88. Kerr in MacDougall, *Voices from Work*, 93.

89. He 'did work for the Communists' and went camping with the local YCL. Carroll in MacDougall, *Voices from the Hunger Marches*, 360–1.
90. Allison in MacDougall, *Voices from the Hunger Marches*, 131.
91. Caplan, *Memories of the Gorbals*, 55–6; Guy Bolton in MacDougall, *Voices from the Hunger Marches*, 346.
92. Crichton in MacDougall, *Voices from Work*, 92; Davidson in MacDougall, *Voices from the Hunger Marches*, 255.
93. McVicar in MacDougall, *Voices from the Hunger Marches*, 179.
94. Crichton in MacDougall, *Voices from Work*, 92.
95. Lennox in MacDougall, *Voices from the Hunger Marches*, 390.
96. Baxell, *British Volunteers*, 6.
97. For example Bob Morrison, 'How the British Communist Party and British Working Class are Helping the Spanish Workers', 31 December 1936, RGASPI, 495/14/213/79–80.
98. One exception was a circular written by the Socialist League leader H. N. Brailsford. This was unusually indiscreet, despite the letter noting that 'nothing must get into the press; it should be done by letter and word of mouth'. As noted in the margin of a CPGB copy, being so explicit made it '*illegal*'. Circular, 9 December 1936, RGASPI, 495/14/213/42.
99. Indirect calls to arms in the pages of the *Daily Worker* – such as by praising those already in Spain and commenting on the desirability of making the contingent 'stronger' – became common from December 1936 onwards, but crucially did not provide information about how to volunteer. For example *Daily Worker*, 12 December 1936, 1. An overview of the shifting rhetoric employed is found in Baxell, *British Volunteers*, 38–40.
100. 'Further Report by The Procurator Fiscal, Glasgow, as to Walter Anderson (Foreign Enlistment Act 1870)', 1937, National Records of Scotland, HH1/595.
101. Antipathy to MacDiarmid surfaced several times, notably in 1937 when the Scottish District attempted to expel him. 'Membership Appeals' CPGB Conference May 1937, RGASPI, 495/14/227/183. Although he successfully appealed, MacDiarmid's erratic behaviour finally led to his expulsion in 1939. CPGB Central Committee Meeting, 18 February 1939, RGASPI, 495/14/265/254.
102. For a comparative perspective on communist political communities in Scotland and Britain, see Morgan, Cohen and Flinn, *Communists and British Society*, 56–76.
103. With unemployment and the NUWM especially, the communists were able to build on grassroots resistance to government policy, see Hughes, *Gender and Political Identities*, 193–8.
104. Fern in Ian MacDougall, *Voices from the Hunger Marches*, 137.
105. *Daily Worker*, 1 May 1939, 1.
106. Kenefick, *Red Scotland!*, 7.
107. Malcolm Petrie, 'Unity from Below?', 311–12.

108. Norman LaPorte and Matthew Worley, 'Towards a Comparative History of Communism: the British and German Communist Parties to 1933', *Contemporary British History* 22:2 (2003), 234; see also Morgan, Cohen and Flinn, *Communists and British Society*, 7–8.

109. Byrne, 'From Brooklyn to Belchite', 72–82; Petrou, *Renegades*, 10–27.

110. Skoutelsky, *Novedad*, 181–2.

111. Baxell, *British Volunteers*, 48–9. For a comparative perspective, see Arielli, *Byron to bin Laden*.

4

Scots in Spain: Continuity, Change and Politics

James Donald and Malcolm Sneddon deserted their comrades in May 1937. This was not, it must be admitted, an entirely unusual occurrence: more than ninety Scots deserted from the International Brigades over the course of the conflict, over one-sixth of the total contingent.[1] Donald and Sneddon's case is in many ways quite typical. Their desertion is hard to view as a moral failing so much as a reflection of the immensely difficult conditions the volunteers were serving under, as a report on their eventual capture made clear.

> They complained of frightful disorganisation in their battalion, the quartermaster running away with their money and no proper command in battle. Once 9 (!) men were sent out to follow up a tank, but the tank got frightened and turned back leaving the men in front of it. Most of them were killed. Donald and Sneddon just walked away after that, one can't really blame them.[2]

Like so many of their comrades on the Jarama front, Donald and Sneddon were casualties of the extraordinary nature of the situation. The International Brigades were a spontaneous undertaking, organised and led haphazardly in a multitude of languages, fighting in a brutal war for which they were poorly trained and equipped. The strain on the volunteers was immense. Even though they were for the most part genuine, sincere and committed anti-fascists, political belief was no inoculation against the realities of battle. Though their organisation improved over time, the frequency with which the International Brigades went into combat meant that desertion caused by stress and disillusionment continued to be a problem throughout the war.

Donald's and Sneddon's experiences are illuminating beyond highlighting these sober realities. Building on the previous chapters' focus on volunteers' origins, cases such as this one demonstrate that these contexts were never entirely irrelevant. Both Donald and Sneddon came from the small town of Methil, in East Fife. They volunteered there together in January 1937. From there, they journeyed to Spain together via London and Paris, they joined the International Brigades together, and they trained and fought alongside one another. In the end, they ran away together. These continuities suggest that perhaps the importance of volunteers' origins did not become moot upon their reaching Spain. In other words, despite never serving in their own national unit, it may be possible to explore a distinctively Scottish experience in Spain, based on the same social and political networks that underpinned recruitment.

In attempting to locate this experience, it is important to avoid the same traps of national exceptionalism discussed in previous chapters. There is no evidence, for instance, that Scots made especially effective fighters in Spain, whatever the contemporary reputation of Highland regiments. Indeed, as Gerben Zaagsma has pointed out, these common claims have all too often relied on uncritical repetition of wartime propaganda.[3] Rather, a Scottish experience is likely to emerge in different realms, shaped by the nature of the informal personal and political connections that permeated the contingent. Just as Scottish political cultures can be seen as leading not to a uniquely Scottish recruitment process but to a particularly intense manifestation of broader phenomenon, so too did their later experiences reflect how the International Brigades tended to work more broadly. In other words, it is in their social and political life that we can reasonably expect to find a distinctively Scottish perspective on the International Brigades.

In this sense, the Scots offer a rather useful window into the lived experience of volunteering in Spain. The very nature of the International Brigades made these particular factors more important than they might have been. Politics, obviously, was a central preoccupation of the leaders of the International Brigades, and political considerations were intertwined with virtually all aspects of the volunteers' lives in one way or another. Yet perhaps less obviously, the social interconnections between volunteers also mattered a great deal more than they might have done in any other contemporary military context. Rather than being scattered throughout the Republican Army, almost all Scots served within the same battalion. Even beyond this, however, the aforementioned haphazardness of the International Brigades' organisation acted to preserve social networks to a greater extent than might be expected. Bureaucracy and procedures were created as needed, where needed. As such, the allocation of volunteers into smaller units usually followed the path of least resistance and kept existing groups together, or proved flexible when individuals sought to transfer to serve alongside their friends, family and colleagues. This scope to choose one's own immediate comrades, combined with recruitment among relatively small communities, opened the door for volunteers organising themselves on the basis of their own preferences. As a result volunteers tended to serve alongside those with whom they already shared mutual acquaintance, trust and shared identities. Even when separated by duty or circumstance, however, they still found ways in which to keep in touch and leverage their social and political connections. When, like Sneddon and Donald, volunteers faced death, desertion and punishment, these connections remained important.

Continuities and Connections

Few Scots journeyed to Spain by themselves. Although it was most pronounced in late 1936, when entire busloads of volunteers departed together from Glasgow, even as recruitment slowed it remained common practice for small groups of volunteers to travel together from Scotland. This acted to multiply the connections discussed in the previous chapter. Travelling together to Spain could both cement existing bonds and help develop new ones, a process doubtless aided by renewed awareness of cultural commonalities in the face of domestic and international travel.

Such a process is indicated in the testimony of Donald Renton, as shared acquaintance as well as local and regional identity bound this group of volunteers for their journey, even with an unusually heterogeneous mix of Party affiliations.

> Among the men who left Edinburgh in November 1936 there was my very, very good friend George Watters and a number of others: Harry Fry, who was destined to become one of the commanders of the British Battalion of the International Brigades; George Bridges, who was killed at Jarama, who was not a member of the Communist Party but of the British Section of the International Socialist Labour Party; and a lad called Forrester, who also was a member.[4]

In this particular case, evidence suggests not only that this group embarked together but that it stuck together. Almost all of this Edinburgh group joined the new British machine gun company before the Battle of Jarama. This unit was caught out of position by the Nationalist advance, and surrounded after taking severe casualties. The survivors' accounts make it clear that the group that had travelled together remained largely intact going into action, and that they shared in the trauma to come.

Our Company at the beginning of that encirclement probably had around 120 men. When we finally were in Fascist hands there were only some thirty of us left, the bulk of whom in one way or another had been knocked about rather badly. I'd been wounded in the legs, Harry Fry had a broken arm, shattered with machine gun bullets, Jimmy Rutherford was battered soft, George Watters had gone down.[5]

Watters recalled the death of his friend in the same action.

My mate from Prestonpans, he was badly wounded just the day before we were surrounded and I advised him to wait on them comin' up wi' the ambulance men that would take him down on stretchers. But he felt the stretchers were needed for men that were more severely wounded than he was. He didn't realise how bad he was and unfortunately he died.[6]

Similarly, Donald Renton remembered the 'bad' death of another Edinburgh volunteer in this action, Robert Mason, who succumbed to severe burns.[7] Of the volunteers who left Edinburgh in December 1936, five perished at Jarama and five more were captured together. Only one Edinburgh volunteer served in the battle without being captured, wounded or both.[8] Their accounts indicate that this high toll among a specific geographical subset of volunteers was due to the majority of Edinburgh volunteers serving together in one of the most dangerous areas of the battle. Other instances, such as that of one shell killing three volunteers from eastern Scotland, also indicate that, even or perhaps especially in the heat of battle, volunteers sought out those with whom they shared connections based on shared origins, identities and social circles – in other words, Scots tended to stick together while in Spain.[9]

This Edinburgh group was part of the flood of volunteers that left Britain in the winter of 1936-7.[10] Groups could be defined by precise point of origin, with those from Aberdeen or Edinburgh travelling within a larger Scottish contingent. Later, as the number of volunteers dwindled and departures grew less frequent, such specific local clusters became less common. However, Scots usually still travelled together, as recounted in a letter describing Tom Murray's journey in April 1938.

There are thirty-five leaving Paris tonight including 11 Scots. Birt Smith of Kirkcaldy and I have been appointed Group Leaders + he has five Scots + I six Scots to pilot over the frontier. In my lot are two youths from Glasgow, the two Dundee fellows who offered their services when I was there and an Aberdeen fellow.[11]

Other volunteers provided less detail about their travel arrangements, but made it clear that they travelled to Spain accompanied by other Scots. The Fife volunteer Tommy Bloomfield journeyed with a Glaswegian who 'got us out of difficulties when we were passing through southern France because he spoke Esperanto'.[12] Tom Clarke recalled leaving Dundee with two other local volunteers.[13] Eddie Brown, living at the time in Perthshire, remembered that he went 'to Glasgow and said I wanted to volunteer . . . There was a group o' people with us, in fact I was along wi' an Aberdeen fellow, John Londragan.'[14] Of 482 volunteers for whom details are available, over four hundred travelled alongside other Scots.[15]

Although it is natural that volunteers who left together travelled together, it is less obvious that these associations continued to matter in Spain. Yet evidence suggests they did. Steve Fullarton, for instance, implied that it was unusual for one's immediate companions not to be those you arrived with, as well as confirming that the majority of these in his case were fellow Scots.

> I was associating with Dusty Miller from Alexandria, Benny Richardson from North of England, Jimmy Glavin from Glasgow, who hadn't been in the same gang as me going out, and another man – I think he was from Dundee.[16]

Making the journey together was not the only way in which shared identity bound Scottish volunteers together in Spain. Volunteers could actively seek out those with whom they shared personal bonds after arriving. Alec Park arrived in Spain on 12 January 1938 with a large group of Scots, including six who hailed from near where Park lived in Glasgow's East End.[17] Park wrote several times to his wife upon arriving, reassuring her that he was 'in a British Company and [Tom McWhirter] is my section leader further all of us who left together are in the same company' and that he enjoyed 'the comradeship of most of our Glasgow Group'.[18] In Park's case, there was clear synergy at work. He departed with several local comrades, who were immediately welcomed into a pre-existing 'section' of individuals they knew from home. Park's comments about the existence of a 'Glasgow Group' are echoed in a different context in Tony Hyndman's complaints of the 'drunken loutishness' of a mob of Glaswegians, provoked by his perceived effeminacy.[19] As well as perhaps reinforcing stereotypes of Glaswegian masculine identity, this incident serves to confirm Park's experience of Glaswegians sticking together in Spain, for better or worse.

The limitations of the British Battalion records hamper sweeping conclusions about who served with whom, and when. However, there was one 'official' subunit where it is possible to see these trends in practice. May 1937 saw the formation of a British Anti-Tank Battery. Commanded by the enigmatic Malcolm Dunbar, the Anti-Tank battery was initially dominated by Scottish volunteers. Eddie Brown, an early recruit, remembered half the unit being Scots when it was formed, chiefly from the east of Scotland.[20] A snapshot of unit personnel from February 1938 reveals that although the number of Scots had thinned, their early dominance had cemented their position in the unit hierarchy, with Scots making up three out of five non-commissioned officers, the Political Commissar (and acting commander), as well as the clerk and quartermaster.[21]

Brown was not the only Scot in the Anti-Tank battery who gave testimony: George Murray, John Dunlop, Hugh Sloan, John Londragan and Bill Cranston were also interviewed by Ian MacDougall, while Arthur Nicoll's recollections were preserved by the Imperial War Museum. Their complementary descriptions of their journeys to Spain and the formation of the unit confirm that the process was similar to that hypothesised above. Londragan noted that the unit was formed chiefly from the group of sixteen that he arrived with.[22] As with those discussed above, this arrival cohort was characterised by pre-existing personal, political and geographic connections. Londragan, Brown, Dunlop and Murray, for instance, knew each other through a combination of prior activism, CPGB branch membership and, in Brown's and Murray's cases, having grown up together.[23] Another group led by the Dundonian Arthur Nicoll featured similar patterns of political and personal acquaintance. Nicoll knew Hugh Sloan through the NUWM, while Sloan himself knew the Kirkcaldy volunteer Fraser Crombie from protests against the Means Test.[24] Personal connections also played a role in selecting newcomers to the unit. Arthur Nicoll pulled strings to get his brother Peter assigned to 'my own unit' to 'keep him in sight' when he arrived in October 1937.[25] Like Alec Park above, this suggests that, for volunteers with the right connections, there was a degree of choice involved in assignment. The natural choice was to serve alongside friends and family.

Local or national identities were of course not the only ways volunteers could make connections in Spain. The vast majority of Scots had working-class backgrounds, a shared identity which likely also influenced their collective preferences when it came to recreational and cultural pursuits. Unlike the Americans or Welsh, however, for them occupational ties proved less important, likely because, as discussed in Chapter 1, the trades union movement was never an effective forum for recruitment. Several Scots, notably Wilfred Macartney, came from more privileged backgrounds, which could distance them from other volunteers, with occasionally significant consequences. Macartney, for instance, was sent home after commanding the battalion during its initial training period, with Communist Party officials citing the gulf between Macartney and the volunteers as a major reason.[26] The testimony of other middle-class volunteers indicates that, while they retained many connections to Scots in the International Brigades, they were more adventurous in seeking out new acquaintances. John Dunlop, for instance, recalled a much wider circle of associates in the International Brigades than many of his working-class comrades. As well as mentioning several 'English chaps' he got on well with, Dunlop also frequently chose to eat with the 'Spanish group' of his unit.[27] Working-class Scots also made friends on the basis of other shared connections. Tom Clarke, for instance, recalled that he 'pal-ed up' with the Liverpudlian Alex Alexander, apparently on the basis of a mutual appreciation for Spanish wine.[28] Yet equally, it is difficult to find Scottish volunteers whose precise origins did not play some role in shaping their immediate social context once in Spain.

Deserting the 'Good Fight'

Desertion offers a striking and counterintuitive way in which these connections continued to matter once in Spain. All too often, desertion was a collective rather than individual decision, as it was with James Donald and Malcolm Sneddon. In November 1937, four Scots – Alexander Elder, Charles Scott, John Crate and Alistair McDonald – were apprehended together after deserting and stowing away on a ship bound for Gibraltar.[29] In perhaps the most extreme case of such clustering, all three volunteers who had once lived together at 106 Parliamentary Road in Glasgow deserted together following the Battle of Jarama. More holistically, these patterns are also indicated by the uneven geographic spread of desertion cases across Scotland. Several locales saw distinctly higher than average clusters of desertion – still others saw far fewer than the norm (Table 4.1).

Perhaps the most infamous such case relates to the two volunteers from Port Glasgow, Alex Kemp and Patrick Glacken. Kemp and Glacken had attempted to desert to Nationalist lines, allegedly with information about the Battalion's positions that would aid the enemy.[30] Whilst both were sentenced to death for this crime, according to several accounts Kemp's

Table 4.1 Regional patterns of desertion

Locale	Total volunteers	Deserters (no. and %)
Glasgow	199	33 (16.6)
Edinburgh	48	5 (10.4)
Dundee	57	9 (15.8)
Aberdeen	23	3 (13.0)
Airdrie	10	3 (30.0)
Alexandria	13	4 (30.8)
Clydebank	11	2 (18.2)
Greenock	17	3 (17.6)
Kirkcaldy	12	2 (16.7)
Cambuslang	7	2 (28.5)
Paisley	8	2 (25.0)
Bellshill	8	1 (12.5)
Scotland	520	96 (18.5)

age and superior rank led to the view that he was the ringleader and had persuaded Glacken to go along with his scheme, so Glacken's sentence was commuted. This incident was highly unusual – unlike Spanish troops, foreign volunteers almost exclusively deserted to the rear rather than to the enemy.[31] Bob Cooney pointed to this in justifying the sentence – the punishment was 'not for desertion', but 'because in order to carry out his desertion he was prepared to betray the lives of his comrades'.[32] Aside from explaining the harsh punishment, this difference makes it difficult to portray the decision as a product of Stalinist cultures.[33] This was betrayal and treason in any understanding, and Kemp would likely have received the same sentence in any contemporary military.

Glacken's case was more ambiguous. Several scholars, including Richard Baxell, have argued that despite the apparent clemency shown to Glacken, he was deliberately exposed to enemy fire in an effort to get him killed in action, a fate supposedly shared by several other 'troublesome' volunteers.[34] Yet if his death was deliberate, it is unclear why. Glacken was given a very public chance at redemption – his commuted sentence and the logic behind it were published as a Special Order to the entire 35th Division.

As to the Corporal Patrick Glacken, considering the service he has previously rendered, the sincerity with which he admitted his crime, and the plea that he be given the opportunity to atone for his failing . . . I order that the death penalty be commuted to demotion . . . and atoning for his crime by means of loyal service and work.[35]

This stress on atonement through service was a common formulation, and, given the consistent emphasis on rehabilitation in International Brigades discipline, there is little reason to assume these orders were euphemistic.[36] There are few other similar cases where the death of a Scottish volunteer appears to be the result of foul play.[37] One candidate is the Glaswegian William Meeke, whose case James Hopkins noted as suspicious as he was 'shot whilst attempting to escape prison'.[38] However, Foreign Office records indicate that he eventually turned up in a camp in France, and Security Service surveillance confirmed his repatriation in February 1939.[39] His International Brigade file reveals further detail apparently missed by Hopkins. He was shot during an incident in which other prisoners attempted to escape – a ricochet off a wall struck him near the left ear – but he survived and recovered in hospital.[40]

The overall picture does not suggest that there was any deliberate policy of trying to dispose of troublesome volunteers by deliberately placing them in harm's way. Even exceptionally awkward individuals, such as the pseudo-Scottish actor James Justice, who mismanaged the base at Madrigueras and was found to be addicted to morphine, were generally expelled from Spain rather than 'gotten rid of'.[41] The gulf between the extremes of imagined repression and what the British Battalion was willing to countenance is also highlighted in a June 1937 incident, where the Scottish officer William Meredith called for 'drastic action' against volunteers who were found drunk in action, as an 'example to the rest of the Battalion'. 'Drastic' punishment turned out to mean ten days in a labour company, and five days' pay stopped.[42] Furthermore, the British Battalion and XV Brigade often evidenced a desire to keep judicial procedures – and harsher punishments – away from outside authorities. In one report on the conditions faced by internationals in Spanish prison, Paul Somogyi argued that such cases should be kept away from Spanish authorities, as he did not 'think that Spanish judges would show much understanding for the special problems and mentality of English speaking people'.[43] In particular, several sources are adamant that executions were vigorously opposed, including George Aitken, who claimed to have resisted suggestions from his superiors that the British 'execute a few' deserters, pointing to the 'catastrophic' reaction that such news would engender 'if it ever got back to Britain'.[44]

The potential reaction in Britain was often raised when it came to the treatment of transgressors. In an interesting reversal, one volunteer coming to the end of a prison sentence wrote to Aitken in May 1937 with a subtle threat: approve his request for repatriation, or his wife might get 'worried over my position and [seek] other methods to get me home'.[45] In the context, there is little doubt that this was a threat to go to the press, albeit couched in the language of loyalty to the Party and professing inability to stop his wife acting of her own accord. In other cases, the CPGB itself raised the issue with Spanish counterparts. One letter to the PCE made the case in November 1938 that prisoners in Republican jails should be repatriated along with the rest of the volunteers. It claimed that whilst those who had committed military offenses would 'receive very little sympathy in this country' and that their interest was 'by no means due to any concern with the men themselves', there was a danger of 'embittered' relatives who might 'exploit a grievance', as well as 'anti-Republican influences' who would 'make propaganda' out of the situation.[46] This careful wording was doubtless intended to pre-empt any accusation that the CPGB was unwilling to approach such matters with the discipline required of true Bolsheviks. Yet whether motivated by pragmatism or humanitarianism, it is clear that opinion at home was of considerable concern to the CPGB, and limited its willingness to take Stalinist disciplinary practices to their extreme.

These conclusions are borne out by the actual fates of deserters. Of more than ninety Scots who deserted or attempted to desert, just seven died of any causes during the war, compared to over a quarter of non-deserters.[47] This suggests that committing crimes actually made volunteers safer, especially as most of these seven did not perish during punishment assignments. International Brigade labour companies, unlike the infamous Soviet penal units, were not simply used as expendable manpower, and it is possible that historians have been overly keen to read later Soviet euphemisms into the terminology employed by the International Brigades. What seems more likely is that labour battalions were just that – an effort to get useful work out of defaulters, either as temporary punishment or as an acknowledgement that further front service would be counterproductive. Casual references to such units tend to support this interpretation, such as an October 1937 letter from Mick Economides to Bill Paynter, which mentioned that 'rotters and other weak types [had been] put together in a special section which does odd jobs in the base'.[48] Whilst a few may have died while serving in these units, deaths were much more uncommon than in combat units, and were likely the result of exposure to indirect dangers such as bombing or artillery fire.

If nothing else, the sheer numbers of deserters precluded especially harsh treatment – and requires some explanation. Research in other contexts has highlighted that pre-existing connections between soldiers, notably in the context of the American Civil War, made them more rather than less likely to desert. Having continued, close relationships with those around them made such a course of action more rather than less attractive.[49] Not only could the topic be broached and discussed with less fear of official or unofficial censure, the persistence of such relationships was in some ways a challenge to volunteers' wholehearted commitment to their role as soldiers. The presence of friends and family was a constant reminder that life existed outwith the immediate unit. The wartime trope of fire-forged bonds made between soldiers in battle was, in this case, subverted, as interpersonal relationships were to a large degree already defined.[50] This combined with other factors – not least the harsh losses and conditions but also the prospect of escaping judicial punishment altogether once they had left Spain – helps explain the severe rate of desertion among the Scottish volunteers.

Post, Party, Politics

Regarding Jimmy Riddel, I have no personal effects belonging to him, he went from my section to the [unclear] on the 9th July, during the Brunete offensive, about the 12th or 13th July they were bringing food up in the *camion* when they were strafed by a plane, Cde Woodhouse was killed, Jimmy was wounded, he got better of the wound but died of some internal trouble in Murcia, Cde John Angus, who is with me just now was there wounded and has given me the information. Tell Mrs Riddel her son was a brave anti-fascist fighter both at Jarama and Brunete. At Jarama Johnny and I went over together and lay behind the same olive tree. I wrote Aitken a few days ago. I have seen Bob Middleton who is with Battalion just now, Bobby Ball is training here. You have to find out if Johnny Young's wife is writing, he has had no word from home for some time, he is in the Maryhill local.[51]

This letter, written by William McGregor of Maryhill, Glasgow, is typical of much of the volunteers' correspondence. Scholarly literature on soldiers' wartime letters highlights their ambiguity as a source into individuals' thoughts and feelings. Letters must be understood as performative, projecting a desired self-image to an audience. As seen in Chapter 3, this has particular pitfalls when considering letters as evidence of motivation and ideological commitment – just as First World War letters attempted to convey the image of the dutiful, patriotic and carefree warrior to those at home, so too did volunteers in Spain attempt to convey the ideological purity of both their cause and themselves.[52] In this context, however, it is the nature of the audiences that these performances were designed to reach that provide insight. The public nature of these letters, read not just by the recipient and the censor but by a wide audience of acquaintances at home – in some cases even intended for public use as propaganda – is part of their very fabric. The intended and actual uses of volunteers' letters therefore reflect the needs of communication, patronage and political manoeuvring.

What is striking about the letters of volunteers like McGregor is the extent that they were given over to gossip. Pages were filled with news of injuries, deaths and captives, changed addresses, chance encounters and visits to mutual friends and family. Rather than simply being idle chatter, this gossip fulfilled an important function in the absence of reliable lines of communication. Information was often not personalised; it was passed on from a wide circle of acquaintance on both ends, in the knowledge that, of several letters sent, only one might arrive in good time, or at all. These connections served purposes beyond the sharing of vital personal information. For senior communists, who often had the best-developed networks in Spain, this correspondence served as an informal backchannel for advice, feedback and political direction. Scottish networks also offered a means of surveillance both within and without Spain, allowing for individuals' morale to be monitored and manipulated, the identification of and co-ordination against dissenting voices and effective promotion of the International Brigades at home.

McGregor's letter blends news from the front and rear with messages for friends and family, from both himself and others. Aside from exchanging details unavailable through official channels, such as the circumstances of Riddel's death, McGregor also makes it clear which friends he has seen lately, where they are and what support they needed. The recipients of the letters was not the final destination. Rather, they acted as a node through which information could be distributed further, just as the writer collected information from those around them. McGregor's network happens to have been particularly well preserved. Its members were Glaswegian Communist Party activists who occupied key roles within English-speaking units, with Peter Kerrigan, Scottish District Leader and sometime CPGB representative in Spain, at its centre.[53] Others, such as Thomas McWhirter, were junior officers, whilst Alec Donaldson was in charge of propaganda for the British contingent.[54] Information about individual Scots, especially Glaswegians, was constantly gathered and exchanged. Donaldson was explicit in regarding Scottishness as the key connection, making 'a point in getting in touch with the Scots lads' in his vicinity.[55] They often demonstrated a paternal outlook for the Scottish volunteers in Spain, keeping track of their progress and well-being. McWhirter kept a special eye on those from his district, Govan.

> Bobby Shields is in hospital at present, a slight chill of the usual acclimatising nature, the four Govan boys are settling down. I'll keep my eye on big H—R, he is doing ok so far.[56]

The reliance on gossip even among high-ranking, well-informed members of the Communist Party is indicative of just how reliant all volunteers were on these informal networks for information. Often, this was the only way for those at home or in Spain to hear of casualties among friends.

> I was sorry to hear about Ralph Forrester and really surprised that such an apparently physically strong comrade should die like that. I can remember him very well in the Calton district when he really had a unique standing among the warring religious factions. I will let the Glasgow comrades know about his death.[57]

Here, the network served to inform Donaldson of the death of a colleague, and allowed him to transmit this information locally among other 'Glasgow comrades'. This particular episode highlights the extent to which these networks complemented the existence of smaller groups of Scots within the International Brigades, with exchanges of information taking place both within and between such groups. Networks were both horizontal and vertical; information passed down the line through Communist Party leaders like Donaldson could be disseminated widely through the ranks. It was not just bad news that was shared. The discovery in early 1938 that the Clydebank volunteer Robert Beggs was alive and had been in a Nationalist prison camp for nearly six months spread quickly among the Glaswegians across Spain and Scotland.

> We have just received word from Spain from Bobby Beggs that he is alive. He is a prisoner of Franco and this apparently is the first letter he has been able to get through from the time he was captured at Brunete.[58]

Tellingly, it was Donaldson, not the recipient of the letter William McAulay, who replied to Kerrigan.

> A couple of days before your letter arrived McWhirter and myself were discussing Beggs and it was suggested that there was still a possibility of him being alive. I am glad that this is so because he was a good steady comrade here and now that his capture has been established it ought to be possible to get his release.[59]

The movement of individuals between front, rear and home also played an important role in keeping networks informed.[60] Thanks to censorship and occasional need for delicacy, visits in person could be considerably more candid and informative. Writing to a fellow Blairgowrie communist, William Gilmour made clear the limits of communicating by letter.

> There are many things to tell you, things which it would never do to write upon, things that are only meant for the private conversation, and observance of two class conscious individuals, and I will if I ever reach home endeavor to enlighten you on some of the subjects, many of which have pleased, and others which have troubled me.[61]

Morale could also be managed proactively. After several repatriated Glasgow volunteers allegedly spread 'rumours' in early 1938, Tom McWhirter put together a rejoinder signed by the Glaswegians in his unit, which was duly sent back to help refute negative claims.[62] In this case, the speed with which information could travel along unofficial lines of communication, combined with the large cluster of Glaswegians McWhirter served alongside, enabled an effective response. In other cases, the networks functioned to send appraisals of those around them. Annie Murray, for instance, provided snippets about her co-workers.

> Nurse Susan Suton, Glasgow trained, Violet met her, she came out with me. She speaks Spanish and French well, is a very good nurse has been brought up in very bourgeois circles but is now much improved politically and very popular with everybody and so smart and clever. Then a nurse Mary Slater, very political . . . She is not a good mixer and is ever so happy on night duty or with someone untrained and really needs a bit of tactful handling but is a good worker too.[63]

Peter Kerrigan's Glasgow network was used for similar ends. Alec Donaldson was particularly forthcoming on such matters, writing to Kerrigan
about volunteers such as Andy Anderson, who was 'a very good lad with
some weaknesses', and 'McDougall, McWhirter, O'Connell', who were
'real gems'.[64] He saved his most fulsome praise for the Aberdonian Bob
Cooney.

> Recently I met Bob Cooney for the first time in my life. He impressed
> me tremendously and I am of the opinion that he is the best political
> man out here. He is popular and balanced. I think he shall go to the
> Brigade and not the Battalion. It is better so because we have too many
> good comrades as battalion commissars.[65]

Such informal observations underpinned a broader system of formal evaluations in Spain, assessing the strengths and weaknesses of each volunteer,
and their capacity for future progression in the Party.[66] With hundreds
requiring appraisal, word of mouth took on a vital role in ensuring that the
Party was kept up to date with volunteers' personal qualities. A network
of peers whose opinions they could rely on was of clear utility – not least
because it helped safeguard their own status in the Party.

Networks could also act as an informal backchannel through which
advice, concerns and suggestions could be aired without fear. As discussed
further below, openly expressing disagreement with Party policy was difficult. In informal and private settings; however, communication tended
to be relatively frank.[67] However, in situations where informal face-to-face
meetings were impossible, personal correspondence bridged the gap. A
striking element of the correspondence of Kerrigan's network is the familiar and informal tone. It is jarring to read of Kerrigan, the most important
Party official in Scotland, referred to as a 'big bear with a sore nut' by
McWhirter.[68] Alec Donaldson used humour to deflect criticism – when
Kerrigan raised concerns about the 'gloomy' tone of his propaganda output, his 'revolutionary soul was temporarily crushed'.[69] He could also be
brutally honest:

> [I] was considerably cut up after the Brunete events. The fact that our
> best comrades went 'down' in that offensive upset me tremendously.
> That, perhaps, is the best comment on your estimation of my 'cynicism'.[70]

Alongside justifying and defending their actions to their superiors, these
mid-ranking Party members also felt comfortable offering criticisms and

suggestions themselves. In February 1938, Donaldson complained about stifling censorship and the poor screening of volunteers, writing that there was not 'good enough control of the type of people being sent', with 'one or two scandalous types who managed to get through'.[71] McWhirter was even more explicit in his opinions on repatriation of 'useless' volunteers.

> The so-named 'Repatriates' are on the way back up, definitely a disgrace on political grounds . . . and I don't believe it is in the best interests of the struggle. Naturally, I have not discussed it except here. I warn you as I am sure it will have repercussions at home, but I suppose your enquiries will be manifold.[72]

McWhirter's displeasure was abundantly clear, but his lack of opportunity to discuss it openly highlights the importance of correspondence in the absence of trusted colleagues. Donaldson also made delicate political suggestions, notably in the case of the Maryhill volunteer Johnny O'Connell. A YCL member and seasoned campaigner in the NUWM, O'Connell had come to Spain in early January 1937 and fought at Jarama.[73] Owing to 'his youthfulness, death of personal friends and disgust at leadership', he deserted at Brunete but was soon caught. Despairing at the loss of his comrades and unable to 'forgive himself' for deserting, O'Connell was demoralised and despondent for months.[74] Donaldson petitioned Kerrigan to get O'Connell repatriated.

> Personally I am worried about Johnny O'Connell and I think you aught to whisper into somebody's ear. Only the mechanical approach to the subject by the person now responsible for this work is holding him back.[75]

The leniency shown to O'Connell is striking. He avoided punishment and was sent instead to the Battalion kitchen, away from the front.[76] Moreover, his Party standing suffered relatively little, likely thanks to his connections. Donaldson himself wrote O'Connell's official evaluation, referring to his desertion in very understanding terms and classing him as 'good'.[77] A second evaluation, written by non-Scottish officials, was harsher, downgrading his rating from 'good' to 'fair' and referring to his personal conduct as 'not satisfactory', although most deserters were classed as 'weak' or 'bad'.[78] While there were limits to the benefits volunteers like Johnny O'Connell could gain from their connections, he was still much better off than many others. For many deserters or otherwise 'deficient' volunteers, not being able to put a word in the right ear could have concrete negative consequences.

Perhaps the most extreme such case was that of Alec Marcovitch, one of relatively few Scots to be openly politically persecuted while in Spain. James Hopkins used Marcovitch's case as the centrepiece of his condemnation of the British Battalion's politics. Hopkins combined Marcovitch's testimony, given in an extensive interview in 1977, with declassified personnel records held in Moscow to paint a dark picture of the fate of dissenters in the British Battalion.[79] His case is used to confirm the worst possible interpretations of the International Brigades' political culture, showing that the Stalinist ways of thinking translated to a repressive and dangerous atmosphere for non-conformers.

> Marcovitch's story is important because, as the Moscow archives of the International Brigade reveal, there were many like him who became disaffected, often deserted, and were conveniently summarized as being 'demoralised' or 'undisciplined' or 'inactive' ... Marcovitch would have agreed with John McGovern, the ILP leader, who predicted in 1937 that communism 'would still the tongues, shackle the limbs, and mould the robot minds in every militant fighter throughout the world'.[80]

Hopkins's interpretation is not unproblematic. To assume, for instance, that Marcovitch agreed with McGovern is a stretch, especially as Marcovitch himself rejoined the Communist Party during the Second World War and voiced considerable contempt for the ILP in his interview.[81] More fundamentally, it homogenises the experiences of others who deserted or became demoralised. While desertion cannot be viewed as entirely distinct from politics, most deserters do not conform to the picture of 'dissent' painted by Hopkins. Marcovitch himself, as shall become clear, was very much an outlier.

Aside from the question of whether Marcovitch's experiences were at all typical, his testimony needs to be treated more critically than Hopkins allows. Whilst Hopkins implies that Marcovitch's account is confirmed by de-classified Comintern records, the reality is much more ambiguous. Aside from providing different reasons for Marcovitch's persecution – his Comintern file claims he was advocating for all volunteers' right to repatriation – the dates and locations in his file are incompatible with his claims to have been assigned to a special operations unit operating behind enemy lines as punishment in advance of the Ebro offensive in July 1938.[82]

Whilst Comintern records should not be assumed to be inherently trust-worthy, the discrepancies indicate a need for caution in accepting the more peculiar of Marcovitch's claims.

Interestingly, there may be another version of Marcovitch's story available from an unlikely source. Ralph Glasser's autobiography con-tains a section on his influences growing up during in 1930s Glasgow, including his friendship with a young communist agitator, 'Bernard Lipchinsky'. Lipchinsky's description fits Marcovitch neatly – a young, talented, well-known orator, part of the Gorbals Jewish commu-nity.[83] Although impossible to prove definitively, it is very likely that Lipchinsky was an anonymised version of Marcovitch, and Glasser was recounting a story told by a childhood friend. If so, the similarities and divergences between these two versions of Marcovitch's tale are telling. Both are thematically similar – covering political enthusiasm, disillusionment with petty corruption of higher-ranking officials, and persecution for unclear and unexplained reasons.

However, the details of each are wildly different. Whilst Marcovitch cast himself as a guerrilla fighter in his testimony, Lipchinsky is a 'mind policeman', who frets at his dirty deeds and the 'lads [who] would never get back across the water because of me'. Eventually, he himself is targeted for 'removal' at the hands of a former comrade, whose ambush he escapes and he manages to shoot in self-defence.[84] As with the claim to have joined a secret special operations unit, this narrative lacks plausibility. Very few British volunteers were executed for political or other offences.[85] Whilst several volunteers worked with Republican military intelligence, none described anything like the atmosphere indicated in Glasser's account.[86] Notably, both stories paint Marcovitch as a heroic, dashing figure despite his persecution. Marcovitch's stories might be best understood as a reac-tion to what he anticipated being his starring role in life becoming an essentially dull, unheroic experience. The most likely version, borne out by International Brigade records, is that he was sent to a labour camp prior to the Ebro offensive, and was briefly released back to the Battalion during the offensive, before being imprisoned once more, this time in a Republi-can jail.[87] In other words, whilst Marcovitch's claims of victimisation are certainly true, he likely invented or exaggerated some key details.

Marcovitch's troubles also point to the continued importance of the various communist networks. He, by his own account, saw himself as an outsider in both Spain and Glasgow, cultivating 'grassroots' connections ahead of relationships with more senior or influential figures, several of whom he mentioned falling out with.[88] Strikingly, Marcovitch's testimony never touches on friendship – even the 'grassroots' figures he speaks of were faceless and anonymous, evoking a crowd that he felt he could influence, but not individuals with whom he connected. This suggests that Marcovitch understood the Party as a political space, but did not grasp the social bonds that underpinned the politics. Without friends in good standing who could speak for him and vouch for his benign intentions, it was much more likely that others would assume the worst. Put another way, Marcovitch, despite his apparent brilliance as a political orator, was a difficult character. This, as it would in many organisations, made him a much easier target for official displeasure. This is not to say that he deserved the consequences, rather that it is difficult to imagine an individual more likely to face the ire of the International Brigades' political establishment.

Marcovitch's fall from grace also sheds light on how political non-conformity was handled within the British Battalion. His case indicates that fluency in Stalinist modes of communication was vital for volunteers who sought to be part of any substantive discussion about the International Brigades themselves. Marcovitch, by both his own and his superiors' accounts, did not conform to either the expected language or conventions required to successfully and safely communicate internal criticism. While Marcovitch clearly understood the precepts of democratic centralism – he recognised political meetings as an appropriate space to voice criticisms – he appeared to have a weaker grasp of how Stalinist norms operated in practice.[89] Marcovitch was simply not constructive – his key 'failing' was not framing his criticisms in a way in which their solution could be understood as reinforcing rather than disputing Party authority. His public, self-admittedly 'impetuous' complaints also militated against their being downplayed by his superiors.

Less politically experienced individuals were more likely to run afoul of these unwritten rules. An outsider's perspective is found in the memoir of the Spanish conscript Fausto Villar Esteban, who served in XV International Brigade. He recalled a fraught experience when asked his views on strategy by some American communists. After hesitating but deciding to 'speak [his] mind', for most of his talk 'all of the Brigaders are nodding approval, but the moment I mention the chances of Franco striking out for the Mediterranean, a chorus of murmurs goes up labelling me a defeatist and even a fascist'. Although his friends smoothed the incident over, Esteban learned his lesson, and was careful to frame his observations more prudently afterwards.[90] Charles O'Neill, an inexperienced Glaswegian communist, also stumbled over these unwritten rules. In O'Neill's case, he was required to make an abject apology to the Political Commissar Dave Springhall for 'allowing my personal feeling to get the better of me' and 'neglecting his CP line'.[91] However, his 'political honesty' and good front service worked in his favour, and O'Neill received generally positive evaluations, albeit not regarding his future as a complex political thinker.[92] Such incidents confirm not just the existence of opaque boundaries to 'acceptable' criticisms but also the importance of personal standing and strong relationships in mitigating the consequences of overstepping.[93]

Status and unwritten rules also defined more formal meetings, characterised by Cooney as 'where our weaknesses were thrashed out in a spirit of healthy self-criticism'.[94] This can be understood as further evidence of democratic centralism in practice, with meetings acting as acceptable spaces for criticisms to be voiced. However, not all such discussions could be mediated strictly by Stalinist norms. Tom Murray was candid in acknowledging the reactive nature of some such meetings, particularly when confronting simmering issues like repatriation.[95] One report from August 1937 noted that, once the volunteers were withdrawn from the line, 'almost every form of complaint began to be heard at once, combined with cynical expressions about the conduct of the war, the offensive, and the government'. Even 'good' Party members took part, hinting at a dynamic where collective discontent provided cover for questioning military and political leadership.[96] Such incidents recurred throughout the war. An 'extraordinary meeting' of XV Brigade Commissars in September 1938 discussed the ubiquitous and open complaints regarding exhaustion and desire to return home, even among officers.[97] Such examples suggest that enforcing Stalinist norms required collective understanding and policing of the boundaries, and as such could not simply be imposed upon an unwilling group. While the leadership was naturally concerned about such views, so long as they were commonly held there was little they could do.

In some cases, however, the Party was very successful in shaping the boundaries of acceptable discourse, notably in the response to the May 1937 fighting in Barcelona between communist-backed government forces and the anti-Stalinist *Partido Obrero de Unificación Marxista* (POUM), which favoured a more revolutionary approach to the war effort.[98] The CPGB had especial reason for concern, even beyond the usual obsession with 'Trotskyists'. The small British contingent in the POUM militia, as well as the presence in Barcelona of other non-communist activists, meant that other versions of events spread to Britain – a particular concern in Scotland, with several prominent Scottish ILP members and anarchists, notably Ethel MacDonald, able to provide alternative versions of events.[99] Ignoring or downplaying the incident might have allowed space for these anti-Stalinist critiques of the communist role in Spain to take root among less ideologically committed volunteers.

The response was a swift and unprecedented propaganda campaign. Within days, the XV Brigade newspaper published articles on the 'revolutionary face of fascism', containing unprecedented vitriol.

> Following months of patient explaining, the Government has finally determined to tolerate no more 'leftist' sabotage in the rearguard. Not sabotage alone, but thinly disguised banditry alienating the sympathies of the peasant and small trader from the Republic . . . Against the Fascist inspired terrorists the central Government made its hand felt, taking full responsibility for public order in Catalonia . . .
> The hour for physical extermination of Trotskyism has arrived.[100]

This marked a distinct departure from the usual language of unity and the Popular Front. It is a sign, perhaps, that the extremes of Stalinism were only lightly buried, that the leap to the politics of extermination was uncomfortably small. Any volunteer with connections to the Communist Party knew and understood the 'Trotskyist' label as signifying an enemy within, even before coming to Spain. As the Battalion was never called into direct action against the 'Trotskyists', it is difficult to say whether these labels would have served their purpose in legitimising liquidation. Hugh Sloan recalled his newly arrived group being asked whether they would be willing to 'help put an end' to the 'situation in Barcelona', to which 'the whole group agreed'.[101] What was meant and understood by this is vague, but ominous.

Such language made it impossible to formulate any sort of legitimate dissent or criticism when it came to the POUM. A firm line had been drawn around acceptable discourse, and crossing it would mean setting oneself against not only the Party but also the Republican war effort itself, which all volunteers agreed was sacrosanct. That is not to say that these attacks should be viewed entirely cynically. Private and public records indicate that the British leaders wholeheartedly believed what they were saying about the POUM. Casual references in private letters between communist loyalists follow the public line closely, such as one message from William McGregor to Peter Kerrigan, commenting on how the POUM and ILP had engineered the 'rising in our rear at Barcelona'.[102] For Party activists, these attitudes dovetailed neatly with their views on the ILP contingent. Even months after the controversy in Barcelona, William McAulay reacted bitterly to what he saw as the ILP's attempt to piggyback on the International Brigades' reputation.

I showed your letter to several of the lads, and what surprised all of them, was the reference you made to the ILP speaking about an ILP section of the International Brigade. I have been in Spain now for 11 months and have never heard about it until I read your letter. We were all disgusted to hear that the ILP are attempting to cash in on the name of the International Brigade.[103]

Such letters reflect the success of efforts to define political discourse surrounding the POUM and ILP. This was the result of persistent efforts to promote this line across all means possible. William Gilmour, for instance, wrote about one particularly effective lecture from the American communist Bob Miller, who 'simplified the recent Barcelona disturbances, the intricacies, facts and figures were all proved to us by documents and newspaper cuttings', producing 'all that condemned the Trotskyites, and Fascists'.[104] Articles continued to appear regularly in the Brigade press, such as a supposed first-hand account entitled 'Trotskyist Traitors' by the ILP volunteer J. A. Franford detailing the 'suspicious' activities he had witnessed while in the POUM militia, illustrated by a menacing caricature of Trotsky.[105] Even a year later, in June 1938, Tom Murray wrote home about the political meetings he organised about how Trotskyism 'attempts to operate in Spain'.[106] Even in oral history interviews decades later, there was often unwillingness to deviate far from these views. For some, the vendetta against the POUM and Orwell would last a lifetime.[107]

Conclusions

Being Scottish mattered while in Spain. That Scots banded together and sought each other out at every stage of the volunteering process is testimony to the value placed on maintaining existing relationships in difficult and testing conditions, and the continued importance of the Communist Party networks that underpinned recruitment. Yet this is not simply a question of nationality and imagined common ground between Scottish volunteers – locality is particularly vital in understanding the way in which volunteers sought out companions in Spain. These comrades did not just volunteer together; they travelled, fought and died together. At no point in the volunteering experience did their prior relationships become irrelevant. However, Scots should not be regarded as inherently exceptional in this regard. What distinctiveness they showed is for the most part a matter of scale – groupings and networks grew from pre-existing relationships fostered by the particularly active political communities that existed in the hubs of Scottish recruitment for the International Brigades. The absence of banal signifiers of national identity – aside from one volunteer who attempted to bring bagpipes to Spain, to general amusement – indicates that the arguments presented in this chapter are likely applicable to any grouping that saw especially concentrated recruitment within specific communities.[108] As such, it is likely that local and regional identities influenced the lived experience of volunteering in the International Brigades, regardless of nationality.

These conclusions also point to the enduring power of personal and political connections in the International Brigades. Even when they were physically separated, being part of the right networks influenced many aspects of volunteers' experiences in Spain. It determined how quickly and from whom they and their family received news, shaped perceptions of their reliability and character among communist elites and allowed for safe and productive informal discussions. As a result, having the right connections offered tangible benefits, while lacking them meant intolerance, suspicion and less support from the Party. As shall be seen in the next chapter, the influence of these networks could also bridge the gap between Scotland and Spain.

Notes

1. A detailed study of civil war desertion has been written by Pedro Carrol, though the reliance on Spanish sources makes the discussion of foreign desertion less useful. Pedro Corral, *Desertores: La Guerra Civil que nadie quiere contar* (Barcelona, 2006). See also Stradling, 'English-speaking Units', 757–64. I am particularly grateful to Professor Stradling for providing his sourced list of British desertions. Whilst some few cases appear to be mistakes, the vast bulk are not, and helped confirm the figures provided here.
2. H. O. Knester, 'Report on deserters, Donald and Sneddon', 9 May 1937, MML, Box 39, File A/9.
3. Gerben Zaagsma, '"Red Devils": the Botwin Company in the Spanish Civil War', *East European Jewish Affairs* 33 (2003), 92.
4. Renton in MacDougall, *Voices from the Spanish Civil War*, 21.
5. Renton in MacDougall, *Voices from the Spanish Civil War*, 25–6.
6. Watters in MacDougall, *Voices from the Spanish Civil War*, 36.
7. Renton in MacDougall, *Voices from the Spanish Civil War*, 26.
8. The other surviving Edinburgher, Charles O'Neill, had travelled to Spain earlier as part of a Glaswegian group. 'Biografia de Militantes: Charles O'Neill', RGASPI, 545/6/181/65.
9. These were George Jackson (Cowdenbeath), Malcolm Smith (Dundee) and Charlie McLeod (Aberdeen). Tom Murray to McLeod, 23 October 1938, NLS, TMP, Box 1, File 6.
10. Baxell, *British Volunteers*, 11.

11. Tom to Janet Murray, 4 April 1938, NLS, TMP, Box 1, File 1.
12. Bloomfield in MacDougall, *Voices from the Spanish Civil War*, 52.
13. Clarke in MacDougall, *Voices from the Spanish Civil War*, 57.
14. Brown in MacDougall, *Voices from the Spanish Civil War*, 108.
15. This is likely an underestimate as different sources recorded different dates, most often either departure from Britain (Security Service surveillance) or arrival in Spain (Battalion records). TNA, KV 5/112-31; RGASPI, 545/6/91.
16. Fullarton in MacDougall, *Voices from the Spanish Civil War*, 294.
17. 'Entradas de voluntarios del dia 12 de enero 1938', RGASPI, 545/6/36/15-16.
18. Alec to Annie Park, 20 February 1938 and 21 February 1938, MML, Box A-12, File Pa/10-11.
19. Stradling, *History and Legend*, 28.
20. Brown in MacDougall, *Voices from the Spanish Civil War*, 112.
21. 'AT Battery', AGGCE, PS-Aragon, Box 6, File 13, Doc. 17.
22. Londragan in MacDougall, *Voices from the Spanish Civil War*, 172, 174.
23. Dunlop and Londragan in MacDougall, *Voices from the Spanish Civil War*, 118, 171.
24. Sloan in MacDougall, *Voices from the Spanish Civil War*, 197, 205; Nicoll, TLS, MS, Tape 956.
25. Nicoll, Tape 956.
26. Hopkins, *Heart of the Fire*, 168-71; Baxell, *British Volunteers*, 67.
27. Dunlop in MacDougall, *Voices from the Spanish Civil War*, 131-2.
28. Clarke in MacDougall, *Voices from the Spanish Civil War*, 60-1.
29. El Ministerio de Defensa Nacional to the Comandante de la XV Brigada, 21 November 1937, AGGCE, PS-Aragon, Box 6, File 11, Doc. 3.
30. Baxell, *British Volunteers*, 140-1.
31. 'Actividades del dia', 18 September 1938, RGASPI, 545/3/435/167.
32. Cooney, quoted in Corkhill and Rawnsley, *Road to Spain*, 121.
33. Baxell cites an article in *Nuestro Combate* referring to a meeting that voiced 'complete approval' of the sentences, indicating that Stalinist norms were not entirely absent. However, I have been unable to locate the cited issue. Baxell, *British Volunteers*, 197n.
34. Baxell, *British Volunteers*, 141. Another was Bert Overton, a disastrously incompetent English officer. It is plausible that Overton was indeed 'gotten rid of'. Yet the underlying evidence is strange. Hopkins made only a short, unsourced claim that 'some wondered' if getting Overton killed was an 'expedient' method of removing a 'dangerous embarrassment'. Baxell quotes this passage, but does not clarify that it was unsourced, attributing the words to 'several brigaders', whilst others have quoted Baxell, in Ben Hughes's case muddying the waters further by claiming these were the words of 'one veteran' who 'openly admitted' the foul play. Whilst there may be a primary source underpinning this chain of references, it is not clear what. Hopkins, *Heart of the Fire*, 268; Baxell, *British Volunteers*, 80; Hughes, *They Shall Not Pass!*, 182.

35. Orden Especial del Dia, 11 January 1938, RGASPI, 545/3/4/103.

36. Kirschenbaum, *International Communism*, 117–20.

37. Another semi-mysterious case is James Donald discussed above. Donald was transferred to Madrid for 'interrogation' in May 1937. Baxell argues that the official claim that Donald died at Belchite was impossible, as he was still in prison. However, other evidence suggests that he was returned to the British Battalion and assigned to a labour company at Tarazona in late 1937. He was likely drafted back into a frontline unit and killed during the Aragon crisis. His hometown acquaintance, Hugh Sloan, mentioned witnessing his death in March 1938. Baxell, *British Volunteers*, 143; Sloan in MacDougall, *Voices from the Spanish Civil War*, 236; Malcolm Sneddon to British Consul (Valencia), 28 May 1937, TNA, FO 889/2/38; 'English in Spain' [November 1937?], RGASPI, 545/6/89/50; 'Relacion de combatientes hechos prisioneros', 1938, RGASPI, 545/6/98/4.

38. Hopkins, *Into the Heart of the Fire*, 268. Original quote is from 'MEEKE, WM', 17 October 1937, RGASPI, 545/6/172/6. Meeke is listed as Irish in several sources, but the bulk of primary material has him born and living in Glasgow.

39. Baxell, *British Volunteers*, 198n. This is confirmed by Security Service records, 'MEEKE, William', KV 5/127.

40. 'William Meeke', 4 July 1938, RGASPI, 545/6/172/4.

41. 'JUSTICE James', n.d., RGASPI, 545/6/156/19.

42. Meredith to Copeman, 11 June 1937, RGASPI, 545/3/451/49.

43. Paul Somogyi, 'General Remarks', [1937?], RGASPI, 545/3/451/159.

44. Aitken, quoted in Cook, *Apprentices*, 82–3.

45. James to Aitken, 31 May 1937, RGASPI, 545/3/444/10–11.

46. CPGB to PCE Secretariat, 17 November 1938, RGASPI, 545/6/87/27. A similar 'line' was proposed in another case. Kerrigan to Pollitt, 13 August 1938, MML, Box C, File 24/6.

47. Just 21 Scottish deserters were fully successful in escaping Spain, meaning those who were caught (and presumably punished) were still thrice as likely to survive as non-deserters.

48. Economides to Paynter, 14 October 1937, RGASPI, 545/2/256/376.

49. Peter Bearman, 'Desertion as Localism: Army Unit Solidarity and Group Norms in the U.S. Civil War', *Social Forces* 70:2 (1991), 321–42.

50. A comparison can be made with some British forces in the First World War – both the famous 'Pals' Battalions, and certain socially cohesive territorial regiments. See Helen McCartney, *Citizen Soldiers: The Liverpool Territorials in the First World War* (Cambridge, 2005), 57–117.

51. McGregor to Kerrigan, 19 November 1937, MML, Box 50, File McG/1.

52. On wartime letter writing, see Michael Roper, *The Secret Battle: Emotional survival in the Great War* (Manchester, 2010); Kate Hunter, 'More than an Archive of War: Intimacy and Manliness in the Letters of a Great War Soldier to the Woman He Loved, 1915–1919', *Gender & History* 25:2 (2013), 339–52; Bruno Cabanes, 'Negotiating Intimacy in the Shadow of War (France, 1914–1920s):

New Perspectives in the Cultural History of World War I', *French Politics, Society & Culture* 31:1 (2013), 8–11.

53. Baxell, *British Volunteers*, 10.
54. McWhirter to Kerrigan, 2 November 1937, MML, Box 50, File McW/1; 'DONALDSON Alec', RGASPI, 545/6/125/61.
55. Donaldson to Kerrigan, 2 October 37, MML, Box 50, File Dn/6.
56. McWhirter to Kerrigan, 16 February 1938, MML, Box 50, File McW/12.
57. Donaldson to Kerrigan, 15 February 1938, MML, Box 50, File Dn/5.
58. Kerrigan to McAulay, 29 January 1938, MML, Box 50, File McA/2.
59. Donaldson to Kerrigan, 15 February 1938. See also McWhirter to Kerrigan, 16 February 1938.
60. For example Kerrigan to McGregor, 1 December 1937, MML, Box 50, File McG/2.
61. Gilmour to Paterson, 17 August 1937, MML, Box 50, File Gl/30.
62. McWhirter to Kerrigan, n.d., MML, Box 50, File McW/13–16.
63. Annie to Lily Murray, 3 April 1937, NLS, TMP, Box 1, File 3.
64. Donaldson to Kerrigan, 17 January 1938 and 2 October 1937.
65. Donaldson to Kerrigan, 4 November 1937, MML, Box 50, File Dn/3.
66. Skoutelsky, *Novedad*, 328.
67. Private openness is apparent in surveillance records, e.g. 'Glasgow Chief Constable's Report', 12 October 1937, TNA, KV 3/391/195.
68. McWhirter to Kerrigan, 9 November 1937, MML, Box 50, File McW/2.
69. Donaldson to Kerrigan, 17 January 1938, MML.
70. Donaldson to Kerrigan, 2 October 1937, MML.
71. Donaldson to Kerrigan, 15 February 1938, MML.
72. McWhirter to Kerrigan, 16 February 1938, MML.
73. 'O'CONNELL John', RGASPI, 545/6/180/25–6.
74. 'John O'Connell – Evaluation', 19 October 1938, RGASPI, 545/6/180/27.
75. Donaldson to Kerrigan, 15 February 1938, MML.
76. 'John O'Connell – Declaration', RGASPI, 545/6/180/31.
77. 'John O'Connell – Evaluation', 19 October 1938, RGASPI.
78. 'John O'Connell – Evaluation', 5 November 1938, RGASPI, 545/6/180/28.
79. Hopkins, *Heart of the Fire*, 258–64.
80. Hopkins, *Heart of the Fire*, 264.
81. Marcovitch, Tape 182.
82. See especially Marcovitch's own declaration, 3 September 1938, RGASPI, 545/6/168/11.
83. Occupation (cutter) and age (a few years older than Glasser himself) also match closely. Glasser, *Growing up in the Gorbals*, 34. As discussed in Chapter 2, few, if any, other Gorbals Jews fought in Spain, and there was certainly no 'Lipchinsky'. 'Marcovitch' itself was not a pseudonym, as his father wrote to the Foreign Office under that name. Marcovitch to Lord Halifax, 29 January 1939, TNA, FO 371/24122/223–4.

84. Glasser, *Growing up in the Gorbals*, 115–17.
85. Baxell, *British Volunteers*, 140–3. This is contested by Pedro Corral, who claims it was more frequent than imagined, but is unable to point to concrete examples. Corral, *Desertores*, 487–8.
86. Tellingly, such accusations are absent from Fraser, *The Truth*. Fraser – who converted from devoted communist to devoted Catholic in the 1940s – wrote extensively on the supposedly totalitarian, Soviet-inspired structures of the International Brigades, having served in military intelligence.
87. RGASPI, 545/6/168/5–15.
88. Hopkins claims Marcovitch was adamant that his previous disagreements with Peter Kerrigan led to his ill-treatment. Hopkins, *Heart of the Fire*, 263–4. This is a curious reading of Marcovitch's testimony – the interviewer asked whether Kerrigan was behind things, and Marcovitch conceded it was possible. Marcovitch, Tape 182. According to Cooney's unashamed testimony, he and Bill Rust orchestrated Marcovitch's persecution. Cooney, IWMSA, Tape 804/5.
89. Marcovitch, Tape 182.
90. Villar Esteban, *Un valencianito*, 60–1.
91. O'Neill to Springhall, nd, RGASPI, 545/6/181/73.
92. 'Charles O'Neill – Evaluation', 19 October 1938, RGASPI, 545/6/181/67.
93. Another case was Arthur Nicoll, the AT Battery Political Commissar. His positive evaluation on leaving Spain noted occasional 'thoughtless criticism of high command', indicating both that such criticism was noted and considered significant, but also that it was outweighed by Nicoll's standing and service. 'Arthur Nicoll – Evaluation', 5 November 1938, RGASPI, 545/6/178/34
94. Bob Cooney, *Proud Journey*, 53. Bill Paynter characterised meetings similarly in *Volunteer for Liberty*, 25 October 1937, 3.
95. Murray in MacDougall, *Voices from the Spanish Civil War*, 314–15.
96. 'Report on Morale of XV Brigade', 8 August 1937, RGASPI, 545/3/435/72–3.
97. 'Parte extraordinario', 6 September 1938, RGASPI, 545/3/435/141–3.
98. These incidents were famously, and controversially, chronicled in George Orwell, *Homage to Catalonia* (London, 1986), esp. 148–69. A more recent overview is Helen Graham, *The Spanish Republic at War 1936–1939* (Cambridge, 2002), 254–315.
99. Jackson, *British Women*, 151.
100. *Nuestro Combate*, 8 May 1937.
101. Sloan in MacDougall, *Voices from the Spanish Civil War*, 199.
102. McGregor to Kerrigan, 19 November 1937, MML, Box 50, File McG/1.
103. McAulay to Kerrigan, 19 November 1937, MML, Box 50, File McA/1.
104. Gilmour to Paterson, 7 June 1937, MML, Box 50, File Gl/24.
105. *Volunteer for Liberty*, 13 September 1937, 9–10.
106. Tom to Janet Murray, 16 June 1938, MML, Box D-4, File My/14.

107. For example Clarke, Brown and Sloan in MacDougall, *Voices from the Spanish Civil War*, 64, 109, 198–9, 234. For an 'official' example of lingering animosity, see Bill Alexander, 'George Orwell and Spain' in Norris (ed.), *Inside the Myth. Orwell: Views from the Left* (London, 1984), 85–102.

108. According to Robert Walker, it was 'a pity' the promised piper never turned up, as 'a good loud lament on the bagpipes might prove the decisive factor in putting the fascists to flight'. Walker to Kerrigan, 16 April 1938, MML, Box 50, File Wk/3.

5

Between Fronts

The 'Home Front' has long been the subject of historical research into modern conflict. In the case of transnational mobilisations, however, the term is inherently ambiguous. The volunteers' home societies were not mobilised behind the war effort, and the relatives they left at home did not experience 'wartime' material conditions, much less any particular danger from invasion or bombardment. However, this situation had drawbacks as well as advantages – for instance, the absence of governmental arrangements designed to mitigate the absence of breadwinners or facilitate communication between home and the front. Leave home was difficult to obtain, if not downright impossible. For the volunteers and their families alike, navigating the situation presented a series of unusual problems. For the Communist Party, managing these unexpected responsibilities was also challenging, and maintaining morale at home and in Spain involved overcoming a series of organisational and cultural hurdles, sometimes with only mixed success.

The ways in which these challenges developed and were addressed have received less attention from historians than might be expected. In existing history writing, studying the 'Home Front' is usually taken to mean domestic political and humanitarian activism on behalf of the Spanish Republic, implying a neat division between volunteering for the International Brigades and 'Aid Spain' movements at home. Yet from the perspective of the volunteers and their families, their participation in the conflict raised issues that were distinct from the usual concerns of pro-Republican activism. The emotional and practical strains of separation were considerable, but, outwith the Communist Party itself, there were few channels through which they could be addressed or ameliorated. This lent the Communist Party a degree of power in managing communication between Scotland and Spain, not to mention when it came to the sticky subject of leave and repatriation. Here – as with the political benefits discussed in the previous chapter – being integrated into the right networks could pay dividends, though desired outcomes were far from assured, even for otherwise well-connected Party members. Moreover, the persistence of personal and political networks could also pose problems for the Party in fostering the impression that decisions regarding leave and repatriation were based on patronage rather than need or fairness.

Yet by far the biggest issue, for the families of volunteers and the Communist Party alike, was financial. Though the initial intention had been to recruit only unmarried men without dependants, this policy was never consistently implemented, and the carnage at Jarama laid bare the reality that some volunteers would return home unable to earn a living due to their wounds. This was a burden that the financially precarious CPGB could not hope to meet, either immediately or in the long term, but also could not be avoided for political as well as moral reasons. Significant sums would need to be raised in Britain to support the International Brigade volunteers' families, as well as any disabled veterans who returned home. Importantly, this was viewed initially as a short-term commitment – once volunteers returned home, they could resume supporting their dependants, whilst it was expected that Republican victory would mean that a grateful Spanish government could grant pensions to disabled foreign volunteers. In the short term, however, a broad sustained effort was necessary to raise money to meet these obligations. The resulting campaign – formalised in June 1937 as the International Brigades Wounded and Dependants' Committee (WADC) – occupied a unique space in the wider British Aid Spain movement, offering perhaps the most direct way for British-based activists to support the Republic war effort.

In the light of this, this chapter takes a two-pronged approach to the question of how a transnational war effort was supported and administered, conceptually bringing the narrative back from Spain to Scotland. The first section deals with communication and movement between Scotland and Spain. Once again, the analysis points to the continued importance of pre-existing networks among the volunteers, though it is here that some of their ambiguities and dangers emerge. Aside from the problems faced by those who were less well integrated into the 'right' circles, the potential for real or perceived manipulation became apparent as the conflict went on, proving an enduring challenge to the Communist Party's moral authority. The second section turns to domestic efforts to support the International Brigade volunteers' families and wounded. Aside from playing an important role in facilitating recruitment for the International Brigades, the WADC offers a unique window in the nature of pro-Republican solidarity across Scotland and Britain, allowing us to map not just where support for the International Brigades was coming from but also the organisations that were taking a forthright political position on the issue of Spain, highlighting important regional and institutional divides across the country.

Between Scotland and Spain

Perhaps the most obvious way in which the International Brigade volunteers could be supported from Scotland was through their friends and relatives. Volunteers, as with soldiers abroad in any context, were hungry for news and contact from home, a desire reflected not only in their own correspondence but in the recurring and vociferous complaints regarding the efficiency of the International Brigades Postal Service.[1] These communications, as discussed in the previous chapter, came to reflect conscious strategies to communicate effectively in difficult circumstances, particularly as 'official' channels were either slow or non-existent. For volunteers and their loved ones at home alike, news was a precious commodity in short supply, and personal connections at home and in Spain went a long way towards mitigating this situation.

Equally, however, uneven access and integration into these networks could lead to uneven outcomes when it came to communicating and moving between Spain and Scotland. Moreover, the overlap between social and political spheres meant that these networks served a variety of purposes, not all of which were completely benign. In seeking to proactively manage the flow of communication to and from Spain, official and unofficial censorship acted to shape morale and perception on both ends. The results could be morally ambiguous – the line between maintaining a positive image of the International Brigades abroad and actively misleading both volunteers and their families could be a thin one. In the eyes of certain Party activists, at least, political necessity justified interference in their comrades' personal affairs. The perception, in turn, that personal connections were used to channel patronage and favouritism proved to be an enduring challenge to volunteers' morale in the British Battalion.

The Murray family, with three members in Spain and several others active in solidarity movements at home, provides an excellent example of how boundaries blurred between Scotland and Spain. Thanks both to their standing in the Party – they came from a good 'CP family' – and their migration throughout Scotland during the 1930s, the Murrays formed the backbone of a diverse network connecting Spain and Scotland.[2] Annie Murray, in Spain as a nurse, often relied on information from Scotland to keep abreast of events elsewhere in Spain.

> I am sorry to hear that Bridges and Mason were killed. I did not know that either was out. Is it little Mason of the party? I hope not he was such a good lad and such a hard worker. I am also very sorry about Donald Renton's plight. Tell their people in Edinburgh that I send my sincerest sympathy.[3]

Similar information about family and friends was communicated among Murray siblings spread throughout eastern Scotland.

> The Moirs have at last heard from Jim who is safely in Spain and has met George and Eddie. Jim's mother and father were overjoyed to get word from him. Mrs Brown has also heard from Eddie who is feeling better and he mentions that George has not yet received one letter from any of us.[4]

Jimmy Moir's story is a tragic demonstration of the utility of belonging to such networks. He remained an active part of the network up to July 1937, corresponding with his friends and family across Scotland and Spain.[5] However, Moir went missing during the Battle of Brunete, with Annie informing her family that, while there was no 'definite word' yet, she was 'afraid he is lost forever'.[6] It was another month until the 'official' channels caught up.

> We heard officially that Jim Moir was lost on the 23rd of July when a big offensive was on and the members of the Brigade were asked to retreat . . . they hold out really no hope of Jim's being alive – except on the very, very frail chance of his being a prisoner.[7]

Correspondence concerning Moir highlights not just the way that news of individuals could be tracked and communicated using unofficial networks but also the extent that these networks operated considerably more efficiently than official channels. For those without such networks, news was often slow and unreliable. The wife of the Glaswegian Alex Harvey, for instance, heard nothing for nearly six months after his death at Jarama.[8] As a non-communist who was in Spain for less than a month, Harvey lacked similar connections to Moir or the Murrays. Without anyone to communicate news of – or perhaps even notice – his death, his wife was left completely uninformed through 'official' channels.

Other cases show more clearly the subordination of Scottish networks to Communist Party needs. Networks were used to monitor repatriated volunteers, informing Party members in Scotland of potential issues and developing strategies to deal with troublemakers. After Tom Murray left for Spain in April 1938, his wife Janet wrote regarding two returned volunteers.

> I also want [Smith] to see Fred to refute if necessary any stories that Gembles might be spreading about things that might give a wrong impression. Smith's story and his do not tally and his stories about superior food the officers are getting (all lies I know) could cause a lot of harm.[9]

The object of the Murrays' concern was 19-year-old Thomas Gembles, who had been repatriated following a truck accident, which had left him half-blinded 'with the mentality of a boy of 13'.[10] Somewhat more justifiably, not least because they had sold their stories in the tabloid press, William Gilmour wrote home about several former comrades who had escaped Spain in April 1937.

> The names of the 'deserters with the yellow streak' were McDonald of Kirkcaldy, Craig of Glasgow and Parker of Dundee, I believe you would do something to expose the Parker renegade as I believe he was an erstwhile member of the CP. They were all yellow. They ran away while the fight was at its worst. There is some excuse for men whose nerves go under the strain. But there is no punishment severe enough for men who desert their comrades in the thick of the fight, and then go home to Britain pertaining to be the bearers of a petition bearing the names of 32 of our comrades who wanted to go home. These men have deliberately tried to destroy our principles by [missing] lies and the sorry part of it all there are a section of the public will believe it.[11]

Such efforts complemented broader efforts to control the flow of information to and from Spain. The International Brigade Censorship Section explicitly saw its purpose as preventing the 'sending of demoralising mail by the volunteers' as well as intercepting 'mail that is harmful and destructive to volunteer morale'.[12] Such decisions were often framed in terms of sparing families unpleasant news, such as when Glaswegian James McKissock died in early 1937.

He fell out of a window and fractured his skull. You had better not let it be known in this way however, as my reports are he was drunk and fell out, hardly inspiring for his relatives, or politically.[13]

It is telling that what was 'best' for the relatives so often coincided with what was best for the political image of the International Brigades. John Dunlop, discussing the execution of Alex Kemp, used a similar formulation.

Needless to say this was not reported at home. They were both mentioned as having died in action as it was reported in the *Daily Worker*, which would save their families the shame of knowing.[14]

Managing relatives' reactions at home was a perennial concern for the International Brigades and Communist Party leadership. When framed by 'correct' political understandings, these relatives could be powerful symbols. The mother of a Glasgow volunteer, Tom McWhirter, who died during the Aragon offensives in March 1938, wrote to the *Daily Worker* in June to encourage their readers to 'carry on' the fight and contribute money to the cause.

I know if he was here and had his wish what he would say, 'Mother, carry on, help the boys who fought along with me.' I can truthfully say he never regretted going to Spain and his letters were always full of hope for victory. So I will say, 'Good luck boys, carry on.'[15]

While McWhirter's mother did not hide or downplay her own grief, her acceptance of the cause her son had died for was a welcome refrain for the Party. In other instances, relatives could be far less accepting of circumstances. The mother of the Bathgate volunteer James Arthur consistently pushed for his return, writing in early 1938 that 'I often think they might let you home now I think you have done your bit' and 'I am beginning to weary for it all to finish and see you back home safe'.[16] Similarly, Arthur's wife complained of 'the pain you have caused me', and that his time in Spain 'could have been spent in a more happier way if only you had stayed at home'.[17] While feelings such as these were rarely publicised, they were far from uncommon among the families of volunteers, and were a source of ongoing worry for the Communist Party. This is hinted at in discussion among the Murray clan regarding Jimmy Moir's death at Brunete.

I am glad Jimmy's people have reacted the way they have. Do you ever see his sister now? When I was in hospital I opened a letter addressed to Jimmy to see if the writer had any news of him. It was from his mother who was, she said, 'perplexed and hurt' that he should have been leading a life of which she knew nothing and that he had gone away to fight in a war which could have nothing to do with him! She seems to have a very limited vision.[18]

George Murray's concern was more explicit in another letter urging his brother Tom to arrange a visit to Moir's family to head off any potential difficulties.[19] The case of Eddie Brown, a friend of the Murrays who had travelled and fought alongside George, is particularly revealing in terms of how far such interventions could be taken. In late 1937, while Brown was hospitalised due to wounds, the Murrays learned that Brown's wife, pregnant with the child of a fellow Perth communist, had eloped to London.[20] Several weeks of frantic communication across Spain and Scotland ensued, discussing the crisis behind Brown's back. Annie Murray wrote to her brother in Scotland that

[Eddie Brown] has not heard anything from his wife and I have told him nothing. He seems quite happy and resigned to his 'letterless fate'. I expect that he has his sleepless nights of worry but he seems much less worried.[21]

Even by mid-January 1938, the Murrays were still concealing the news from Brown.[22] The deliberateness of this approach is suggested by Brown's file, which highlighted potential mental health concerns, labelling him as 'hypochondriacal'.[23] Previous bouts of low morale are also alluded to in earlier letters.[24] Viewed charitably, the incident reflects the qualitative difference of serving alongside friends and family, who could not only provide a support network but had intimate knowledge of their comrades' situation and needs. Viewed cynically, however, the Murray network was being used to control the flow of personal information in order to manage an individual's morale for the good of the Party.

Party influence over the lines of communication between Scotland and Spain also extended to the physical movement of the volunteers themselves. As Richard Baxell has noted, the lack of access to leave or repatriation was one of the single most significant factors in driving discontent and desertion in Spain. Of particular concern was the perception – whether accurate or not – that senior communists eluded restrictions that forced many volunteers to stay in Spain indefinitely.[25] Many volunteers had been promised repatriation after a certain period of service, and demands to return home multiplied from mid-1937 onwards.[26] The Scottish Political Commissar George Aitken in particular struggled to cope with the volume of cases that needed to be 'fobbed off'.[27] The lack of repatriation opportunities was particularly egregious for the severely wounded. William Gilmour, for instance, grew bitter at being forced to remain even after wounds left him unfit for frontline service.

> Every time there is a possibility of me getting home something always seems to happen, and I am left high and dry, and disappointed . . . The part that rubs me is the fact that men who have not got half the service in, as good service, are managing to get home with comparative ease.[28]

Gilmour's complaint reflected the belief that while less well-connected volunteers languished in Spain, senior communists came and went much more freely. Baxell challenges the basis of this view, pointing out that the most famous such case, which saw several senior officers recalled to Britain to answer for the poor state of the Battalion's morale and organisation, was hardly a holiday for those involved.[29] Yet however unpleasant the experience of being dressed down by the CPGB General Secretary Harry Pollitt, it is unlikely to rival the privations dealt with daily at the front, or the frustration felt by those languishing in Republican hospitals. The characterisation of their return in the Battalion's newspaper, *Nuestro Combate*, as a 'well-earned rest' likely did not appease those remaining behind in Spain who justifiably felt that they also deserved a rest.[30]

Beyond this infamous example, some seemed to face fewer obstacles in coming and going. Sydney Quinn was open about the strings pulled to get him home.

> A certain comrade came to me, he says 'there's five of you going on a propaganda leave.' Well, I was never a propagandist but apparently we would never have got away if we just said you're going home, they had do something to satisfy the authorities. Now I wasn't running away, neither was the rest of them, but we thought we'd done our share.[31]

Robert Middleton, the brother of the prominent Glaswegian communist George Middleton, also managed to obtain repatriation in slightly dubious circumstances. One account – which may have been unduly coloured by his subsequent falling out with the Party – claims he was sent home due to being drunk at the front.[32] Other sources indicate that he was wounded at the Battle of Jarama.[33] What appears to have formally sealed his permission to return home, however, were '*raisons de famille*' – his wife had died leaving three children requiring care. This, at least, was what had been told to the Commandant of the Albacete base, who supplied the necessary paperwork, but is not referenced at all in Middleton's own correspondence or biographical details, and did not impede Middleton's return to Spain in October.[34] It is difficult to avoid concluding that Middleton was provided with an acceptable excuse to justify his leave in a similar fashion to Quinn.

Alec Marcovitch – whose complex relationship with Party authority was discussed in the previous chapter – was outspoken on this question in his testimony. He complained that high-ranking Party members, who stayed with the Battalion for a matter of weeks, were going home and getting a 'big middle page article' in the *Daily Worker* 'about their experiences in the Spanish Civil War'.[35] Aside from the implied slight to those who had served for months without publicity, Marcovitch questioned why repatriation could be arranged for them and not those for whom 'if any compassion existed at all' should have gone home.[36] In this case, Marcovitch was far from alone in expressing his dissatisfaction. The English volunteer William Benson made a particularly memorable complaint.

> Between them they sent young Barker back to the line, the one comrade who should have been sent back to England. He will probably get killed and nothing will be said about him, while hero's like Kerrigan, Springhall, Aitken and Copeman, will continue to be headliners in the DW. *shit* [original emphasis].[37]

Both Benson and Marcovitch linked perceived inequities surrounding repatriation to unhappiness regarding Communist Party representations of the volunteers. Whilst most agreed that propaganda about the British Battalion was necessary, they felt frustration that the spotlight often lingered on a select few Party favourites, especially if reporting did not conform to what they had experienced. Such rewards tended to accrue to communists in good political standing, often regardless of the nature of their service – the Glaswegian Alec Donaldson, for instance, was singled out to receive a special signed message from Spanish communist icon 'La Pasionaria' as reward for good service in late 1938, despite never serving at the front and having in fact refused to do so when asked.[38] In another list of 'distinguished' figures in the XV Brigade, only one Briton, the Scot George Murray, was not an officer or commissar – but he was the secretary of the Battalion's Party Committee.[39] While they may all have rendered outstanding service, such lists gave credence to the complaint that public glory was the preserve of a Party elite.

Whether or not these complaints stemmed from perception or reality, it was soon realised that they could be damaging. Writing to the Glasgow communist Thomas Anderson prior to the Battle of Brunete, Political Commissar Wally Tapsell laid out the reasons why he was refused repatriation.

> All leave outside Spain, all repatriation other than grounds of complete physical incompetence for any form of military service, is completely forbidden to Party members. Cunningham with 4 severe wounds, one bullet in his lung and his left arm stiff, leaves today to rejoin the battalion. McDade with more or less permanent paralysis of his left arm ditto.
>
> Reason? There are plenty of lads with grave domestic problems, who have had severe but not incapacitating wounds, who would like either leave or repatriation ... Under the circumstances Communists must be prepared to give a lead. Kerrigan and Springhall were ordered back for political work, but chaps here who are simply anxious to get home also want to do political work. I can appreciate and sympathise with your personal problems – the solution is to take your difficulty to your CO and get allocated some lighter job.[40]

This letter highlights the limits of volunteer networks in a military context. Not only were some requests likely to be impossible, but it was also Party members who were expected to show the lead in terms of sacrifice and discipline. Most volunteers accepted this, so long as the policies were fairly applied. It is precisely when the principle of fairness broke down that the difficulties with repatriation, leave and other treatment emerged. The importance of fairness as an integral feature of communist doctrine and values is drawn upon in a letter co-written by the Dundonian James Doyle to the authorities at Albacete after being imprisoned by the Spanish police for desertion. Doyle and his English companion claimed that, as communists, they had 'always fought against oppression', which they contrasted with the poor treatment they were receiving in prison, at times 'worse than we receive in capitalist prisons where we expect vile treatment'. Both admitted their crimes, but claimed that while 'we deserve punishment', 'we also deserve fairness'.[41] The failure to live up to these values lay at the heart of many volunteers' disillusionment with the Party on their return home. Some left Spain with their faith in the Party itself shaken, such as Thomas Mitchell of Edinburgh, whose 'general political attitude' was that 'Communism is a good thing' but 'individual communists almost without exception are no good', or John Paterson, who bemoaned 'the general contempt held by the bureaucrats for the rank and file in Spain'.[42]

Such responses highlight the potential downsides of the system of personal networks that underpinned recruitment and political organisation alike – in helping well-connected volunteers better navigate the political and organisational landscape of the International Brigades, they also became channels for favouritism and preferential treatment. It should not of course be assumed that these reactions or perceptions were universal, nor that efforts such as Tapsell's to rein in decisions based on patronage were wholly unsuccessful.[43] Moreover, the Party gradually found its power in some areas curtailed, as restrictions on leave and repatriation grew stricter as the war went on, to the extent that even officers were openly seething about delays returning home after September 1938.[44] In understanding these issues, it is worth remembering that Spain represented an organisational culture shock for the CPGB, which was not used to having this level of control – literally life and death – over the lives of its adherents. In the relatively low-stakes environment of British communism, everyday decision-making based on personal relationships and connections had few immediately negative consequences. In Spain, the Party found its power and responsibilities magnified, not just in terms of assuming military and political leadership of the British Battalion, which was readily understood, but also over more subtle aspects of the experience for which the importance of fairness and transparency only slowly became apparent. Here, the transnational nature of the International Brigades made a significant difference to their organisation, augmenting the importance and relevance of the networks and political cultures that underpinned the movement of volunteers and information across borders.

Wounded and Dependants

As the British Battalion went through its baptism of fire at Jarama in February 1937, the CPGB representative in Spain, Peter Kerrigan, wrote to Harry Pollitt about a newly pressing issue.

> The comrades here are raising a question as to what will be done with the lads who come back suffering from some disability. For example

the lad who is the bearer of this letter has lost his eye through shrap-
nel. This is a very big disability and there are political reasons why
something should be done about it.[45]

As casualties among the British volunteers mounted, Party officials in
Spain and Britain faced the reality that maintaining significant numbers of
volunteers in Spain entailed a significant financial responsibility. Though
Kerrigan framed his missive to Pollitt in terms of political necessity, it is
hard to doubt that even hard-bitten Party officials felt the moral imperative to act. Kerrigan knew many of those dying at Jarama personally – he
had led several busloads of volunteers down from Glasgow less than two
months before – and few Party officials would have been spared the loss
of friends and colleagues as the war in Spain dragged on. There was a personal, moral and political need to ensure that the families of the dead and
wounded received support.

Yet it was also clear that the scale of support required was well beyond
the financial capacity of the CPGB itself. A sustained campaign would be
required to meet the growing expenses. First launched as the 'Harry Pollitt
Fund', the campaign was reorganised and rebranded in June 1937, becoming the International Brigade WADC. Though it had a broad range of
sponsors and benefactors, the day-to-day operations were run by Charlotte
Haldane, who, along with her husband (a prominent scientist), had close
ties with the CPGB. Haldane was to spend two tireless years administer-
ing the WADC, co-ordinating not just fundraising and appeals across the
country but also the payment of stipends to returned wounded volunteers
as well as the dependants of those still in Spain. At its peak, this meant
supporting some 1100 families, at a cost of £700 each week.[46]

The WADC occupies a marginal place in existing writing on both the
International Brigades and domestic pro-Republican activism. Yet its support was not insignificant in directly enabling recruitment. Particularly as
the stipend was set somewhat above the rate paid by unemployment benefits, prospective volunteers could be relatively secure in the knowledge
that their decision would not harm those close to them. Michael Clarke
of Greenock, for instance, recalled specifically reassuring his wife on this
point.

They could guarantee would be a better livin' wage for your wife or
dependants . . . you'll be looked efter, you and the kids. Yer rent'll be
paid, I know for a fact, and ye'll get more than anybody's getting oot
the buroo.[47]

The importance of this pledge should not be underestimated – while the volunteers were certainly not mercenaries, it is doubtful that many would have been willing to leave their families destitute, especially as some already faced accusations that they were abandoning their familial responsibilities.[48] One volunteer, the Glaswegian Thomas McColl, went so far to claim while in Spain that, if the Communist Party failed to support his mother adequately, it meant 'the agreement with [him] was broken and no longer binding', justifying his immediate repatriation to support his family.[49] For McColl, and doubtless many others, service in Spain was undertaken with specific expectations and preconditions, and violation was grounds for reassessing their decision.

Beyond its impact in enabling the decision to enlist, the WADC also offers special insight into the dynamics of pro-Republican activism and British radical politics more broadly. For the Communist Party, supporting the Spanish Republic offered a way in which not only to build influence and prestige but also to develop the sort of grassroots connections and coalitions that would be necessary to build meaningful alliances with the labour movement and other progressive organisations.[50] For the CPGB leadership, there was often little distinction between the Aid Spain movement and its strategic goal of laying the foundations for a British Popular Front.[51] Yet its actual success in doing so remains hotly disputed. Lewis Mates, for instance, argues that any semblance of unity was achieved only by adopting a 'predominantly humanitarian campaigning message'.[52] Mates's position built on that of Tom Buchanan, who argued that early characterisations of 'Aid Spain' as a unified movement or embryonic 'Popular Front' ignored the lack of any overarching political common ground, manifesto or organisation among participants.[53] Whilst more recent research has cast doubt upon the binary nature of this debate – could, for instance, humanitarianism not have political dimensions? – these accounts generally support the basic point that earlier triumphant accounts of CPGB-led activism drastically overstated its success in using the Spanish Civil War as a way in which to expand its political influence.[54] Yet while these accounts have generally neglected Scotland, they do tend to acknowledge that Wales's distinctive political cultures led to different outcomes.[55] For these reasons, there remains the possibility that, even if a British 'Popular Front' remained illusory, localised or regional successes may still have been achieved in Scotland.

This possibility is explored in Malcolm Petrie's comparative study of Aberdeen and Dundee, which suggests that Aid Spain coalitions more in line with the communists' aspirations could form in some contexts. He highlights the extent to which British politics was still profoundly local in the 1930s, and demonstrates that the eventual shape of Aid Spain movements depended a great deal on local context.[56] In particular, Petrie emphasises the extent to which the Communist Party considered Aid Spain a part of wider efforts to gain affiliation to the Labour Party in accordance with United Front tactics, the outcome being closely linked to the success or failure of earlier unity efforts.[57] Petrie's approach shows Aid Spain as a useful reflection of the state of progressive politics throughout Britain in the late 1930s. However, this does little to build our understanding of the Aid Spain movement in any collective sense. Without vast numbers of local studies across Britain, there is no way to capture a broader sense of how important and prevalent political co-operation was, in Scotland or beyond.

In this historiographical context, a detailed study of the WADC offers unique advantages. Of the various organisations and causes that solicited money on a nationwide basis, it was indisputably the most politicised. While providing clothing, medicine and food to Spanish Republicans could be framed as humanitarianism, directly enabling the presence of volunteers fighting for the Republic could not, to say nothing of the Committee's obvious ties to the CPGB.[58] Individuals and groups who contributed to the WADC, in other words, can be safely assumed to have done so with political intent, intent that was at least to some extent aligned with the Communist Party's position on the Spanish Civil War, and combating fascism more broadly. The successes and failures of the WADC, in other words, reflect the successes and failures of CPGB influence more broadly. Moreover, its unique methods of record-keeping and generating publicity has reserved a source base that enables a detailed comparative approach, both within and beyond Scotland

Many dedicated Aid Spain organisations left behind few internal records, which are supplemented unevenly by what can be gleaned from the contemporary press, the archives of collaborating organisations and individual testimonies. Estimates of the sums involved – let alone where and how they were raised – are therefore imprecise at best. Uniquely, the WADC published detailed financial statements, including breakdowns of totals received from various types of organisations.[59] Most important, however, was its practice of publicly acknowledging donations received in the pages of the Communist newspaper, the *Daily Worker*. From the Committee's launch in June 1937 until the campaign became more sporadic around April 1939, the WADC published a near-daily selection of its receipts, usually including the precise amount and origin for each entry. Aside from providing a detailed map of Aid Spain activity throughout Britain, these data allow us to chart just how successful the Communist Party actually was in using the International Brigades and Aid Spain as a way in which to build grassroots institutional support across the country.

This account uses a sample of these columns across thirteen months from 1937–9, with each month's acknowledgements transcribed into a database, a total of 2645 contributions with a collective value of £10,824.[60] This represents roughly a quarter of the WADC's total income derived from organisations, which is consistent with the sample size.[61] This figure excludes contributions from individuals, as the detail provided was much more inconsistent and scanty, as well as being difficult to confirm using other sources. This last point is an important one. Given the close ties of the WADC and *Daily Worker* to the CPGB, it is reasonable to question whether the figures given in this column were wholly accurate or reliable. However, for organisational totals at least, there are several reasons why the amounts listed are dependable. Firstly, the records of multiple contributing organisations have been consulted, and in every case the *Daily Worker* figures were corroborated in terms of both amount and timing.[62] Secondly, there is little indication that figures were massaged to maintain Party prestige – indeed, when financial difficulties were experienced the Committee made no pretence otherwise, with multiple columns taking a begging, even desperate tone.[63] Finally, while there is evidence that the Party channelled funds to the WADC covertly, this was unlikely to have been concealed by faking donations from real organisations, especially as the column made no pretence of acknowledging all receipts publicly.[64]

It is worth remembering that, like all other national Aid Spain organisations, the WADC itself made little effort to track the regional basis of its fundraising. In this sense, a comprehensive regional breakdown is already a unique starting point for analysis, and reveals immediately that overtly politicised Aid Spain activity was spread evenly across Britain. Support for the WADC campaign was largely absent in many places, notably in the South-West and East of England and Northern Ireland, and relatively little came from other parts of England outside the capital, even in industrial regions. That is not to say that there was little Aid Spain activism outside the hubs of London, Scotland and Wales, but rather that, as per Mates's observations in the North-East, humanitarian-focused campaigns were preferred as a way of mobilising support in these areas, putting causes such as the WADC at a disadvantage.

Table 5.1 Contributions to the WADC by region

Region	Total (£)	Percentage of UK total	Number of contributions
London	2923	27.0	785
Scotland	2062	19.1	606
Wales	1780	16.4	230
North-West England	794	7.3	204
Midlands	483	4.5	165
North-East England	412	3.8	99
South-East England	300	2.8	120
Yorkshire	243	2.2	94
East of England	172	1.6	77
South-West England	92	0.8	37
Northern Ireland	1	0.0	1
International	479	4.4	21
Miscellaneous	1083	10.0	206
Total	£10,824		2645

The figures in Table 5.1 show parallels with the strength of the CPGB itself, with London, Scotland, Wales and North-West England representing the regions where it had a substantial membership base by the late 1930s. Indeed, by September 1938, nearly three-quarters of the Communist Party membership resided in those four districts, which as shown above contributed nearly 70 per cent of all contributions to the WADC – more than 80 per cent if international and other miscellaneous contributions are discounted. Whilst this represents a logical correlation, as with recruitment for the International Brigades discussed in Chapter 2, the relationship is again not completely straightforward. By September 1938, London's membership was double Scotland's, but contributed considerably less than double the Scottish total. The North-West had seven hundred more CPGB members than Wales, yet contributed much less.[65] Further complexity is hinted at by the variance in individual contributions, with Wales in particular seeing a surprisingly small frequency of contributions despite their large total. Divergences are even more apparent when regional contributions are divided by organisation type.

Table 5.2 Contributing organisations in major regions: £ (% of the total for each region)

Organisation	London	Scotland	Wales	NW Eng.	Midlands	NE Eng.	UK total
Trade Union	437	744	1106	120	86	221	3265
	(15.0)	(36.1)	(62.1)	(15.1)	(17.8)	(53.7)	(30.2)
Factory Collection	1019	150	69	28	28	1	1458
	(34.9)	(7.3)	(3.9)	(3.6)	(5.8)	(0.2)	(13.5)
Co-operative Society	21	19	3	16	34	0	126
	(0.7)	(0.9)	(0.1)	(2.1)	(7.0)	(0.0)	(1.2)
Public Meeting	778	65	115	81	24	25	1504
	(26.6)	(3.1)	(6.5)	(10.2)	(5.0)	(6.2)	(13.9)
Spanish Aid	225	628	333	345	119	46	2122
Committee	(7.7)	(30.5)	(18.7)	(43.5)	(24.7)	(11.2)	(19.6)
Communist Party	233	352	28	144	130	13	1086
	(8.0)	(17.0)	(1.5)	(18.2)	(26.8)	(3.1)	(10.0)
Labour Party	76	11	19	21	12	66	253
	(2.6)	(0.5)	(1.1)	(2.7)	(2.6)	(16.0)	(2.3)
Left Book Club	56	12	27	16	2	27	323
	(1.9)	(0.6)	(1.5)	(2.0)	(0.5)	(6.7)	(3.0)
Youth Organisation	3	2	5	9	0	0	46
	(0.0)	(0.0)	(0.2)	(1.1)	(0.0)	(0.0)	(0.4)
Miscellaneous	76	80	75	13	48	12	643
	(2.6)	(3.8)	(4.2)	(1.7)	(9.9)	(3.0)	(5.9)
Total	2923	2062	1780	794	483	412	10824

In Table 5.2, regional differences are revealed not just as a matter of scale but in how money was raised. Different types of institutional support, organisation and collection strategies led to different outcomes across Britain. Wales's large regional total is seen to be the product of influence among Welsh trades unions, while the WADC's success in London was underpinned by its ability to organise large-scale public meetings and regular workplace collections. Such variations point to an Aid Spain movement that looked very different depending on local context, lending substantial support to Petrie's emphasis on the importance of local factors in shaping the nature of activism.

It is useful to see these figures as reflecting the extent and limits of the Communist Party's institutional influence. In Scotland and Wales in particular, the willingness of trades unions to contribute directly from branch funds, or even encourage regular collections among their members, points to significant CPGB influence in the labour movement. Significantly, much of this support was coming not from national bodies but rather from local branches and regional organisations, reflecting the Party's strategy of building grassroots influence. Moreover, contributing to the WADC was contrary to the controversial TUC policy that all Aid Spain activity should be directed through a few officially sanctioned channels, meaning that each contribution from branch funds represented a small act of political defiance.[66] Clearly, these organisations were receptive to supporting a communist-led initiative, and their interest went beyond the humanitarian plight of the Spanish Republic. Moreover, over time these figures improved considerably, going from an average of 48 trades union donations a month with an average cumulative value of £210 in 1937 to 87 donations a month totalling an average of £268 in 1938. Whilst such variations admit multiple possible explanations, they are at least indicative of the campaign gaining momentum.

Yet several limitations are also visible. For one, growth in existing strongholds was not nearly so pronounced, with Wales actually seeing a fall in activity from 1937 to 1938, with a minute increase in the number of donations each month more than outweighed by a sharp decline in the average amount given.[67] Whilst trades union support was still very substantial, contributions from headquarters and branches of the South Wales Miners Federation made up a staggering 98 per cent of Wales's trades union total, which was clearly driven almost entirely by pre-existing CPGB influence within the South Wales Miners Federation.[68] The reliance on communism's traditional support base in Wales indicates that the WADC was capitalising on existing support rather than necessarily expanding its influence in the Welsh labour movement. More broadly, strong, regular activity on the part of trades unions might also be indicative of failure in building coalitions, as substantial and sustained efforts contained wholly within the labour movement may reflect limited opportunity for co-operation with other groups. Given that CPGB strategy emphasised building functional local coalitions, reliance on existing organisational resources would indicate that their preferred approach was not succeeding.

In contrast to the relatively strong support received from trades unions, the tiny sums received from Co-operative societies or Labour Party branches indicate a failure to attract institutional support from these quarters, another sign that communist efforts to use Aid Spain as a vehicle for the Popular Front had limited success. Although this does not preclude the active participation of these organisations' members acting as private individuals, this is nonetheless a sign that CPGB attempts to spread its influence were being blocked not only by a hostile leadership and bureaucracy but also by rank-and-file scepticism. In contrast, Left Book Clubs (LBCs), while composed of sympathetic individuals and an effective tool for spreading communist influence in the late 1930s, were not spaces that fostered activism or mobilisation.[69] Only the East of England saw LBCs contribute a substantial portion of its total, where the LBC summer retreats at Digswell Park provided a social space more conducive to fundraising activity.[70] The other major source of LBC contributions was from their 'Recruiting Scheme', which allowed new members to supplement their initial subscription with a small contribution to the WADC; this provided a steady income for the duration of the fund's existence.[71]

The most important groups for examining the viability of Aid Spain coalitions are Spanish Aid Committees (SACs). A multitude of such committees were formed throughout Britain during the conflict, some affiliated with the National Joint Committee (JC) for Spanish Relief, and many more that were fully or partially separate from this organisation.[72] Their composition could be radically different depending on circumstances. Founding a committee required negotiation, and individuals and organisations would choose whether or not to participate on the basis of their own sympathies, loyalties and priorities. It was not unusual for otherwise sympathetic groups to eschew active co-operation with a local SAC.[73] Negotiation did not end with the choice to participate. With so many major and minor Aid Spain initiatives taking place throughout Britain, the choice of where to channel funds represented key defining moments for such committees, revealing what they saw as their role in relation to the conflict. With the vast majority of such committees leaving behind no internal records, the choice to contribute to the WADC provides an indication of political intent in their work, showing not only that the committee itself supported a more activist stance on the conflict but also that it felt its donors would countenance this use of their money. Regular contributions from SACs to the WADC are therefore an indication that a region or locality had successfully built a sustainable, overtly politicised coalition around supporting the Spanish Republic. Here is the first concrete sign that the Scottish Aid Spain movement was different from that elsewhere in Britain: of the committees that gave at least three contributions to the WADC in the months sampled, fully one-third were found in Scotland. Equally, however, the relatively low number of SACs – 39 – that met this threshold across Britain indicates that CPGB success in influencing the Aid Spain movement directly was fragmented and localised.

Counterintuitively, substantial Communist Party contributions are a likely sign of the Party's failure. With CPGB strategy aimed at building coalitions, relying purely on its own organisation and membership for sustained fundraising represents an inability to foster co-operation. It is especially telling that places with sustained contributions from a local SAC almost never saw simultaneous contributions from a Communist Party branch, and vice versa. Strong CPGB contributions indicate either that communists took part in a local SAC but could undertake political work only independently, or that local efforts to set up a SAC were abortive and there was no committee to work alongside in the first place. It also highlights the Party's limitations in raising money alone: individual SAC donations were on average 50 per cent larger than Communist Party donations.

Once again, the wider pattern of variation is replicated at a Scottish level in Table 5.3, though here the danger of outliers begins to become apparent.[74] The Glasgow total for SACs, for instance, is underpinned by

Table 5.3 Scottish contributions to WADC by region: £ (% of the total for each region)

Organisation	Glasgow	Edinburgh	Dundee	Clyde	Fife	Other	Scotland
Trade Union	354	247	39	39	7	58	744
	(44.9)	(92.5)	(51.3)	(9.8)	(2.6)	(22.0)	(36.1)
Factory Collection	76	1	0	44	17	11	150
	(9.6)	(0.3)	(3.9)	(11.1)	(5.8)	(4.0)	(7.3)
Co-operative Society	1	3	0	2	13	0	19
	(0.1)	(1.1)	(0.1)	(0.5)	(4.7)	(0.0)	(0.9)
Public Meeting	22	4	9	21	9	0	65
	(2.8)	(1.5)	(11.8)	(5.3)	(3.3)	(0.0)	(3.1)
Spanish Aid Committee	264	11	12	122	202	17	628
	(33.50	(4.1)	(15.8)	(30.8)	(75.6)	(6.5)	(30.5)
Communist Party	44	0	8	124	14	162	352
	(5.6)	(0.0)	(10.5)	(31.3)	(5.1)	(61.8)	(17.0)
Labour Party	8	0	0	1	0	3	11
	(1.0)	(0.0)	(1.1)	(0.2)	(0.0)	(1.0)	(0.5)
Left Book Club	1	0	10	0	0	1	12
	(0.1)	(0.0)	(13.2)	(0.0)	(0.0)	(0.5)	(0.6)
Youth Organisation	0	0	0	0	0	0	2
	(0.0)	(0.0)	(0.0)	(0.0)	(0.0)	(0.0)	(0.0)
Miscellaneous	19	0	0	43.2	5	11	80
	(2.5)	(0.0)	(0.0)	(10.9)	(1.9)	(4.3)	(3.8)
Total	789	267	76	397	266	263	2062
	(38.3)	(12.9)	(3.7)	(19.3)	(12.9)	(12.8)	

a one-off windfall of £200 from a Flag Day run by the otherwise inactive Dependants' Aid Committee, leaving just £64 raised as the result of ongoing SAC activity in Glasgow.[75] Without this outlier, SAC income from Glasgow was just 10.8 per cent of the total raised in the city, in direct contrast to the exceptional Fife total for SACs, which saw twice as many individual contributions as Glasgow in the months surveyed, with no single donation above £20. Broadly speaking, however, local patterns conform to the above picture: SAC and Communist Party donations rarely coincided, lending weight to the conclusion that the committees represented among WADC contributors were those in which the CPGB was present and influential. Interestingly, as with International Brigade recruitment, Kilmarnock was once again the exception to this rule, with considerable sums received from both the local CPGB branch and the SAC. Though speculative, it is plausible that the lack of International Brigade recruits meant that there was a larger base of experienced and committed communist activists available for Aid Spain work. Edinburgh also represents an important outlier, for reasons discussed in greater depth in Chapter 6, though it bears noting that the exceptionally high proportion of trades union contributions was driven almost entirely by a group of remarkably reliable and persistent railworkers at St Margaret's Depot, rather than widespread labour movement support across Edinburgh.

Importantly, the data point to a slow expansion of influence in the Scottish labour movement. In Glasgow, for instance, though the average size of each contribution dropped marginally, this was more than balanced by the increased frequency of contributions from local trades union branches, with an average of five per month recorded in 1937 rising to eight in 1938. This was balanced, however, by an ongoing failure to attract support from other mainstream working-class institutions. Whilst, as shown above, the lack of support from the Labour Party, Co-operators and youth organisations was a problem across Britain, it was particularly acute in Scotland. Equally, however, variability across and even within regions indicates that there is not a straightforward, uniform picture across the country.

Taken together, the picture here suggests that Scottish responses to the Spanish Civil War were more politicised than elsewhere in Britain. These efforts resulted in disproportionate contributions to the WADC – nearly 20 per cent of the British total, well out of proportion to the Scottish population. There is no evidence to suggest that this largesse was matched in other areas of fundraising – in fact, Scotland was singled out for being 'unexpectedly bare' in terms of fundraising for the more genteel National

JC for Spanish Relief.[76] In many parts of Scotland – most notably in Fife – Spanish Aid Committees were apparently willing to contribute directly to the Republican struggle rather than couching their purpose in humanitarian terms, suggesting that they were organisations with an explicitly political purpose. Scottish trade unionists also proved more willing than their English counterparts to defy TUC directions and contribute money to a CPGB-associated fund. However, while these are useful starting points, this overarching picture can take us only so far in sketching the contours of the Scottish Aid Spain movement. The contributions received by the WADC indicate that, if a distinctive Scottish response to the Spanish Civil War is to be found, it is likely to be in the interplay between Spanish Aid Committees, the labour movement and the Communist Party. Accordingly, these groups and institutions are the focus of the final two chapters exploring domestic activism, seeking both to confirm whether there was indeed a distinct response to Spain within Scotland, and, if so, to establish what led to this particular outcome.

Notes

1. For example *Nuestro Combate*, 3 April 1937; December 1937 – January 1938, 9.
2. 'Summary and critical survey of my work in Spain', September 1938, RGASPI, 545/6/88/11.
3. Annie to Tom Murray, 16 April 1937, NLS, TMP, Box 1, File 3.
4. Lily to Agnes Murray, 19 June 1937, NLS, TMP, Box 1, File 5.
5. Moir to Lily Murray, 6 July 1937, NLS, TMP, Box 1, File 6.
6. Annie Murray, 18 September 1937, NLS, TMP, Box 1, File 3.
7. Lily to Tom Murray, 12 October 1937, NLS, TMP, Box 1, File 5.
8. Robson to Paynter, 16 July 1937, RGASPI, 545/6/51/10.
9. Janet to Tom Murray, 25 April 1938, NLS, TMP, Box 1, File 2.
10. 'Thomas Gembles', RGASPI, 545/6/138/76.
11. Gilmour to Paterson, 5 April 1937, MML, Box 50, File Gl/17.
12. 'Rapport par le Chef de la Censure', 17 August 1937, RGASPI, 545/2/158/114.
13. Tapsell to Pollitt, [April 1937?], MML, Box C, File 13/1.
14. These were Alan Kemp and Patrick Glacken, though, as discussed in Chapter 4, it is unlikely that Glacken was actually executed. Dunlop in MacDougall, *Voices from the Spanish Civil War*, 151.
15. *Daily Worker*, 6 June 1938, 3.
16. 'Mother' to James Arthur, 31 January and 7 February 1938, AGGCE, PS-Aragon, Box 126, File 6.
17. 'Peg' to James Arthur, 1 and 7 January, 1938, AGGCE, PS-Aragon, Box 126, File 6.
18. George to Lily Murray, 28 December 1937, NLS, TMP, Box 1, File 4.

19. George to Tom and Janet Murray, 21 November 1937, NLS, TMP, Box 1, File 4.
20. Lily to Tom Murray, n.d., NLS, TMP, Box 1, File 5.
21. Annie to Tom Murray, 28 December 1937, NLS, TMP, Box 1, File 3.
22. Annie to Lily Murray, 8 January 1938, NLS, TMP, Box 1, File 3.
23. 'Edward Brown – Evaluation', RGASPI, 545/6/111/56.
24. Annie to Tom Murray, 8 August 1937, NLS, TMP, Box 1, File 3.
25. Baxell, *Unlikely Warriors*, 247-50.
26. Baxell, *British Volunteers*, 138-9.
27. 'Repatriation and Allowance Requests', [May 1937?], MML, Box 39, File A/12.
28. Gilmour to Paterson, 20 March 1938, MML, Box 50, File Gl/36.
29. Baxell, *British Volunteers*, 139.
30. *Nuestro Combate*, 34 (October–November 1937), 4.
31. Quinn, TLS, MS, Tape 202.
32. 'MIDDLETON, Robert', [1938?], RGASPI, 545/6/173/19.
33. Middleton to Kerrigan, 2 March 1937, RGASPI, 545/6/173/6.
34. These details were laid out in a letter from the commandant authorising a cash advance to Middleton on his journey home, 21 April 1937, RGASPI, 545/6/173/20.
35. Marcovitch, Tape 182.
36. Marcovitch, Tape 182.
37. Benson to 'Jud', 18 March 1938, RGASPI, 545/6/105/103.
38. 'Camaradas para recibir el mensaje de Pasionaria firmado', RGASPI, 545/6/39/146. On Donaldson's refusal to transfer to the front, see 'DONALDSON Alec', RGASPI, 545/6/125/61.
39. 'List of distinguished comrades in the 15th Internationals', 23 October 1938, RGASPI, 545/3/452/78. Concerns about equitable coverage were not exclusively aimed at high-ranking communists. Regarding press coverage in early 1937, for instance, Tapsell reported that volunteers 'rightly object to deserters and imposters being warmly welcomed and getting a public when they don't deserve it'. Tapsell to Pollitt, 25 April 1937, MML.
40. Tapsell to Anderson, n.d., MML, Box 39, File A/14.
41. 'Note de Service no. 16428', 8 June 1937, RGASPI, 545/3/451/47.
42. Paterson to Murray, 12 May 1939, NLS, TMP, Box 4, File 4.
43. Strikingly few volunteers – about a third – were willing to immediately engage with the Party-sponsored veterans' organisation, the IBA, on their return. While this doubtless had multiple causes, it likely reflects widespread dissatisfaction with Party organisations. CPGB Central Committee Meeting, 19 March 1939, RGASPI, 495/14/265/49,53.
44. 'Parte extraordinario', 6 September 1938, RGASPI, 545/3/435/141-3. See also Fred Thomas, *To Tilt at Windmills* (East Lansing, 1996), 168.
45. Kerrigan to Pollitt, 16 February 1937, MML, Box C, File 10.
46. Alexander, *British Volunteers for Liberty*, 140-1.
47. Clarke in MacDougall, *Voices from the Hunger Marches*, 167.

48. For example Nicoll, TLS, MS, Tape 956.
49. McColl to 'Mother', 25 August 1938, RGASPI, 545/6/169/58.
50. Mates, *Spanish Civil War*, 188.
51. For example 'Material on Spain', April 1937, RGASPI, 495/20/74/83-4.
52. Mates, *Spanish Civil War*, 192.
53. Buchanan, 'Britain's Popular Front?', 62-72. See also Fyrth, 'Aid Spain Movement', 153-64.
54. See especially Mason, *Democracy, Deeds and Dilemmas*; Kerrie Holloway, *Britain's Political Humanitarians: The National Joint Committee for Spanish Relief and the Spanish refugees of 1939* (PhD Thesis, Queen Margaret University of London, 2017).
55. Mates, 'Durham and South Wales Miners', 373-95.
56. Petrie, 'Unity from Below?', 308.
57. Petrie, 'Unity from Below?', 318-25.
58. Mates, *Spanish Civil War*, 188.
59. This account uses the same organisational categories as the WADC reports themselves, although, as the definitions used by the WADC were never made clear, figures are not directly comparable. 'Dependants' Aid Committee Annual Report', 1939, NLS, TMP, Box 3, File 2.
60. These months, chosen randomly from the period from June 1937 to April 1939, were: June, July, August, September and November 1937; January, March, April, June, July, August, November 1938; January 1939. This provided a sample of 294 individual columns, and included months when the Battalion was in heavy action, away from the front or had left Spain entirely.
61. This consistency also rests on the fact that generally up to half of contributions received were publicised. For example, the Edinburgh JC had donations of £25 acknowledged, whilst its own records indicate they gave £50 in total. 'Edinburgh Joint Committee for Spanish Relief, Statement of Accounts 8.8.1938-30.6.1939', NLS, TMP, Box 2, File 3.
62. Alongside the Edinburgh JC mentioned above, see also Foundry Workers West of Scotland District Committee, Balance Sheets, 1937-1938, NLS, Acc. 5010, File 160; AUBTW Glasgow 1st Branch Minutes, 24 June 1937, 22 September 1937, 24 November 1937, 16 March 1938, 24 August 1938, 19 October 1938, GCA, TD675, Files 3-4.
63. For example *Daily Worker*, 6 October 1938, 3.
64. £4350 was provided from 'funds available from the Party' up to July 1938. However, given the vagueness surrounding individual donations, and the open practice of providing only a sample of receipts, concealing this subsidy by faking contributions from real organisations would have been unnecessarily complex and risky. 'Wounded and Dependant's Committee', (October 1938?), RGASPI, 495/14/262/189-90.
65. 'Party Membership', (1939?), RGASPI, 495/14/265/23.

66. Despite attempts to convince them otherwise, the TUC leadership insisted that all Aid Spain activity be directed through their own 'International Solidarity Fund'. See 'History of Case: Spanish Rebellion – International Brigade', 1938, TC, 292/946/35/1; TUC to William Elger, 2 November 1938, TC, 292/946/34/172. See also Buchanan, *British Labour Movement*, 161.

67. This was chiefly due to a decline in the second half of 1938, with the first half of 1938 showing a small but significant improvement over the 1937 figures.

68. By December 1936, a communist (Arthur Horner) was president of the South Wales Miners Federation, and the Party had five members on the Executive Committee. See 'Report on Basic Measures for the Growth of the CPGB', 3 December 1936, RGASPI, 495/14/215/12.

69. This was openly acknowledged at the time, see 'Left Book Club', CPGB Scottish District Congress, 45 September 1937, RGASPI, 495/14/263/9.

70. In August 1937, for example, the LBC Summer School at Digswell Park managed to raise over £22, in part by contributing 'the entrance fees for the tennis tournament'. *Daily Worker*, 14 August 1937, 1.

71. For example, the scheme raised £10 in November 1938. *Daily Worker*, 11 November 1937, 4.

72. Fyrth cites a report claiming 850 National JC-affiliated bodies. Jim Fyrth, *The Signal Was Spain: The Spanish Aid Movement in Britain, 1936–1939* (London, 1986), 203.

73. For example, for nearly a year the Glasgow TC refused to send a delegate to the Glasgow JC for Spanish Relief, for reasons explored in Chapter 6. See Glasgow TC Executive Committee Minutes, 8 March 1938, Glasgow City Archives [GCA], (uncatalogued).

74. 'Clyde' covers regions adjacent to Glasgow, including Ayrshire, Renfrewshire, Lanarkshire and Dunbartonshire. 'Other' includes regions not otherwise listed, as well as donations from national organisations (e.g. 'Scottish District of the Communist Party').

75. *Daily Worker*, 26 June 1938, 1.

76. *Spanish Relief Bulletin 9*, October 1937, 1.

6

Coalitions of the Willing: Spanish Aid Committees in Scotland

In January 1937, an extraordinary meeting took place at Lochgelly Town Hall. Activists crowded the room, hearing how a new committee formed in the mining town of Bowhill had started to organise local responses to the Spanish Civil War. Communist Councillor Abe Moffat spoke movingly of

> The assistance the Spanish Government forces were receiving from Fife. Sacrifices had been made by the poorest of the poor. In the mining villages of West Fife, poverty stricken mothers had contributed what they could in food and materials. He appealed for assistance from all parts of the County. In the course of his speech he revealed that miners from Fife were fighting in Spain for the Government forces.[1]

This last point resonated with those present. Sixteen volunteers from Fife were already serving in the International Brigades, and this very local connection helped capture the imagination of the audience. The meeting resolved 'to form Spanish Aid Committees in every town and village to support the dependants of British workers who are voluntarily fighting for democracy, and for the relief of the civil population in Spain'.[2] The organisations founded in response to this appeal were some of the first SACs in Scotland, and provided the impetus for what would prove to be a particularly vibrant grassroots Aid Spain movement across Fife.

Yet the same meeting featured distinct elements of opposition. The newspaper account noted that 'speakers received a considerable amount of heckling from two questioners'.[3] These hecklers pointedly questioned the position of the clergy in both Fife and Spain, ridiculing arguments that Catholics could support the Republican cause. Not to be silenced by the jeers of their peers, this opposition continued in the local press, with one letter sarcastically noting that

> This harping on the religious string is becoming a habit with our tame reds. If they don't become religious themselves there is a serious danger that people might begin to imagine that Communism is not militantly atheist.[4]

This opposition from local Catholics was just one difficulty faced by the Fife Aid Spain movement, and reflected problems faced by Aid Spain activists across Scotland. Despite the conclusions of Daniel Gray, who claimed that Scotland had 'nailed its colours to the mast' when it came to supporting the Republic, the reality was that Scottish pro-Franco opinion was neither marginal nor silent during the conflict.[5] In particular, many working-class districts of Glasgow – the heartlands of Labour and ILP parliamentary representation – were home to large Catholic communities, the product of generations of Irish immigration.[6] Navigating divided loyalties between religion and politics proved exceptionally difficult at times. Whilst pro-Franco opinion was less effectively mobilised during the conflict, and the activities of groups such as the 'Friends of Nationalist Spain' were often met with widespread disgust, the consequences for pro-Republican activism cannot be ignored. In particular, they threatened the viability of SACs – the coalitions of sympathetic organisations and individuals, who pooled resources, ideas and efforts in order to expand and intensify local or regional efforts. The success and failure of these committees across Scotland are vital for understanding the character of the Aid Spain movement more broadly.

Yet it was not opposition from conservatives or Catholics that proved to be the greatest barrier to co-operation. Rather, those on the pro-Republican left were often more than capable of sabotaging a united front on Spain by themselves. Counterintuitively, the very strength and diversity of pro-Republican feeling in Scotland acted against efforts to foster collaboration. It is perhaps unsurprising that SACs proved to be variably effective across Scotland, but effectiveness often did not reflect whether a given locale was more or less ardently in favour of the Spanish Republic. Rather, what mattered more was the local electoral calculus. In particular, for SACs to function effectively, local politics needed to be relatively stable. Co-operation could happen only when prospective partners did not need to fear one another's real or imagined schemes to use Aid Spain as a vehicle for local political success. However, this meant that Scotland's fractured political landscape – particularly on the left – often did not allow for SACs to function as effectively as has often been assumed.

This broad picture is reflected in the records of national organisations. The National JC for Spanish Relief, which controlled the single most successful British Aid Spain fund, enjoyed only modest returns in Scotland despite being chaired by the Duchess of Atholl, a Scottish Tory MP. Even by October 1937, Scotland was singled out by this body for the perceived lack of activity, with 17 Scottish towns and cities noted as having no committee.[7] Even when such committees existed, the pages of its regular Bulletin reveal that Scottish committees rarely bothered to inform the National JC of their activities.[8] Overall co-ordination was also poor. A Scottish JC, eventually set up under the direction of Brian Campbell in December 1937, was not noted for its effectiveness. Janet Murray, the chairman of the Edinburgh JC, regarded him as 'hopeless' and 'rather a handicap than a help', even going so far as to completely ignore his Scottish Committee when she later took the lead in encouraging Scottish Co-operative societies to revitalise their Milk for Spain programme.[9]

While simple at its heart, the argument here has several important implications for understanding the Scottish – and British – response to the Spanish Civil War. For one, it reaffirms the importance of locality. Spain was often understood and framed from perspectives that were local as much as international or transnational. In the same way that it was possible for many International Brigade volunteers to see their decision as a logical extension of their struggle against unemployment, so too could domestic activists understand the civil war as a reflection of their own political lives. Secondly, this explanation places a renewed emphasis on the centrality of the Communist Party. It has become common in recent historiography to decentre the CPGB, highlighting that Aid Spain was a broad, diverse set of movements, and the need to be wary of the Party's tendency to take credit for movements 'which probably would have occurred, in some form, anyway'.[10] Yet by focusing on the CPGB's role here, the intent is not to resurrect a triumphant Party narrative, but rather to explore how the Party's efforts had mixed, often unintentional outcomes in shaping these key local dynamics of co-operation.

The Party's centrality in this process stemmed less from its absolute numbers, or even its vaunted campaigning energy and organisation, but rather from the fact that its political position and strategy demanded a coalition-based response to the Spanish Civil War. This reflected the current Comintern line and the turn towards the 'Popular Front' in the years prior to Spain, as well as the more local need to build relationships with the labour movement to expand CPGB influence and membership.[11] Yet Labour Party and trades union leaders were for the most part unwilling to entertain any notion of an agreement with communists, rebuffing any and all attempts to foster high-level discussions and agreements of the sort which had led to successful pacts elsewhere.[12] The remaining route for the CPGB was local – building influence and thereby delegate votes at the Labour Party conference, town by town and branch by branch. Aid Spain, from this perspective, offered a vehicle through which progress towards this goal might be made. This meant that almost invariably, regardless of their actual numbers or influence in a local sense, communists were among the earliest and most consistent proponents of setting up Spanish Aid Committees across Britain. These committees would ideally also be willing to support communist goals, policies and fundraising priorities, but this was less important than creating spaces in which the CPGB might meaningfully co-operate with those in the official labour movement and beyond. While Aid Spain activism may well have occurred, in some form, anyway, that it so consistently and quickly took on a coalition-based, committee-style character owed a great deal to the catalyst provided by communist activists up and down the country.

This chapter examines how these dynamics actually affected the establishment, nature and success of SACs across Scotland, as well as exploring some of the intersections and tensions between class, gender and politics in their day-to-day functioning. The chosen case studies highlight the adaptability and diversity of these bodies, and show that their organisers used a wide range of messaging and tactics that they felt would resonate best with their particular audience and advance their own political priorities. This, it is suggested, requires something of a revision to existing scholarship – efforts to characterise SACs collectively, whether as embryonic Popular Fronts or as humanitarian efforts devoid of political meaning, cannot be sustained even within one city or region, let alone across all of Britain. Instead, this account proposes that, whilst the committees themselves took on many forms, it is possible to identify common factors that shaped these dynamics across contexts.

Fife's Spanish Aid Committees

Building on the Lochgelly meeting in January 1937, at least ten separate SACs were formed in Fife during the conflict, more than in any other region of Scotland.[13] Many were located in working-class districts or towns, often in mining areas with a long association with leftist politics. However, it should not be imagined that these committees were homogeneous, or that radical political traditions sufficed to ensure that a committee would be successful. Towns not traditionally associated with militancy also formed local committees. Even Dunfermline, regarded dismissively as 'patriotic' by the local communist leader Bob Selkirk, had its own committee by the end of the war.[14] More than the sheer number of committees, it is this variation that makes Fife a particularly useful case study for examining the nature of SACs in Scotland and Britain.

Whilst the Fife coalfields cannot be seen as homogeneously radical, there is no doubt that in places like Lumphinnans, Bowhill and Methil the Communist Party played a major, if not dominant, role in political life in a way that was rarely replicated elsewhere in Britain. In these towns, which had all been strongholds of the CPGB-affiliated United Mineworkers of Scotland (UMS), the Party could count on a level of political influence that belied their small Party membership.[15] This offered considerable advantages for local Aid Spain efforts. Based on distinct, politically unified communities, communists had a simpler task in convincing local institutions and individuals to accept their lead. In Bowhill, for instance, the SAC brought together local miners, the Co-operative Women's Guild and the Communist Party.[16] This reflected the extent that local and community identity had become intertwined – belonging meant not only living in the village but also participating in these forms of collective solidarity. Importantly, their choice of beneficiary did not need to reflect the opinions of apolitical or moderate allies. With the entire community united in a radical interpretation of the conflict, these committees often chose to give a far larger portion of their income to the WADC than elsewhere in Scotland or Britain.

However, locales in which the Communist Party was able to exercise enough influence to guarantee a cohesive, united response were not the norm, even in Fife. Particularly in larger, more diverse towns, communists could not hope to build a committee purely on their own terms. Kirkcaldy provides a particularly interesting example that defies neat categorisation. The Kirkcaldy SAC was formed in February 1937, with Labour Councillors Dall and Wright providing the public face of the Committee, as Chairman and Treasurer respectively, while the local communist James Ord acted as 'Organiser'.[17] The Committee made its partisan political take on the conflict clear from the outset, stating that its purpose was to 'aid the Spanish Workers and the International Brigade volunteers'.[18] This stance drew considerable criticism. The conservative *Fife Free Press* delighted in editorialising on the inadvisability of these forms of fundraising, as well as publishing letters from 'eyewitness' correspondents who ridiculed the Committee for its stance.[19] Instead of retreating into inoffensive humanitarianism, Dall and Wright responded in kind, leading to several angry public exchanges focusing on the political meaning of the conflict.[20] Despite constant criticism, Kirkcaldy SAC maintained a consistent level of activity, holding regular whist and dance evenings and soliciting weekly donations from subscribers.[21] The Committee raised a respectable £270 in 1937, reaching £500 by September 1938, and, as promised, sent much of this money to the International Brigade fund.[22]

Kirkcaldy presents a rare example of a locale where the Labour Party was willing to co-operate actively with the Communist Party in setting up and running an SAC. Labour involvement with the Committee was above board, with Councillor Dall even presenting a report on its activities to the 1937 annual meeting of the District Labour Party.[23] This reflects the open-mindedness of the local Labour establishment. The MP for Kirkcaldy was outspoken on the need for co-operation with other parties, claiming that 'for all his life in politics he had stood for the United Front'.[24] The Kirkcaldy SAC Treasurer, Councillor Wright, was also known for his willingness to co-operate with unofficial groups, such as by addressing an NUWM rally in October 1936.[25] However, Labour's willingness to collaborate with communists can also be understood as a product of the relative weakness of the Communist Party in Kirkcaldy compared to elsewhere in Fife. Unlike in other towns such as Cowdenbeath, communists held no Town Council seats in Kirkcaldy.[26] This meant the local Labour Party could take a more relaxed attitude towards the Communist Party, allowing already sympathetic representatives more leeway in their choice of allies.

As Petrie found in Aberdeen, this success built on previous co-operation, yet there is little doubt that Spain afforded the Communist Party an opportunity to deepen and regularise local ties with Labour. Yet this outcome was predicated on the extent which Labour enjoyed local hegemony over left-wing politics, and was able to co-operate with communists without fearing the electoral consequences. In contrast, Cowdenbeath provides an example of how an unsettled political context could undermine attempts at forging a working-class Aid Spain coalition. It had been a major UMS stronghold, and communists such as Bob Selkirk had been elected to the Town Council, challenging Labour from the left.[27] Indeed, Cowdenbeath directly contradicts Fyrth's argument that a history of unemployed 'organisation' and 'demonstrations' provided the foundation for successful working-class action on Spain.[28] The local chapter of the Cowdenbeath NUWM, which was as well-organised as any in the area, attempted to compensate for the lack of a local SAC, with little success. After one such attempt, a local NUWM representative noted

> that there is unfortunately no Spanish Aid Committee active in Cowdenbeath at the moment. The NUWM decided to run an all-night dance in order to send assistance to the Spanish workers. That effort was a failure.[29]

That is not to say that no fundraising at all took place in Cowdenbeath. The local Communist Party branch was active in supporting the International Brigades, sending regular £2 contributions to the fund throughout 1937 and 1938. Bob Selkirk remembered the 'period of the Spanish Civil War' as when the local Party organised its 'most successful mass Marxist lectures'.[30] Clearly, Cowdenbeath had a significant communist presence that was able to mobilise support for the Spanish Republic, yet, equally clearly, it influence was limited in isolation. Other working-class organisations proved unwilling to follow their lead, which in turn limited the scale of Aid Spain activity that could take place under communist leadership. The gulf between the Communist Party acting alone and the capabilities of the Cowdenbeath labour movement more broadly was demonstrated by a one-off effort led by local Co-operative societies and Labour Party branches, which raised £65 in cash and £50 in goods in just two weeks in April and May 1938 for a campaign in support of the British Youth Peace Assembly.[31]

The picture is once again different in locales where neither Labour nor the CPGB held sway in local politics. Despite its radical reputation, Fife was home to many pockets of well-off, Tory-voting areas. This, however, was not necessarily an impermeable barrier to Aid Spain activism, and committees were formed in places such as Dunfermline and St Andrews – neither a natural home for leftist politics. However, both locales had groups that were positioned well to provide some initial impetus. Dunfermline hosted an active LBC branch, while St Andrews was home to a small group of student socialists and sympathisers.[32] Of the two committees, St Andrews was more active, with student volunteers regularly raising considerable sums in St Andrews and Dundee, alongside one-off events such as concert nights.[33] In contrast, Dunfermline SAC was formed much later in the war, with its bourgeois credentials bolstered by the appearance of the Duchess of Atholl at its inaugural meeting.[34] Neither St Andrews nor Dunfermline SAC contributed any money to the International Brigades, unlike most committees in Fife, although Charlotte Haldane spoke in Dunfermline in September 1937 under the auspices of the Fife Dependants' Aid Committee.[35] Just as the success of Spanish Aid Committees in more traditionally radical areas was predicated on a degree of local dominance of one particular party, these committees can be seen as the product of middle-class political hegemony, with the priorities of the committees that emerged reflecting the preferences of their more genteel members and donors.

The proliferation of similar committees throughout Britain belies the extent to which their formation was not an inevitable outcome. In the successful examples discussed above, a common factor is the local dominance of one party or social group, which defined the committees' purpose and agenda. In each case, this dominant group could co-operate with other interested parties without fearing that they were weakening themselves or strengthening their rivals. Timeliness also emerges as an important concern – whilst a more decorous committee could emerge somewhere like Dunfermline without any obvious CPGB or other radical involvement, it took over two years to actually happen, leaving the committee little time to actually achieve anything. Moreover, in places like Cowdenbeath, where local politics were fiercely contested, co-operation on the issue of Spain was much less likely. Inter-class tension or political rivalry could undermine the viability of SACs even in locations where there was broad support for the Spanish Republic. This was to prove especially significant in Glasgow – where widespread enthusiasm for the Republican cause was tempered by an unsettled political context.

Spanish Aid Committees in Glasgow

According to most existing understandings of the British Aid Spain movement, Glasgow should have provided fertile soil for pro-Republican activism. With a famously politically active working-class population, and a well-known history of mobilisation and activism, Glasgow appeared to be the natural hub for Scottish Aid Spain efforts. Yet, curiously, direct evidence of such leadership is often missing. That is to say not that pro-Republican activism was absent in Glasgow – far from it – but rather that there was less in the way of co-ordination and organisation than might be expected. This is reflected in the frequent ineffectiveness of SACs in a Glaswegian context. Such committees were often short-lived, raised relatively little money or proved unable to provide leadership or co-ordination

to wider efforts. This section explores the activities of several such committees, and examines the factors that led to their success or failure. It
is argued that political disunity, combined with a legacy of inter-class
suspicion, meant that the only committees capable of sustained, successful
action were those based on local working-class coalitions, which required
careful negotiation of competing political interpretations of the conflict.
The difficulty of achieving such unity, even on a local level, in such a
diverse and highly charged political environment led to few successful
committees being formed.

Glasgow's case reinforces the conclusion that co-operation was not an
inevitable outcome of widespread sympathy for the Spanish Republic.
As discussed in previous chapters, Glasgow was still a fiercely contested
political space in the 1930s, with the disaffiliation of the ILP leaving a
much-weakened Labour Party competing with a diverse and vibrant set
of radical alternatives. Yet in the immediate aftermath of the military
uprising in Spain, it did seem as if Spain might be an issue that could bring
Glasgow's left together. Early mass demonstrations usually featured most
major left-wing groups in Glasgow, frequently including the Labour Party
despite official proscriptions against sharing a platform with communists.[36]
Informally, the ILP and the communists often co-operated in organising
early demonstrations and public meetings, and presented a united front on
the problems caused by the Catholic Church in key working-class neighbourhoods.[37] It was common for ILP members to contribute to Communist Party funds, even those supporting the International Brigades.[38] This
co-operation is in stark contrast to earlier campaigns such as the Hunger
Marches, which were more often characterised by mistrust and bickering
between the two parties.[39] Some echoes of this legacy were still visible
after the outbreak of the Spanish Civil War, including a communist boy-
cott of an ILP 'flag day' in August 1936. This, however, was itself a sign of
just how keen the CPGB was to foster an alliance with the official labour
movement – the dispute arose as the ILP aimed to send the funds raised to
its political allies in Spain, rather than the TUC-backed ISF.[40]

Although such episodes ultimately did not undermine the willingness
of Glasgow's left to work together, the ILP's contradictory attempts to pursue an independent anti-communist policy in Spain, while simultaneously
seeking a domestic alliance with the Communist Party, eventually proved to
be untenable.[41] The events surrounding an alleged anti-government uprising
in Barcelona by the POUM and others in May 1937 brought matters to a
head. The communist version of events, in which anarchists and Trotskyists
staged an uprising in support of Franco, largely held sway in much of Britain,

resulting in minimal impact on the political arrangements supporting the Aid Spain movement.[42] This was not the case in Glasgow, however, where local activists had strong ties with the POUM and other anti-Stalinist groups in Barcelona. They soon received very different accounts of events, namely that the Communist Party forcefully suppressed rival political groups in order to destroy the workers' revolution in Barcelona.[43] Although the ILP hesitated at abandoning the common front on Spain, the relentless attacks on them and their allies in the communist press forced their hand.[44]

Although sporadic defences of the ILP position appeared from mid-1937, clashes began in earnest following the return from Spain of the ILP MP John McGovern and the publication of his sensational pamphlet *Terror in Spain*.[45] He claimed that Stalinism had taken root, ushering in censorship, secret police and the suppression of other radical groups.[46] Unfortunately for the ILP, this was seized upon by the right-wing press as confirmation of the Republic's inherent flaws, justifying its consistently neutral or pro-Franco stances.[47] This in turn was used by the Communist Party to portray the ILP as aiding reactionary forces in destroying the Spanish Republic.[48] Whilst the pamphlet was intended to expose the betrayal of what they saw as a once-pure revolution, the ILP's complex message was quickly and unfavourably reinterpreted by left and right alike. The issue was clouded further by the mysterious death of the ILP activist Bob Smillie, who had served in the POUM militia alongside George Orwell. Smillie was well-known and liked in Glasgow, and accusations of foul play soon emerged, fuelled in particular by the return from Spain of the Glasgow anarchist Ethel MacDonald, who claimed Smillie had been tortured and murdered by the Communist Party while in prison. Over much of 1938, vitriolic accusations regarding Smillie were traded between local communists, anarchists and the ILP, forestalling remaining prospects of radical unity in Aid Spain campaigns.[49]

From a communist perspective, co-operation with the ILP on Spain was in any case secondary. Gaining access and building influence within the Labour Party was of considerably higher importance, and the ultimate goal of CPGB policy in the period. Yet even aside from the difficulties in overcoming official barriers to co-operation, the question of how to respond to the Spanish Civil War could cause acute internal divisions within Labour itself. One Labour magistrate was forced to resign after publicly supporting Franco and attempting to hinder pro-Republican fundraising activities in Glasgow. The local Labour paper, *Forward*, commented that 'in such circumstances resignation was possibly the best way out ... Labour in Glasgow is definitely 100 percent on the side of the

Spanish Government.'[50] This, as it turned out, may have been somewhat optimistic.

Catholic opposition to the Spanish Republic, as well as active support for Franco, had been present in Glasgow and elsewhere in Scotland from the earliest days of the conflict. The ILP *New Leader* noted the disruption of its Glasgow flag day in September 1936 by 'religious folks [convinced] by capitalist organs that the Spanish workers are an unruly mob, beset on murder'.[51] The Glasgow district of the Ancient Order of Hibernians had also laid the groundwork for bureaucratic efforts to stymie pro-Republican fundraising, resolving in August 1936 that

> Catholic members of the trade unions and kindred organisations to see and determine that none of the funds to which they contribute shall be used in support of a campaign having for its objective the extermination of Christianity in Spain or any other country.[52]

It is difficult to say how far these efforts were successful, though the local Catholic press pointed to concessions extracted from the Co-operative movement, including the Scottish Co-operative Wholesale Society itself.[53] That these campaigns were at least somewhat effective in preventing the full participation of otherwise sympathetic organisations in pro-Republican fundraising is indicated by an article in the *Daily Worker* in late 1936, which noted 'instances of reactionary opposition (mainly of a Catholic character) to aid for Spain making itself manifest in the Trade Union movement'.[54]

The founding of a Glasgow chapter of the 'Friends of Nationalist Spain' brought these tensions to a head in early 1938. Scattered violence at their inaugural meeting was expected to escalate at a larger meeting planned in St Andrew's Hall in March. Following the Glasgow Chief Constable's warning that police were unable to guarantee the safety of public property given the likelihood of 'disturbances' organised by pro-Republican groups, Glasgow Labour magistrates revoked permission for the planned meeting.[55] The ruling prompted an immediate outcry from the Catholic press against the 'Corporation Hitlers' who made the decision.[56] Their outrage found some resonance, with a broad cross-section of opinion viewing it as an attack on free speech. The *Glasgow Herald* letters page featured numerous condemnations of the local Labour Party, including one correspondent who without any apparent irony called on the military to 'do something' about Labour in order to prevent fascism in Britain.[57] Aside from external criticism, several Labour representatives broke party lines and voted against the decision.[58] One such rebel defended himself, claiming that

I did not surrender my liberty as a free man and a free citizen when I
joined the Labour Party. I do not intend to surrender it now. Nor do I
intend to allow the Labour Party to be put in the position of curtailing
the liberty of others.[59]

In a tense meeting, the Glasgow Labour Party decided against expelling
the rebels, settling on a motion of censure.[60] Given the earlier resignations
over the issue, further high-profile expulsions could well have resulted in
a split of the Glasgow Labour Party.

Political divisions on the left were not the only factor militating against
the development of a broad Aid Spain coalition in Glasgow. The local politics
of class also made it more difficult to imagine the kind of elite participation
that often characterised efforts in England. Although Glasgow is often
seen as an archetypical working-class city, it 'had a complex social structure
with all classes – from the very poorest to the super-rich – living within
its boundaries'.[61] Yet memories of open class conflict in Glasgow were still
fresh in the 1930s. The 'Red Clydeside' in particular was very much a part
of living memory, though it is not intended here to contribute to the long-
running debate over the nature of Red Clydeside. For this account, it is
enough that Red Clydeside cemented the perception that Glasgow was a
hotbed of revolutionary activity, a perception that many on Glasgow's left
encouraged. Ramsay MacDonald, then Labour leader in 1925, remarked that

Glasgow is a fearful bogey to the outside world and I am not sure
sometimes but that our movement there is more concerned to keep up
the hair-raising reputation than is good for it.[62]

In 1936, the year of the outbreak of the Spanish Civil War, the recently
elected Communist MP William Gallacher released his own account of
the Red Clydeside, helping cement the perception both within and outside the labour movement that Glasgow was the revolutionary hub of
Britain.[63] Although its intention was linking the CPGB more closely with
Glasgow's radical history, such efforts had the inevitable effect of stoking
middle-class fears.[64] These long-established anxieties meant that convincing Glasgow elites to co-operate with working-class political groups was
always going to be difficult, especially on an issue with so many revolutionary implications as Spain.

Conversely, the mythology surrounding Glasgow as the 'Red Centre'
of the British Empire also encouraged the belief among Glasgow workers
that they did not need elites to take effective action. In one of Britain's

largest cities, with a strong and politically aware working class with a history of mobilisation and activism, appealing explicitly to local elites was not necessarily desirable in the eyes of Glaswegian activists. Indeed, when co-operation did take place, such as with the February 1937 concert held to raise money for the Scottish Ambulance Unit, it was Sir Daniel Stevenson that made the initial overtures to the Glasgow TC, and even then labour movement leaders were initially equivocal in their response.[65] While Patrick Dollan's view that 'the wealthy people of Scotland who organised the [ambulance unit] ought to produce the finance', as it was 'the only thing they have done on behalf of democracy in Spain' was extreme, the lack of support Stevenson received from elites and workers alike is an indication of the especial difficulty faced in generating cross-class support in Glasgow. The February 1937 concert, for instance, raised just £44 despite months of planning, whilst Stevenson felt 'very annoyed that his business associates had let him down' and revealed that less than £1500 had been raised in total by November 1936, against operating costs of £10,000.[66] It is likely that Stevenson made up much of the difference himself, as well as seeking grants from non-Scottish Aid Spain organisations. This was certainly his approach later in the conflict; after mentioning a large £1000 donation in a letter to the *Manchester Guardian* in February 1939 in an effort to secure support from 'our well-to-do friends', Stevenson admitted in private correspondence that the £1000 was his own contribution, on top of thousands of pounds already borrowed against his name.[67] Stevenson had more success in soliciting funds from the British TUC than from the Scottish labour movement, securing grants totalling £2200 made from the ISF, compared to grants of £1900 made to the much larger London-based Spanish Medical Aid Committee.[68] Whilst the amount raised through direct fundraising in Scotland was hardly inconsequential, it is also clear that there was significant popular and institutional scepticism towards Stevenson's project.

The Scottish Ambulance Unit's troubles reflected the extent that large-scale, inter-class co-operation was unlikely to succeed in its home town of Glasgow. Yet proving the absence or failure of Aid Spain activism is methodologically fraught. Few Aid Spain organisations systematically preserved their own records or ephemera. Newspaper coverage was highly uneven, tending to focus on more respectable, high-profile forms of activism. Few column inches were given over to local committees or events. This poses a conundrum when evaluating their success: without detailed or consistent coverage, do we assume that large amounts of day-to-day activity are simply missing from the historical record, or that there was less such activity than might be expected? While the former is not unreasonable, and is doubtless true in some instances, the scattered available material in the press or records of other organisations indicates that the latter explanation may be closer to the truth in Glasgow.

Although few records of local committees survive, WADC donations can once again be used to sketch out when and where some committees existed. In some cases, Aid Spain committees could emerge naturally from pre-existing groups. The Southern Anti-Fascist Committee, for instance, was a pre-existing organisation formed of ILPers, communists and trades unionists, with the committee deciding in December 1936 to concentrate on organising and expanding 'activities on behalf of Spain'.[69] Although little is known of the continued operations of this body, it remained active until at least January 1938, making several sizeable donations to the WADC in this time.[70] It is notable that this committee, which at least began as a model example of coalition-building, was not affiliated to the National JC for Spanish Relief. Given the overtly political stance of the organisation, the choice of WADC as a major beneficiary and the emphasis on working-class coalition-building, the Southern Anti-Fascist Committee represents a more Glaswegian embrace of the older United Front concept that had little space for middle-class liberals or moderates.

A similarly robust committee was formed in Shettleston, a working-class district in the Glasgow's East End. Despite being home to a significant number of International Brigade volunteers, the Aid Spain movement faced considerable difficulties in fostering unity. Shettleston was home to a large Catholic population. Almost uniquely – not just in Glasgow, but across Britain – the local ILP MP, John McGovern, took a combative approach to Catholic criticism of the Spanish Republic, declaring that 'if I had a thousand seats, I would lose them on this issue'.[71] As a result, Shettleston became a flashpoint in the simmering tension between working-class Catholicism and pro-Republicanism. A major confrontation was sparked by the publication of a pamphlet written by McGovern justifying Spanish anticlericalism in December 1936.[72] Many Shettleston Catholics, backed by the local Catholic press, rose to the challenge, heckling McGovern at meetings and confronting pro-Republicans in the streets.[73] Events culminated in a public debate between McGovern and the Catholic intellectual Douglas Jerrold in June 1937. With four thousand spectators split evenly between camps, both the Labour newspaper *Forward* and the *Lanarkshire Catholic Herald* noted that the Catholics in the audience were louder and more assertive than their socialist counterparts.[74] Organising Aid Spain activities in Shettleston, therefore, meant facing opposition from working-class Catholics already mobilised against the Spanish Republic. The very name of the organisation that emerged, the 'Shettleston United Spanish Aid Committee', hints at the difficulties that were faced and overcome by its organisers, though its regular donations to the WADC – and the lack of similar donations from the Shettleston branch of the CPGB – indicates that local communists had taken the lead.

Both of these committees managed to unite disparate political groups, navigating increasing conflict amongst left-wing groups over the course of the war, and, in Shettleston's case, the threat of working-class sectarianism. Yet these groups remained the exception to the rule. Other working-class districts failed to organise similar bodies, leaving local Aid Spain movements in the hands of individual organisations. That is not to say that the Aid Spain movement lacked enthusiasm in districts without committees. When the International Brigade Foodship Convoy visited Glasgow in January 1939, it visited several such districts, including Springburn, the Gorbals and Govanhill, raising £400 in a single day.[75] Yet the absence of SACs meant that the Aid Spain movement in these districts remained limited in scope and no local body had the capacity to organise large-scale, sustained schemes on its own initiative.

The delays and difficulties in setting up the Glasgow JC for Spanish Relief are a further sign of just how challenging it could be to co-ordinate Aid Spain efforts in a city like Glasgow. The founding of this committee in early 1938 has usually been seen as being necessary in order to 'get together' the many local committees of this type already operating successfully in Glasgow.[76] Yet it is far from clear that this was actually the case. According to a list of Scottish SACs compiled by the Edinburgh activist Tom Murray, many areas of Glasgow actually had no dedicated committee, including working-class areas that saw significant recruitment for the International Brigades such as the Gorbals, Springburn and Govanhill.[77] Moreover, of the Glasgow committees listed, several overlapped in their coverage. The north-western suburbs of Anniesland and Knightswood, for example, had three separate committees listed, each with a different contact.[78] Either these committees competed for donations and resources, undermining the purpose of SACs as co-ordinating bodies, or they survived only for short periods, with replacement committees founded at later junctures. Whilst Murray's list may have been incomplete, the lack of reference to the work of such committees in the press or records of other local or regional organisations is also telling. The First Glasgow Branch of the Amalgamated Union of Building Trade Workers provides an illustrative example. Branch minutes from 1936–9 record discussions of Spain on no fewer than 32 occasions, including donations for International Brigade dependants, foodships, the Basque children and other schemes. Only once, in January 1939, was any contact with a Glaswegian SAC recorded.[79]

The Glasgow JC should therefore be seen in a quite different light. Rather than an attempt to manage existing local committees, as assumed by Fyrth, its aim was to co-ordinate the activities of a myriad of organisations acting almost completely independently. Early signs were somewhat promising in this regard. Focusing on cross-class appeal and humanitarianism, the new committee was launched in February 1938.

> In the new campaign throughout the length and breadth of Scotland, which has been announced in your columns, Glasgow must play its part. A joint committee for that city and district, with representatives of over seventy organisations, is now in existence. Our motto is: 'Help Spain Now'. In the name of humanity we urge every man and woman in Glasgow who has shuddered at the accounts of the bombing of Barcelona to come to the help of innocent sufferers in Spain.[80]

Yet despite such grand calls to action, the new committee does not appear to have had much immediate impact, particularly when it came to engaging with existing working-class efforts. The Glasgow TC refused to be represented on the new committee, relenting only in early 1939.[81] Yet even when the local Amalgamated Engineering Union (AEU) offered 'ample support', the only communication it ever received in return was a generic letter suggesting that they write to local MPs about the arms embargo on Spain.[82] The bulletin of the National JC refers to just one event held in Glasgow, a joint meeting held in conjunction with the Youth Peace Council in February 1938.[83] The only other major initiative known to have taken place was a Spanish Fiesta and Fair, which was held in February 1939, raising an impressive £1400.[84] However, the publicity surrounding this event makes all the more telling the organisation's absence in both the media and the records of sympathetic organisations for the preceding year. Aside from the particular difficulties of joint action in Glasgow, this likely also reflected a key problem with committees founded in the later stages of the war: it took time to build the experience and contacts necessary to operate effectively. However, the Glasgow JC's one apparent success, the Spanish Fiesta, demonstrated clearly the sort of financial impact that such bodies could achieve when they managed to bring together and co-ordinate different groups, and secure cross-class support. Whilst this kind of success proved fleeting in Glasgow, this was not necessarily the case elsewhere in Scotland.

The Edinburgh Joint Committee for Spanish Relief

Edinburgh is hardly famed for its radical political heritage, and perhaps as a result has tended to be dismissed as a site of pro-Republican activism.[85] Yet, equally, Edinburgh did not share Glasgow's recent history of acute inter-class tension or sectarianism, nor did Edinburgh see a particularly meaningful rivalry between parties of the left in the 1930s. In other words, the impediments to effective coalition building that existed in Glasgow were not reflected in Edinburgh. The result was that – despite its 'genteel' reputation – Edinburgh was home to what was likely the most effective SAC in Scotland: the Edinburgh JC for Spanish Relief. Alongside exploring the basis of this committee's success, this section looks more closely at the internal workings of this committee, highlighting in particular the way that the Aid Spain movement challenged the boundaries of women's involvement in political activism.

The committee's first chairman was the Labour Town Councillor Tom Murray. As a respectable local authority figure with bipartisan connections in local government, he was a sound choice in appealing for middle-class support. Murray was also one of four clandestine communists among Edinburgh's Labour Councillors.[86] As such, Murray could appeal to both Edinburgh's elites and to Labour and Communist Party activists who could be relied upon to provide a core of enthusiastic volunteers when necessary. The eventual composition of the Committee reflects the emphasis placed on building a broad coalition of support. A 'great' meeting of the Committee might involve thirty or more delegates; before major events this number could rise to over seventy.[87] All local unions with TC affiliations were invited to send representatives, although some chose not to or delayed doing so until later in the conflict.[88] Groups such as the Fabian Society and Quakers were represented, as were local Liberals and churches.[89] The local LBC also provided useful contacts with Edinburgh's middle-class fellow travellers.[90] As the new committee began work in mid-1937, it was soon apparent that the Edinburgh JC had succeeded in forging a coalition with broad, cross-class appeal, the first and most effective of its kind in Scotland.

In April 1938, Tom Murray stepped down from his position as chairman of the committee to join the International Brigades in Spain, and was replaced by his wife, Janet Murray. Despite her relative inexperience, Janet Murray's tenure as chairman proved exceptionally successful. Her letters to her husband in Spain chart her growing confidence and success as an organiser and public speaker, as well as the personal and organisational problems she faced. This section discusses her role as the leader of the Edinburgh JC, which saw the Committee take a prominent role in the Scottish Aid Spain movement, and marked a shift away from the tactics used by the labour movement. In particular, it focuses on the role of gender in shaping the strategies and effectiveness of the Edinburgh JC under her leadership, and examines the implications of this for the wider Aid Spain movement in Edinburgh.

The interwar period is often seen as a nadir of women's roles in modern British political life, with gender dynamics shaped and reinforced by the traumas of the Great War and economic depression. Despite contending that Scottish women did maintain active political identities during the period, Annmarie Hughes acknowledges that 'women's political agency was largely confined to domestic issues'.[91] Similarly, Alan Campbell argues that women's 'primary political function was to raise election funds through raffles, songs and Burns Suppers, and to act as auxiliaries in the next election campaign'.[92] Scholarship dealing with women's role in the Aid Spain movement rightly highlights the extent to which women were able to challenge these limitations, though it says less about the difficulties such women faced.[93] This section complements the work of Angela Jackson by examining women's roles within specific organisations rather than exploring a range of individual activists.[94] Janet Murray's position as leader was shaped by entrenched gender norms, yet she was able to pioneer forms of fundraising and activism that often proved more effective than those employed under other leadership. However, Janet Murray faced consistent pressure to conform to others' expectations of what women's roles in activism should be.

Gender also played an ambiguous role in perceptions of Janet Murray as an orator. She herself modestly downplayed her early successes in her letters; she allowed only that 'I must have done all right' or that 'I suppose I was effective'.[95] By June, however, she relished the opportunity of matching up against Sir Walter Citrine in competing events in Dundee, and took pride in her 'reputation for cadging money at these meetings'.[96] This reputation was well-earned; her record of £106 for a single collection was only broken once, by Sir Stafford Cripps.[97] Her eminence as an orator led to committees throughout the region inviting her to speak, notably in Kirkcaldy and Dundee, where she returned several times. This helped the Edinburgh JC to establish itself as the principal Aid Spain organisation in the east of Scotland and play a prominent role nationwide.

However, Janet Murray's success as a speaker was still perceived in ways that implicitly diminished her contributions. Her husband, Tom

Murray, interviewed years after her death, recalled her success in eliciting donations in very specific terms.

> She raised enormous sums of money for Spanish relief. She always appeared, you see, as the wife of an International Brigader. Naturally, that created a bit of a response.[98]

This explanation places the credit for Janet Murray's success squarely upon his own actions, implying that it was his volunteering in Spain that underpinned Janet's accomplishments, limiting her role to that of a dutiful wife rather than an ardent campaigner in her own right. Yet while initially modest, her own letters contain rather different explanations of her success.

> I have been getting commendation all round for the way I took the collection in the Usher Hall on Tuesday. £106 of a collection seems a bit of a record. I feel so intensely about the urgency of the need in Spain that I suppose I was effective.[99]

Janet Murray consistently linked her activism and oratorical success not to her husband but to her own passion for the cause. She was, in her own words, 'living, thinking and dreaming Spain all the time and really devoting all my energies and time to stirring up public opinion'.[100] Given the variety of causes for which she spoke, such as Basque Children and Medical Aid as well as Dependants' Aid, and the demand for her services throughout eastern Scotland, it is apparent that Janet Murray's success was primarily due to her own talent and drive as a speaker, and not just her husband's volunteering in Spain.

Janet Murray's organisational strategies were also a departure from earlier efforts, which favoured collections at public meetings and demonstrations. She ran weekly medical aid meetings where volunteers folded bandages and packed medical supplies for Spain and set up two 'Spain Shops' to receive donations and goods as well as disseminate propaganda and sell Spanish oranges and toys.[101] Major events included a 'Spanish Birthday Party' in 1939, a tea party and dance, with each table 'hosted' by a prominent local citizen.[102] The largest single event, however, was the Spanish Fiesta and Fair in December 1938. The list of organisers and stalls reveals that women, particularly from local Labour Party organisations, played the largest role in running the event, with most of the £1000 raised coming from the stalls and games run by Edinburgh women.[103] These

events, alongside a range of smaller initiatives such as whist drives, drawing room meetings and dances, paid significant dividends. This success,
and that of women up and down the country in supporting the Spanish
Republic, reflected the reality that the skills required to fundraise effectively for Spain were also those which were honed in traditional 'women's
work' in the labour movement – raising the funds to support political campaigns – though the newfound prestige and perceived importance of this
work offered opportunities to women such as Janet Murray to challenge
and transcend these boundaries. Particularly in CPGB circles, the fact that
many male activists were away in Spain also led indirectly to more opportunities for women to take on more responsibility in domestic campaigns,
a process highlighted by the means through which Janet Murray became
the chairman of the Edinburgh JC.

The new prominence of women in the Aid Spain conflict was not
uncontested, and Janet Murray faced considerable difficulties in winning
over labour movement support that her husband had been able to take
for granted. The Edinburgh TC reacted condescendingly to Janet Murray's
informal request to sell badges at their meetings, deciding that in response
to the 'lady in charge of Spanish Aid Shop', they would 'grant [the] request
but that in future all such requests be made in writing'.[104] Trades union
elements within the committee also presented difficulties. The executive's
unified purpose gradually deteriorated; 'bickering and squabbling' replacing
'harmony'.[105] Tensions were stoked by perceived imbalances between the
often middle-class Executive and the working-class rank-and-file of the
committee. The secretary position, for example, was held first by Mrs
Geddes, the wife of a prominent local doctor. She was replaced in 1938
by Andrew Finlayson, who later admitted to taking the position not out of
interest in Spain but as an opportunity to impress his activist girlfriend.[106]
His one redeeming quality, in Janet Murray's eyes, was that he owned
a car, although she continued to complain about his lack of enthusiasm
throughout his tenure.[107]

Simmering tensions led to open conflict by July 1938. Janet Murray
and other executive committee members were not seen to be doing their
fair share of work in running the two 'Spain Shops'. Her chief antagonist,
an AEU representative named Bell, was 'terribly critical and pugnacious'
in meetings, demoralising Janet Murray to the extent that she offered to
resign as chairman. It is clear though that Janet Murray was no shirker.
She noted that her detractors seemed to disregard 'the number of jobs I
am tackling', which involved speaking at multiple meetings each week and
organising one-off events, as well as handling day-to-day correspondence

and appeals.[108] Bell's criticism of her focusing on high-level organisation and oratory was an implicit double standard, especially given his earlier wholehearted support for Tom Murray undertaking the same duties as chairman. Whilst it was acceptable for a man with established status within the labour movement to concentrate on organising and oratory, Janet Murray lost legitimacy by not conforming to expectations of what 'women's work' entailed in labour movement activism. They could not argue with the numbers, however: in its first year, before Janet Murray became chairman, the committee raised around £500, compared to approximately £2800 in the fifteen months afterwards.[109]

Janet Murray had succeeded in multiplying the funds raised by the Edinburgh Joint Committee several times over, a remarkable achievement by any measure. Yet financial success is not the only measure by which the effectiveness of Spanish Aid Committees should be judged. The Spanish Civil War could not be won by humanitarian aid, and supporting the Republic required campaigning for political change as much as raising money. Lewis Mates claims that Spanish Aid campaigns 'that looked like de facto popular fronts used predominantly humanitarian language', sacrificing political impact for the sake of raising money.[110] At first glance, Edinburgh's committee resembles this characterisation. By the time Janet Murray became chairman in April 1938, the JC resembled the archetypal organisation described by Mates: a broad coalition united on humanitarian terms and largely apolitical in its appeals, despite the clear pro-Republicanism of its leaders. The justifications for adopting a humanitarian strategy – to appease more conservative elements of the committee and appeal to new potential supporters across class boundaries – correspond closely with those postulated by Mates.[111]

Whilst the Edinburgh JC had always aimed to garner such support, the process gathered pace under Janet Murray's leadership. In promoting her medical campaign, Janet Murray highlighted the participation of corporate and professional partners such as the British Medical Association, Pharmaceutical Society and local wholesale firms.[112] She also frequently sought to reassure middle-class supporters by emphasising their humanitarian remit, reminding 'those with political scruples that in medicine and nursing the only criteria of service are suffering and need'.[113] Similarly, at a November 1938 concert, her speech focused on the 'thousands of children' who 'would die this winter'; her co-host claiming that it 'was not ultimately a political issue but a human one'.[114] The 'Spain Shops' went even further, displaying notices claiming 'that the Committee is non-political' and 'humanitarian in its attitude to the victims of war'.[115]

Murray's choice of benefactor was also cautious, with the vast majority of funds channelled to the National JC, with only small, occasional grants made to politicised funds like the WADC.[116] This was despite her own strong views on Spain. Murray's private letters reveal her frustration with labour movement inaction on Spain, referring to their 'rotten leadership' and struggling to contain her sarcasm when interacting with the more staid and 'ignorant' wife of the Scottish Labour Party Secretary, Barbara Woodburn.[117]

In late 1938, the Edinburgh JC itself acknowledged that the political aspect of its work was unsatisfactory. It decided to sponsor a new organisation, the Edinburgh Spain Emergency Committee. This new group was the result of collaboration with the Edinburgh TC, with the TC providing the public backing and the JC the initial funding.[118] Its purpose was solely political; over its short existence, it sent deputations to the Italian and German consulates as well as local organisations and politicians, organised demonstrations and public meetings and gathered twenty thousand signatures for an anti-Franco petition.[119] Following the defeat of the Republic several months later, the organisation was quietly disbanded, although the JC itself continued to campaign on behalf of Republican refugees until mid-1939.

The JC's role in founding the Emergency Committee has ambiguous implications. That the committee backed the new organisation indicates that the committee's leadership was firmly pro-Republican and its leaders clearly saw their role as political as well as humanitarian. However, it was also a tacit admission that the JC could not conduct an intensified political campaign alone, especially given its rhetorical focus on humanitarianism. Additionally, the mild secrecy surrounding the JC's role in financing the Emergency Committee indicates a desire to keep its involvement at arm's length, possibly to avoid tainting its reputation among existing donors. In themselves, the Edinburgh JC's actions do not contradict Mates's argument about the self-imposed limitations of a humanitarian approach, but they do suggest that the picture may be somewhat more complex than he allowed, with humanitarian-orientated campaigns actively seeking out ways in which to achieve their political goals in ways that would not jeopardise their fundraising.

Conclusions

The specific debate over whether Aid Spain represented the beginnings of a British 'Popular Front' has now haunted histories of the movement for decades. It is, as originally formulated, unlikely to be fully resolved. However, the broader question of how far pro-Republican activism was able to bring together different strands of British progressivism in the late 1930s – and, crucially, how far this was a vehicle for Communist Party engagement with the broader British left – remains an important one. The Scottish examples explored here indicate that the overall picture is mixed. Aid Spain coalitions were certainly forged in Scotland, but their character and purpose was far from monolithic. Local politics made for local outcomes, complicating any attempt to build a cohesive picture of a distinctively 'Scottish' Aid Spain movement. However, most examples discussed here did share a common denominator: the role of the Communist Party in providing a catalyst, for better or worse. Whilst SACs could indeed evolve without communist involvement, they tended to do so in the final year or even months of the war, and their impact often began to be felt only as the Republic started to collapse.

How far did Aid Spain coalitions serve their intended purpose in the eyes of the Communist Party? Certainly, activism on behalf of the Republic served the CPGB well when it came to attracting potential recruits – the Party expanded significantly in this period, adding a thousand Scottish members between 1936 and 1939.[120] Yet it is much less clear how far this reflected a successful effort to rehabilitate and integrate the CPGB into the wider Scottish left. Success in co-operating with the Labour Party or labour movement was generally achieved in places where such co-operation had previously been successful, such as in Kirkcaldy, or where co-operation had limited political possibilities – indeed, co-operation could succeed in some places precisely because the stakes were so low. Elsewhere, in the very places where unity held the most potential for integrating Scottish communism into the political mainstream, progress was much harder to come by.

The difficulties of bringing a fractured Scottish left together had significant implications for the character of Aid Spain activism in Scotland. As coalitions grew wider, larger compromises were needed to achieve consensus. Many sympathetic individuals and organisations chose instead to act independently, and had correspondingly greater freedom in expressing their views and choosing the beneficiary of their efforts. For these reasons, a great deal of Scottish Aid Spain activism could consistently be more politicised, and it retained a predominantly working-class character. Yet a price was often paid in terms of scale. Without co-operation, bringing together resources and knowledge into common endeavours, Scottish Aid Spain activism struggled to put together events and initiatives on the same scale as found elsewhere in Britain. Delays in founding local or regional committees also proved a handicap at times. SACs tended to grow increasingly effective over time, perhaps reflecting growing sympathy for the Spanish Republic amid a wider context of fascist aggression across Europe, but likely also the growing capacity and capability of their leaders and activists. Building and maintaining solidarity over such a long period required innovation to succeed – as Janet Murray's tenure as chairman of the Edinburgh JC demonstrated, successful tactics in this new context involved boldly challenging existing mindsets and assumptions, as well as a great deal of hard work. This would also be a lesson learned by the official labour movement in Scotland over the course of the conflict.

Notes

1. *Cowdenbeath and District Advertiser*, 15 January 1937, 6.
2. *Cowdenbeath and District Advertiser*, 15 January 1937, 6.
3. *Cowdenbeath and District Advertiser*, 15 January 1937, 6.
4. *Cowdenbeath and District Advertiser*, 15 January 1937, 7.
5. Gray, *Homage*, 140.
6. On the intersections between working-class Catholicism, Irish immigration, Labour and communism, see Hughes, *Gender and Political Identities*, 70–2.
7. *Spanish Relief Bulletin 9*, October 1937, TC, 292/946/18a/60.
8. Of all Scottish towns, only Edinburgh and Glasgow had events reported in the *Bulletin*, and then rarely. See *Spanish Relief Bulletin 1–11*, 1937–1938, TC.
9. Janet to Tom Murray, 22 May 1938, 22 June 1938, 29 June 1938, NLS, TMP, Box 1, File 1.
10. Buchanan, *British Labour Movement*, 35.
11. On CPGB policy in this period, see Kevin Morgan, *Against Fascism and War: Ruptures and Continuities in British Communist Politics, 1935–41* (Manchester, 1989).
12. For different perspective on the 'Popular Front' across Europe, see Helen Graham and Paul Preston (eds), *The Popular Front in Europe* (Basingstoke, 1987).
13. 'List of Spanish Aid Committees in the Scottish Area', n.d, NLS, TMP, Box 4, File 3.
14. Bob Selkirk, *Life of a Worker* (Dundee, 1967), 38.
15. Campbell, *Scottish Miners*, 386–7; Worley, *Class against Class*, 30–3; Macintyre, *Little Moscows*, 74–5.
16. Mary Docherty to Jim Fyrth, 17 June 1984, MML, Box B-4, File R/2.
17. *Fife Free Press*, 20 February 1937, 1; *Kirkcaldy Times*, 21 October 1936, 4.
18. *Fife Free Press*, 20 February 1937, 1.
19. *Fife Free Press*, 15 August 1936, 6; 13 March 1937 14; 2 April 1938, 11.
20. *Fife Free Press*, 20 March 1937, 3; 27 March 1937, 3; 3 April 1937, 3.

21. For example *Fife Free Press*, 27 February 1937, 1; 17 April 1937, 8.

22. *Fife Free Press*, 1 January 1938, 6; *Daily Worker*, 10 September 1938, 6.

23. *Fife Free Press*, 1 January 1938, 6.

24. *Kirkcaldy Times*, 7 October 1936, 2.

25. *Kirkcaldy Times*, 7 October 1936, 1.

26. *Kirkcaldy Times*, 21 October 1936, 4.

27. Campbell, *Scottish Miners*, 320.

28. Fyrth, *Signal Was Spain*, 209.

29. *Cowdenbeath and District Advertiser*, 1 July 1938, 2.

30. Selkirk, *Life of a Worker*, 38.

31. *Cowdenbeath and District Advertiser*, 6 May 1938, 4.

32. *Kirkcaldy Times*, 20 January 1937, 3.

33. For example *Daily Worker*, 11 March 1939, 3; *Dundee Courier*, 29 May, 1937.

34. *Dundee Courier*, 26 November, 1938, 16.

35. *Dunfermline and West Fife Journal*, 10 September 1937, 5.

36. *Daily Worker*, 25 August 1936, 6.

37. See *Daily Worker*, 25 August 1936, 6; 13 January 1937, 6. On ILP and CPGB co-operation on the Catholic issue, see *Daily Worker* 19 August 1936, 5; *Daily Worker*, 22 December 1936; John McGovern, *Why Bishops Back Franco* (London, 1936), 1. Labour also aided such campaigns to some extent: see 'Catholics and the Civil War in Spain', November 1936, MML, Box 13, File F/10.

38. For example *Daily Worker*, 5 December 1936, 5–6.

39. McShane in MacDougall, *Voices from the Hunger Marches*, 21–3.

40. Flag days were public collections – requiring permission from local authorities – on a particular day, with flags or badges given to donors to mark their support of the charity in question. *Daily Worker*, 1 September 1936, 3.

41. Buchanan, *Britain and the Spanish Civil War*, 77.

42. Buchanan, *British Labour Movement*, 75–6.

43. Angela Jackson claims that Glasgow may well have been the first city outside of Spain to hear the alternative version of events. Jackson, *British Women*, 151.

44. Headlines such as 'Is the ILP For Winning The War Or Aiding Franco?' began to appear from late May 1937. *Daily Worker*, 21 May 1937, 3.

45. John McGovern, *Terror in Spain: How the Communist International Has Destroyed Working Class Unity, Undermined the Fight against Franco, and Suppressed the Social Revolution* (London, 1937).

46. McGovern, *Terror in Spain*, 3–7.

47. The Catholic press was not above gloating. For example *Glasgow Observer*, 15 January 1938, 1.

48. William Gallacher in *Forward*, 1 January 1938, 3.

49. The David Murray Papers (DMP) contain a series of exchanges: Murray and Gallacher in *Forward*, 25 December 1937; McShane in *Forward*, 1 January 1938; MacDonald in *Forward*, 8 January 1938; McShane in *Forward*, 15 January 1938. The feud reignited in August, with Gallacher in *Forward*,

13 August 1938; Murray in *Forward*, 20 August 1938; McGovern in *Forward*, 27 August 1938. An exasperated editorial note in the 27 August issue stated that no further dialogue between the parties would be accepted for publication. NLS, DMP, Acc. 7915, Box 4/5.

50. *Forward*, 13 March 1937, 1.
51. *New Leader*, 4 September 1936, 1.
52. *Lanarkshire Catholic Herald*, 15 August 1936, 1.
53. *Lanarkshire Catholic Herald*, 17 October 1936, 1 and 24 April 1937, 1.
54. *Daily Worker*, 23 November 1936, 2. For an overview across Britain, see Buchanan, *British Labour Movement*, 167–95.
55. *Glasgow Herald*, 28 March 1938, clipping in NLS, DMP, Box 2, File 6.
56. *Glasgow Observer*, 26 March 1938, 1.
57. *Glasgow Herald*, 25 March 1938, clipping in NLS, DMP, Box 2, File 6.
58. According to Fyrth, four out of fifteen magistrates broke the Party line, although he incorrectly states that all were expelled from the Labour Party. Fyrth, *Signal Was Spain*, 282–3.
59. Unlabelled newspaper clipping, 8 June 1938, NLS, DMP, Box 2, File 6.
60. *Scottish Daily Express*, 23 June 1938, NLS, DMP, Box 2, File 6.
61. Smyth, *Labour in Glasgow*, 3.
62. MacDonald, quoted in Ian Wood, 'Hope Deferred: Labour in Scotland in the 1920s' in Ian Donnachie, Christopher Harvie and Ian Wood (eds), *Forward!: Labour Politics in Scotland, 1888–1988* (Edinburgh, 1989), 42.
63. William Gallacher, *Revolt on the Clyde: An Autobiography* (London, 1936).
64. Richard Finlay, 'Continuity and Change: Scottish Politics 1900–45' in Tom Devine and Richard Finlay (eds), *Scotland in the Twentieth Century* (Edinburgh, 1996), 75–6. See also James Smyth, 'Resisting Labour: Unionists, Liberals and Moderates in Glasgow between the Wars', *The Historical Journal* 46:2 (2003), 377–85.
65. Patrick Dollan, 'Memorandum on Scottish Medical Unit', 12 November 1936, TC, 292/946/41/104. See also Glasgow Trades Council Minutes, 2 September 1936, GCA.
66. William Elger, 'Telephone Communication on Scottish Medical Unit in Spain', 12 November 1936, TC, 292/946/41/106.
67. Daniel Stevenson, 'Help For Spain', 24 February 1938, TC, 292/946/41/106; Stevenson to Tewson, 2 March 1938, TC, 292/946/42/84.
68. TUC to Elger, 1 September 1937, TC, 292/946/42/115.
69. *Daily Worker*, 23 December 1936, 3.
70. See especially *Daily Worker*, 26 November 1937 1; 22 December 1937, 5.
71. McGovern, quoted in Gray, *Homage*, 131. More broadly, Buchanan, *British Labour Movement*, 186–8; Gallagher, *Glasgow,* 210–13.
72. McGovern, *Why Bishops Back Franco*, 1–12.
73. Gallagher, *Glasgow,* 211.
74. *Lanarkshire Catholic Herald*, 12 June 1937, 1; *Forward*, 12 June 1937, 1.

75. *Daily Worker*, 28 January 1939, 6.
76. Fyrth, *Signal Was Spain*, 203.
77. 'List of Spanish Aid Committees in the Scottish Area', NLS.
78. 'List of Spanish Aid Committees in the Scottish Area', NLS.
79. AUBTW Glasgow (1) Branch Minutes, 1936-9, GCA, TD675.
80. *Glasgow Herald*, 3 February 1938, 12.
81. Glasgow Trades Council Minutes, 8 March 1938 and 17 January 1939, MML, Box B-4, File Q/6.
82. AEU Glasgow District Committee Minutes, 23 February 1938, GCA, TD1051.
83. *Spanish Relief Bulletin 11*, March 1938, TC, 292/946/39/2.
84. Press Release, 4 May 1939, NLS, TMP, Box 2, File 2.
85. For example Fyrth, *Signal Was Spain*, 209.
86. Tom Murray in MacDougall, *Voices from Work*, 293.
87. Janet to Tom Murray, 3 May 1938, NLS, TMP, Box 1, File 1; Spanish Fiesta and Fair Committee Meeting Attendance List, 7 December 1938, NLS, TMP, Box 2, File 3.
88. For example NUR Edinburgh 1st Branch Minutes, 21 August 1938, NLS, Acc. 4313, File 28.
89. Tom Murray in MacDougall, *Voices from Work*, 273.
90. Edinburgh Fabian Society Minutes, 4 December 1937, NLS, Acc. 4977, File 9. See also Janet to Tom Murray, 25 April 1938, NLS, TMP, Box 1, File 1; clipping from *Daily Worker*, 28 April 1938. NLS, TMP, Box 1, File 8.
91. Hughes, *Gender and Political Identities*, 38.
92. Campbell, *Scottish Miners*, 382.
93. Fyrth, *Signal Was Spain*, 210.
94. Jackson, *British Women*, 48-83.
95. Janet to Tom Murray, 25 April 1938; 28 April 1938, NLS, TMP, Box 1, File 1.
96. Janet to Annie Murray, 22 June 1938, 26 June 1938, NLS, TMP, Box 1, File 1.
97. Edinburgh Trades Council Annual Report (1938), NLS, Acc. 11177, File 48.
98. Tom Murray in MacDougall, *Voices from Work*, 328.
99. Janet to Tom Murray, 28 April 1938, NLS.
100. Janet to Tom Murray, 25 April 1938, NLS.
101. For example Janet to Tom Murray, 22 May 1938 and 29 June 1938, NLS, TMP, Box 1, File 1; Janet to Annie Murray, 22 June 1938, NLS, TMP, Box 1, File 1; Clipping from *Evening Dispatch*, 'Spanish Shop to be opened in Edinburgh', n.d., TMP, Box 1, File 8.
102. Tom Murray (circular), 1 May 1939; 'Invitation to "A Spanish Birthday Party"', 3 June 1939, NLS, TMP, Box 2, File 3.
103. Edinburgh Joint Committee for Spanish Relief, 'Statement of Accounts, 10.11.1938-9.1.1939'; 'List of Labour Stalls at Spanish Fiesta and Fair', NLS, TMP, Box 2, File 3.
104. Edinburgh Trades Council Minutes, 16 September 1938, NLS, Acc. 11177, File 26.

105. Janet to Tom Murray, 8 July 1938, NLS, TMP, Box 1, File 1.
106. Janet to Tom Murray, 2 May 1938 and 12 June 1938, NLS, TMP, Box 1, File 1.
107. Janet to Tom Murray, 22 May 1938, NLS, TMP, Box 1, File 1.
108. Janet to Tom Murray, 8 July 1938, NLS.
109. Edinburgh Joint Committee for Spanish Relief, 'Statement of Accounts, 8.8.1938–30.6.1939', 'Statement of Accounts, 8.8.1938–30.6.1939', NLS, TMP, Box 2, File 3.
110. Mates, *Spanish Civil War*, 192–
111. Mates, *Spanish Civil War*, 160–5.
112. Janet Murray, 'The Need for Medical Supplies', n.d., NLS, TMP, Box 1, File 8. A similar letter appeared in *The Scotsman*, 9 August 1938, 11.
113. Murray, 'The Need for Medical Supplies', NLS.
114. *The Scotsman*, 21 November 1938, 10.
115. *The Scotsman*, 16 May 1938, 9.
116. 'Statement of Accounts, 10.11.1938–9.1.1939', NLS.
117. Janet to Tom Murray, 12 May 1938; n.d. (circa August 1938), NLS, TMP, Box 1, File 1.
118. Edinburgh Spain Emergency Committee, 'Closing Report', 21 March 1939, NLS, TMP, Box 2, File 3.
119. 'Closing Report', 21 March 1939, NLS.
120. 'Party membership', January 1940, RGASPI, 495/14/265/24.

7

Taking the Lead? The Scottish Labour Movement and Spain

It is rare to find records of any Scottish labour movement body – from local trade union branches right up to the Scottish Trades Union Congress (STUC) – that did not respond in some way to the war in Spain.[1] Many gave generously and consistently to the cause, often through the TUC-approved ISF, but also to a wide spectrum of local and national campaigns with varying levels of 'official' sanction. Whilst the Communist Party could perhaps claim to have been even more consistent and persistent in supporting the Spanish Republic, the sheer scale of the official labour movement in terms of membership and institutional resources dwarfed anything the CPGB could muster on its own. If Aid Spain was to achieve political or financial success in Scotland, the labour movement was crucial.

Yet mobilising the resources of this movement was far from straight-forward. Resistance to various forms of activism, or even political or religious objections to supporting the Republic altogether, were always a limiting factor to what could be achieved through the Scottish labour movement institutions. Trades union branches were not always readily mobilised for the type of activism that was required. Responding gener-ously or enthusiastically to one-off collections or demonstrations – given prior warning, of course – was one thing, participating in or leading a persistent campaign that could sustain fundraising and political pressure over time was quite another. The unprecedented magnitude and duration of Aid Spain campaigns in Scotland forced adjustments and innovation of the part of the labour movement. As with even the most successful SACs, this was a process that took time and hard work on the part of labour movement leaders, organisers and activists.

British labour movement responses to the Spanish Civil War have been well-documented, particularly through the work of Tom Buchanan and Lewis Mates. However, Buchanan's focus on the national institutions of the labour movement – the leadership of the TUC and the National Council of Labour, as well as individual unions – means that regional perspectives and variation are less salient than they might be. This chapter builds on Buchanan's work in exploring the tension between the centralising tendencies of the 1930s British labour movement, and what was actually required to build an effective Aid Spain campaign in Scotland.[2] Understanding the labour movement response to the Spanish Civil War once again requires appreciating the importance of locality, albeit in a rather different way from that discussed in previous chapters. Creating and sustaining Aid Spain activism required more than just a good cause and generous souls. To build the kind of campaigns that were required – that could motivate and mobilise people over the course of months and years – inspiration, leadership and imagination were crucial ingredients, which could not be instilled by diktat from head office. The Scottish labour movement gradually learnt this lesson over the course of the Spanish Civil War, in the face of considerable opposition from TUC headquarters in London.

In exploring labour movement responses to the war in Spain, the focus here is on Scottish trades unions, as well as regional Trades Councils. The Scottish Labour Party – and its contemporary affiliate, the Scottish Socialist Party – was hardly politically irrelevant in 1930s Scotland, yet also had not yet filled the holes left by the disaffiliation of the ILP in 1932. As Labour struggled to build a new branch system, the trades union movement remained the key link between workplace, community and wider Labour politics in 1930s Scotland, and as such was often the key site for Aid Spain activism. The trades union movement, naturally, was far from the only working-class civic space in which Aid Spain activity might be co-ordinated.[3] Scottish Co-operative societies, for instance, played a notable role in supporting the Spanish Republic. By the end of 1938, the Scottish Co-operative Wholesale Society alone had donated at least £1700 to the Co-operative Alliance Spain Fund, out of £16,000 nationally.[4] Local Co-operative societies were often represented on SACs, and frequently supported a range of other schemes, with Edinburgh-based St Cuthbert's Co-operative Society alone contributing at least £230 to the national 'Milk For Spain' fund.[5] Yet whilst the Co-operative movement was an important source of funds and support for the Spanish Republic, it was for the most part not a source of leadership for the Scottish Aid Spain movement as a whole. The trades union movement, in contrast, contained both the will and the institutional capacity to lead the Scottish response to the Spanish Civil War.

First responses

The labour movement had several advantages in responding to the initial military uprising in Spain. Even as widespread sympathy for the Popular Front government and the Spanish workers swept the country, there were as yet few immediate ways in which practical aid could be swiftly rendered. Spain was not well integrated into the usual channels of transnational working-class politics and organisation. The ISF – an existing scheme managed by the International Federation of Trade Unions (IFTU), of which the TUC was a key participant – had been set up to support working-class victims of fascism and other right-wing political movements across Europe.[6] This fund was well placed to provide active and immediate support for the Spanish Republicans, and it swiftly became the official policy of the TUC that all British trades union efforts for Spain should be in support of this centralised fund.

Accordingly, trades union branches up and down the country were swiftly circularised with appeals for contributions to the ISF. Most branches could respond within a matter of weeks, either through arranging collections or by making a direct donation from branch funds. The ability to call upon branch funds for such purposes was another key advantage that enabled a swift labour movement response. These funds were often called upon in the name of solidarity – a pit disaster in a Fife mining village, for instance, might result in a deluge of donations from unions across Scotland and Britain from branch funds, supplemented by voluntary collections. The situation in Spain provoked a similar response, following well-established channels and procedures for such action. It is impossible to calculate just how much money was raised in Scotland in these first weeks of the civil war, but it was certainly substantial.

Yet these mechanisms of solidarity, which enabled a swift, effective response to a crisis, were ill-suited to a longer campaign that required sustained effort. From the perspective of the TUC, the formula was a simple one: widespread sympathy for the Spanish Republic existed amongst the trades union movement. If subordinate organisations wished to express this sympathy, they could do so by contributing to the central, officially sanctioned fund. Sympathy, therefore, would translate naturally into money for Spain over time, with the occasional reminder or special appeal generated from the TUC via the central leadership of the major national unions. Yet after initial optimism faded, and it became clear that the military rebellion would not be swiftly defeated by the Spanish workers, it was much less clear how financial support and political pressure might be maintained over months and years. Branch funds might allow for occasional donations and grants, but were not inexhaustible. Whilst particularly motivated individuals might arrange for ongoing collections in their workplace or branch, this was inevitably on a far smaller scale than what had been achieved in the initial rush of enthusiasm. Perhaps above all, the TUC lacked an effective apparatus – or arguably even the desire – for encouraging, much less leading, ongoing fundraising and political activity.[7] Whilst the centralised efforts of the TUC and IFTU had worked well in enabling and co-ordinating an initial response, it was much less clear that these bodies were in a position to provide leadership of a large, sustained movement in support of the Spanish Republic.

This does not mean, however, that nobody in the labour movement sought to provide leadership in shaping the nascent Aid Spain movement. Rather, intermediate organisations – with closer ties to local communities, and perhaps somewhat less doctrinaire views on co-operating with potential allies outwith the official labour movement – sought to step into the breach. Trades councils in particular offered a promising avenue for co-ordinating Aid Spain activity in Scottish towns and cities. Formed of representatives of local trades unions – and, in some cases, the Labour Party – trades councils had long offered a space in which labour movement activity could be co-ordinated locally. While the centralising tendencies of the trades union movement had diminished their function and importance somewhat by the 1930s, they still retained influence at a local level by the time of the Spanish Civil War.[8]

The Glasgow Trades Council was, unsurprisingly, the single largest and most important such body in Scotland. It was also an organisation with considerable political will to provide leadership on the question of aiding the Spanish workers. Whilst the Communist Party's private boast that it controlled a majority of delegates on the Glasgow TC was likely somewhat exaggerated, key figures such as the secretary Arthur Brady repeatedly demonstrated a willingness to work with local communists, and took a bullish attitude towards providing aid to the Republic.[9] The TC explicitly rejected calls to limit speaking roles at their rallies to Labour MPs only, and invited both ILP and Communist MPs to share their platform at times.[10] Yet despite its clear willingness to play a leading role, the TC was caught flat-footed by the pace of events in Spain. The first meeting for which Spain was able to be included in the agenda was not until mid-August, by which point other efforts were already in full swing. Initially, its efforts focused on organising a political response, such as a city-wide demonstration on 23 August, with fundraising measures discussed but not acted upon.[11]

The TC issued an appeal for collections to its affiliates only in November 1936, by which stage many affiliated unions had received similar calls to action through other channels, and saw little point in co-operating with the belated and duplicated efforts of the TC.[12] Whilst the TC had managed to organise several large demonstrations, it had missed the opportunity to co-ordinate the first wave of trades union fundraising in the city.

Poor timing was not the only problem faced by Glasgow TC. It had become clear that acting in the same manner as the TUC – circularising affiliated organisations and awaiting a response – would not have the hoped-for result, and that it would need to be more proactive in seeking new ways to raise money. Yet it faced a steep learning curve. Many of its early fundraising initiatives proved inefficient in actually raising significant sums. Large outdoors demonstrations, while well attended, proved to be poor venues for collecting money – one rally in August 1936, which was attended by up to eight thousand marchers, took in less than £9.[13] All told, the TC demonstrations and other activities raised just £103 up to November 1936, while the new collection appeal in November did little to improve matters, bringing in just £70 over two months.[14] Even a major new initiative, a concert held in St Andrew's Hall for the benefit of the Scottish Ambulance Unit, still did not have the desired results. Despite careful planning, securing the pro bono services of the local musicians' union and weeks of publicity, the concert failed to meet the organisers' expectations financially. The final amount raised was just £44 – £23 after expenses were paid.[15] By March, the ongoing failure of the TC's schemes resulted in a long discussion of the 'ways and means of raising further monies', with Executive Committee members being asked to brainstorm 'what further efforts can be made to raise money' – a tacit admission that their strategies to this point had not been as effective as hoped.[16]

These problems were not particular to Glasgow, with their Edinburgh counterparts also attempting to provide early leadership for local efforts to support the Spanish Republic. The Edinburgh TC was notable for the speed with which it identified the Spanish Civil War as a key issue for the local labour movement to address. By the end of July 1936 it had issued a resolution condemning the 'Fascist attempt to suppress democracy', and demanding that the 'same facilities and credits be granted to the Popular Front Government of Spain . . . as would be accorded to any capitalist government'.[17] This urgency continued into August, with normal business suspended twice to address the question of practical aid.[18] Debate over the response to Non-Intervention continued into September, culminating in a 'very full discussion' that led to condemning British 'neutrality'.[19]

Despite the enthusiasm of some delegates, however, it was soon clear that there was limited organisational capacity for effective action. Only five representatives attended a special 'Spain' meeting in September 1936. Despite the paltry turnout, a plan of action was formulated, which called for workplace collections, a flag day, a mass demonstration and setting up a permanent 'Spain' subcommittee.[20] The results were underwhelming. Collections proceeded slowly, realising just over £50 by March 1937, with fewer than twenty organisations participating.[21] The mass demonstration, held in January 1937 in Edinburgh's largest Music Hall, raised just £29 despite much effort and expenditure on the part of the TC.[22] There was no further mention of the planned flag day, although the Town Clerk's later refusal to grant permission for a similar scheme in 1938 indicates that it may have proved impractical as a result of the Tory majority on the town council.[23]

Although the Edinburgh TC was quicker than its Glasgow counterpart in initiating collections, delays still undermined their efforts. By September 1936, when its collection scheme began, many unions had already received appeals through the national executive and acted accordingly. The Edinburgh Union of Distributive and Allied Workers, for example, upon receiving the TC appeal, resolved 'that no aid be given through [the Trades Council] as same had been granted through Central Office'.[24] Poor communications also hampered their efforts; the AEU Musselburgh Branch, for example, was informed of the Music Hall demonstration only the day before it was held, with the branch responding that, despite its sympathy for the cause, there 'was no time for any member to make arrangements to attend the meeting'.[25] Unlike in Glasgow, however, the relative failure of these efforts led the TC to conclude that a completely new approach was needed. It proposed to conduct Aid Spain work 'on broader lines', paving the way for the establishment of the Edinburgh JC for Spanish Relief in March 1937, as discussed in the previous chapter.[26]

The difficulties faced by the Edinburgh TC was however very different from the failure of its Glasgow counterpart. Whilst in Glasgow the problem stemmed from the TC's inability to assume leadership of diverse, fragmented yet enthusiastic Aid Spain efforts, Edinburgh faced the prospect that the local labour movement was not strong enough to support a successful Aid Spain movement alone. Unlike in Glasgow, there was a clear need to engage with other elements of Edinburgh society in order to sustain an effective campaign. This decision was made easier by the more loosely delineated barriers between working-class and middle-class activism. The Edinburgh Labour Party relied on 'bourgeois socialists' to a much greater extent than its counterpart in Glasgow, reflecting the party's lack of viability as a solely working-class-orientated organisation in Edinburgh.[27] This solution, the founding of the Edinburgh JC for Spanish Relief, was one that capitalised on what was perceived to be the best opportunities for effective work in this context.

Yet whilst the founding of the Edinburgh JC addressed this problem, it came at a cost. The centralisation of Aid Spain activities under the auspices of the JC allowed grander events, but also undermined the internal capacity of affiliated organisations to act on their own. As the JC functioned by attracting delegates from sympathetic local organisations such as trades unions, an inevitable consequence was that the most active Aid Spain proponents in affiliated organisations became delegates to the committee. Particularly enthusiastic delegates might become more involved, helping to organise or administer large-scale initiatives. This inevitably came at the expense of the delegate's activities in their parent organisation. Less enthusiastic delegates might even view attending committee meetings as 'doing their bit', limiting their activity in their own organisations while doing little to enhance the activities of the JC itself. In Edinburgh, where relatively few trades unionists were able and willing to engage in such work, the reduced availability of the most dedicated activists could severely impair many branches' Aid Spain activities. The widespread lull in trades union activity throughout 1937 and early 1938 is testimony to the lack of initiative in the Edinburgh labour movement; the secondment of the most engaged activists to the Edinburgh JC helps explain why this was so.[28]

Roots and Branches

The difficulties faced by Edinburgh and Glasgow TCs in taking the lead on Aid Spain did not reflect wider apathy on the part of the Scottish labour movement. Indeed, some of the most effective organising and fundraising – particularly in the early stages of the war – took place on the initiative of district-level leadership of individual unions. Even local branches were sometimes able to act as focal points of local activism, with railworkers at Eastfield and St Margaret's depots able to maintain a startling level of workplace activism across nearly the entire conflict, each branch raising hundreds of pounds to support International Brigade dependants. Yet, as Tom Buchanan has noted in his study of the AEU, the hierarchical nature of the trades union movement made such consistent efforts the exception rather than the norm.[29] Opinions inevitably diverged between national, district and branch leadership over the best way to respond to the Spanish Civil War. This section explores these issues across two particular case studies, the Fife district of the National Union of Scottish Mineworkers (NUSM) and the Glasgow district of the AEU. The aim is to highlight not only the undoubted achievement of many Scottish trade unionists in politically and financially supporting the Republic but also the extent that divergences and divisions within the trades union movement could hamper this response.

Both the engineers and the miners were noted for their militancy in interwar Britain, and this is reflected by the proportionally large role each played in supporting the official TUC-backed ISF, particularly in Scotland. Their Scottish affiliate, the NUSM, frequently donated impressive sums. In the June quarter of 1937, for example, Scottish districts contributed over a fifth of all Miners' Federation of Great Britain (MFGB) donations to the ISF.[30] Glaswegian branches of the AEU alone managed to raise £82 for the ISF by the end of September 1936, out of £561 contributed by the AEU nationally in that period.[31] The engineers' strong showing for this particular fund continued throughout the war; by the end of November 1938, the Glasgow district had contributed £250 out of total AEU contributions of £1422 to the ISF.[32] This figure, which had reached nearly £400 by the time the fund was wound up in mid-1939, was in addition to other significant contributions to other pro-Republican causes.[33]

Much of this success can be put down to the proactive stance of the local District Committee, which launched its first appeal for Spain to its subordinate branches in August 1936, months before the Glasgow TC managed to do the same. Twenty-three Glasgow branches had responded by early September, along with a number of factory collections.[34] However, it was clear that the Glasgow AEU was far from politically unified on the issue, with Temple Branch requesting that the District Committee support an 'unofficial' ILP initiative in mid-August.[35] It was apparently not alone in pushing these boundaries. By mid-October, the Committee felt it necessary to warn branches against sending 'their contributions to the Spanish Workers through channels other than our own fund'.[36] Problems with unified action continued throughout the conflict, and were most apparent in the particular difficulties faced by two local AEU initiatives.

After being petitioned by the Glasgow 12th Branch and learning that several local AEU members were already serving with the International Brigade, the District Committee decided to create a small fund to support their dependants and pay their union dues, with individual branches asked to pay a small monthly levy.[37] This compromise solution found little favour. The National Executive rebuked the District for supporting an unofficial fund, and only half of the branches which had earlier contributed to the national fund chose to pay.[38] The decision also upset branches like Glasgow 12th, which argued that the levy should instead be paid directly to the newly formed WADC in London.[39] The District Committee initially rejected this approach, preferring to work within the official labour movement and encourage the creation of a TUC fund to support any International Brigade volunteers who were also trades unionists. However, by December 1937 it became clear that the TUC would not support the International Brigades, and the Committee relented and forwarded the scheme's remaining funds to the WADC.[40] However, despite the antipathy towards the scheme, it did prove comparatively effective in mobilising support for the International Brigades locally. By September 1937, only fifty individual AEU branches nationwide had donated directly to the WADC.[41] In contrast, twelve Glasgow branches had contributed to the local fund set up by the District Committee.

The difficulty of taking independent action, even for a large and locally influential union like the Glasgow AEU, is shown also by the district's repeated forays into the Voluntary Industrial Aid for Spain scheme. The concept was simple enough: capitalising on the skill-sets and expertise of Britain's trades unionists, the goal was to buy cheap or broken-down equipment, repair and recondition it, and send the results on to Spain. In mid-1937, a conference of Glaswegian AEU branches decided to embrace the scheme, opting to recondition vehicles for use as field ambulances in Spain.[42] This was endorsed by the District Committee, who encouraged members to work thirty minutes overtime each week and donate the extra pay to the scheme.[43] However, despite this initial enthusiasm, little was achieved in 1937. In April 1938, Parkhead 5th branch sent an angry resolution to the District Committee, demanding that:

> the D.C. to recall the Voluntary Industrial District Committee for Spain already formed a year ago, and [calling] upon the D.C. to pledge its full support for this committee, the failure of the Committee to act last year [being] due entirely to the lack of support from District Committee.[44]

Six other branches sent similar resolutions over the next three weeks, and progress was evidently resumed. However, the scheme still advanced slowly. Working with the local Transport and General Workers Union, just one ambulance and a motorcycle had been bought, reconditioned and dispatched to the Spanish Medical Aid Committee in London by October 1938.[45] On arrival in London, however, it became obvious that the 'van purporting to be an ambulance' was in no condition to be sent on to Spain.[46] The Committee promptly sold the van and motorcycle for just £10, 'which was considered a good price in view of the condition of these vehicles'.[47] Given the success of Voluntary Industrial Aid schemes in other British cities, its failure in Glasgow points to the difficulties faced in channelling the activity of a large, independently minded organisation that at times found itself at odds with both national leadership and individual branches.[48]

Like the engineers, British miners have long been regarded as a source of particularly effective support for the Spanish Republic. The MFGB raised the most of any union for Spain, and regional bodies, particularly those in places such as South Wales, were also prominent in a range of official and unofficial initiatives.[49] Alongside Wales, Fife was particularly known for the militancy of its miners. Yet despite – indeed, because of – this militancy, the Fife, Clackmannan and Kinross Miners' Union (FCKMU) led the most remarkably unenthusiastic Aid Spain effort of any major mining district in Britain. Not only did the union leadership refuse to take any initiative within their district, but its actions verged on obstructionist, viewing even humanitarian aid initiatives with scepticism and attempting to undermine the efforts of its membership and even the MFGB as a whole.

The poor track record of the FCKMU on Spain reflected their leaders' rather distinctive local concerns about the spread of communist influence in Fife. Just a few years earlier, Fife had been the main stronghold for the UMS, a short-lived attempt to set up a communist-aligned trade union. Though the UMS had been disbanded with the turn to the Popular Front in 1935, the CPGB's influence in the region was confirmed by the victory of William Gallacher in West Fife at the 1935 General Election, based on strong support for the CPGB among many of Fife's mining communities. Yet the local cost of these successes was felt in trades union politics. Whilst the UMS had several thousand members at its peak, very few of these miners – just 55 in 1931 – were actually members of the Communist Party, making Party members easy targets for exclusion from the pits and the official union after the UMS folded.[50] With many of their leaders barred, ex-UMS members also faced being substantially outnumbered in the new FCKMU. Moreover, the union leadership, for whom the years of being labelled 'social fascists' by local communists still rankled, had little reason to either like or trust the communists now in their midst. These 'labour bureaucrats' used every means at their disposal to ensure that communists were excluded from the structures of the FCKMU, and were successful in limiting them to a vocal minority in the murky world of trades union representation and officialdom. Even by 1938, the FCKMU remained vigilant in its efforts to curtail CPGB activity in the union, censuring the Kirkford Branch for allowing a known communist to act as a delegate to the local Labour Party.[51] Although Communist Party influence in the mining unions and coalfields would eventually recover, the late 1930s proved to be 'a period in the wilderness' for the CPGB in the Fife labour movement.[52]

The leadership of the FCKMU, therefore, was heavily predisposed towards suspicion of any cause that local communists championed. Their lack of enthusiasm for Aid Spain activities was already apparent by August 1936. The Dundonald and Glencraig branches recommended that the FCKMU provide a grant of £100 to the 'Spanish Government' as a response to the National Council of Labour appeal. The union's bureaucratic apparatus was utilised to delay proceedings, with the Sub-Executive Committee deciding that, before any such grant could be made, MFGB officials must be contacted to explain their policy on Spain.[53] An attempt to challenge this ruling was defeated at a full Executive Board Meeting a week later, with only five delegates dissenting from the decision.[54] These delaying tactics stalled the grant for over two months, with the final motion approved only at the end of October. Moreover, the size of the grant was challenged, and eventually reduced from £100 to just £30.[55] It was clear that any future attempts on the part of subordinate branches to encourage the FCKMU to actively support the Republic would have to overcome an entrenched and unenthusiastic Executive. Such attempts grew increasingly rare over the course of the conflict.

A comparison with the Lanarkshire Miners' Union (LMU) indicates the consequences of Fife communists' earlier confrontational policies for the Aid Spain movement. Like their Fife counterparts, Lanarkshire miners had earned a reputation for militancy. In Lanarkshire, however, the UMS experiment had been largely unsuccessful from the beginning. Forced to work within the LMU from an earlier point, communists were able to establish themselves in the official structures of the union and influence policy much sooner than in Fife.[56] The results for the Aid Spain movement were readily apparent. Regular donations were made to several causes, including the International Brigades, and subordinate branches were encouraged to take collections for Spain, with branches unwilling to co-operate pressured directly by the Executive.[57] Resolutions condemning Non-Intervention and aerial bombing or supporting the International Brigades were approved and, in one case, forwarded to the Prime Minister.[58]

Beyond these broader measures, the Executive Committee also organised collections at its own meetings, raising several pounds each month.[59] The proactive and occasionally inventive approach of the LMU Executive provides a glaring contrast to the bureaucratic obstructionism of its counterpart at the FCKMU.

The extent of the FCKMU's resistance to Aid Spain measures is best demonstrated by its reaction to the MFGB's decision to impose a Spanish levy of 2s 6d per member in June 1938, of which Scotland's total came to £6250. The NUSM Executive decided in July to call upon district bodies to pay £4250 of the total.[60] The response of the FCKMU was furious. After 'considerable discussion', it was resolved to refuse the demand, with just six delegates voting to pay its share of £1250.[61] However, with the NUSM unwilling to overturn the decision, the FCKMU had little option. The payment was remitted in January 1939, along with a resolution

> strongly protesting against the action of the MFGB in granting large sums of money to objects not provided for in the rules of the Organisation and imposing levies without the Districts being consulted or any other effort being made to obtain their opinion as to whether or not grants should be made.[62]

The resistance of the FCKMU members to paying the Spain levy was unparalleled in Scotland. Their challenge not only attempted to avoid financial responsibility, but explicitly questioned the legitimacy of the levy, claiming that it was unconstitutional and implying that they disapproved of the levy's objectives. Other districts were united in rejecting the FCKMU's request that the NUSM pay the full amount, with just four national delegates supporting the FCKMU position.[63] The FCKMU was also alone in using the levy as a pretext for refusing to co-operate with other Aid Spain initiatives. At least two separate requests from Labour Party-sponsored initiatives were refused 'in view of the commitments entered into', with the Executive explicitly refusing to countenance 'further payments from the funds of the Organisation'.[64] The LMU, in contrast, continued to participate with other schemes, donating £25 towards a foodship and £18 towards distributing propaganda leaflets in the months afterwards.[65] The FCKMU finally relented in March 1939, although, similarly to its first grant, the initial proposal for a £30 foodship contribution was reduced to £10 after discussion by the Executive Committee.

It is more difficult to determine the extent to which the FCKMU leadership's tepid response to Spain impacted the activities of individual branches throughout Fife, as no individual branch records from the period survive. Given the impact that proactive district-level leadership could have on branch activity, as shown by both the LMU and the AEU in Glasgow, it is almost certain that such activity suffered in Fife. It is possible that branches such as Dundonald, which was openly critical of the stance taken by the Executive Council, were active locally in organising collections and providing grants.[66] However, the data from Chapter 5 suggest that any such independent activity was minimal, with just one WADC contribution recorded from a Fife FCKMU branch, although some pithead collections were taken in mining villages such as Bowhill.[67] It is more likely that, in the absence of any other local leadership on Spain, miners largely abandoned union-based activity in favour of working with the burgeoning array of Fife SACs discussed in the previous chapter. Whilst these efforts were often successful, being shut out of the institutional and financial resources of the union could not help but limit the broader success of the Aid Spain movement in Fife.

Not 'on powdered milk alone'

In the first eighteen months of the Spanish Civil War, it was far from clear whether the labour movement would ever be able to play a leading role in Scottish efforts to support the Spanish Republic. This was generally not for want of sympathy or effort, aside from isolated cases such as the FCKMU. As Tom Buchanan has noted, the Scottish labour movement had 'consistently taken more advanced positions on Spain than the British Trades Union Congress and Labour Party', yet, as the war continued into 1938, it was far from clear that this was actually being reflected in practical terms.[68] Varied, even innovative methods of supporting the Spanish Republic had been attempted, but the results of local schemes and initiatives had often been broadly disappointing for their organisers. While Scottish trades unions and other working-class organisations had contributed strongly to national schemes, the prospects for locally directed action looked bleak, particularly in places such as Edinburgh where vibrant SACs had established themselves and assumed de facto leadership over local efforts.

This picture was to change dramatically in the spring of 1938, as the Scottish labour movement finally hit upon a formula that could marry widespread – and strongly politicised – feeling about Spain in Scotland with an effective fundraising scheme. The key moment came at a joint meeting of Scottish TCs in April 1938, which set in motion plans to call an emergency conference of Scottish trades union branches on the Spanish issue – itself a measure looked upon unfavourably by the TUC leadership – and, more radically, 'to bring before this conference a proposal to send a munition and food ship from Scotland to Republican Spain'. In the words of the Glasgow TC Secretary, Arthur Brady:

> This war is not going to be won on powdered milk alone. It is going to be won with guns, tanks and airplanes. We know where we can get the munitions, if you raise the money.[69]

This was an immensely ambitious and proactive scheme, and explicitly aimed to bypass the normal channels available through the TUC and STUC, which were perceived as preventing a rank-and-file voice on the Spanish issue. For all of the organisers' pugnacious rhetoric, however, it is far from clear that the Scottish labour movement had the means to carry the scheme out. Brady himself apparently kept his cards very close to his chest. Wilfred Roberts, an English Liberal MP heavily involved with the National JC, made several immediate enquiries north of the border. Most were answered candidly, but his sources were evasive as to how exactly they would proceed.

> As to what is being done to carry the project into effect, the main appeal is being made to the trade union branches in Scotland to send delegates to the Conference of Action which this Saturday meeting agreed upon. I don't know that the financial appeal will be officially opened until the Conference of Action endorses it, but now that the idea has been mooted I think money will begin to come in immediately. There will be little difficulty, I think, about getting a crew to man the ship and Brady appears to have a clear idea about how the whole job can be done.[70]
>
> Munitions come first in importance to the Spanish people at this juncture and though it may seem difficult to help them we believe it can be done. I do not wish to say more, but you can try Brady for anything further.[71]

The announcement of the TCs' munitions ambitions was met with shock and alarm in London. The TUC suspected that their 'old friends', the communists, were behind the scheme – which, given their influence in some Scottish TCs, was not an entirely unreasonable suspicion, though there is little evidence that this was a well-laid CPGB plot.[72] The TUC swiftly convened a meeting of the Emergency Committee of the General Council to condemn the conference's resolutions, claiming that it represented a diffusion of existing schemes.[73] This was a common criticism of local Aid Spain efforts in Scotland and beyond, with the TUC consistently arguing that efforts were best channelled through a single national fund in order to achieve the most overall impact, rather than duplicating efforts or engaging in inefficient practices such as door-to-door food collections. The latter were particularly condemned for increasing shipping costs, as well as representing poor value for money, as it meant that food was purchased at commercial rather than wholesale prices.

In the weeks following the conference and its condemnation, a series of negotiations took place between the TCs and the TUC, with the secretary of the STUC, William Elger, acting as intermediary. The TCs agreed to quietly drop the idea of sending arms or ammunition to Spain, and agreed that any funds raised would be credited to the TUC-sponsored ISF. Despite the TUC making it clear that it expected them to fail, the TCs stuck to the foodship scheme with no further concessions.[74] Eventually, both the STUC and TUC agreed to endorse the scheme officially, which allowed the TCs to begin collecting money in earnest in mid-July 1938.[75]

Although it eventually did not reach its goal of raising £10,000, the scheme represented a significant victory for the Scottish TCs. There was genuine enthusiasm for the scheme throughout Scotland, adding much-needed impetus to local trades union activity. Virtually every Scottish trades union branch or body for which records exist – even the otherwise miserly FCKMU – contributed some amount to the foodship scheme. Often, the amount raised for the foodship was considerably more than a given branch had ever managed to raise previously. In Edinburgh, for instance, the local branches of the National Union of Railwaymen (NUR) succeeded in raising at least £69 for the foodship by October, after their Spain-related activity had slowed to a crawl in the first half of the year.[76] Not only were unprecedentedly large sums being raised for the foodship, the momentum carried through into a broader spectrum of Aid Spain activism. In six months from July 1938, the Edinburgh NUR 1st Branch raised over £30 for Spain, considerably more than it managed over the previous two years combined. Significantly, this money was not just being raised through donations or workplace collections as in previous efforts, but was the result of branch members organising their own initiatives such as a prize draw – which alone raised over £20 – as well as a whist drive and dance.[77] Similarly, collections made by Edinburgh Shop Assistants resulted in over £34 raised for the foodship, alongside £23 in direct grants to Spanish Aid schemes throughout 1938, compared to £10 and £8 for 1936 and 1937 respectively.[78] Across Edinburgh, £500 was raised for the foodship in just a few months.[79] This was a significant turnaround in labour movement activity, which had slumped for over a year after the Edinburgh JC was founded in April 1937. All told, approximately £2500 was raised in Scotland for the foodship, dwarfing the TCs' previous initiatives.[80]

The logistics of the scheme also represented an organisational triumph. The TCs secured free of charge the services of a Scottish ship and captain, which departed Glasgow in September 1938 and reached Valencia without incident. They were also able to persuade the TUC, which was mindful of the adverse consequences of having a TUC-endorsed endeavour appear to fail due to the ship sailing half-empty, to secretly augment the cargo of the ship using £1700 of their own funds.[81] In contrast to its earlier failures, the Glasgow TC managed to spearhead a scheme that was both popular and effective, using internal labour movement politics to their best advantage and making a high-profile political statement on Spain and Non-Intervention. The success of this scheme paved the way for a further foodship organised by the STUC in early 1939, although the funds were diverted to providing clothing for Spanish refugees in France after it became clear that the ship would not depart before the Republic fell.[82]

Despite the TUC's argument that the most efficient way to help Spain was simply to contribute more to the central fund, it was clear that this form of local initiative had much greater appeal than a London-administered fund. Nearly every union branch surveyed in both Glasgow and Edinburgh contributed to the foodship, including unions that had previously been reluctant to engage with the Aid Spain movement. This success also reflected the ongoing attachment found across Scotland and Britain to collecting food door-to-door. Such measures were particularly popular in the poorest working-class neighbourhoods, where a cash surplus might be thin or non-existent, but where a tin might be spared from the family stores. Bob Selkirk, for instance, recalled the exceptional response local activists received when they went 'round the working class rows in our Ward' with 'handbells and wheel-barrows'.[83] These were contributions that would never have been made to a national fund. Quite aside from the question of whether there was cash to spare, collecting money for a distant, abstract scheme in London lacked the same intimacy of collecting and sending food to Spain. The success of foodship schemes lay in their immediacy – not only was it obvious where the money was going, but it was clear exactly what was being achieved. Their local or regional character also made it far easier to rally support, not only tapping into potent local identities but offering the prospect that their specific contribution could be recognised and acknowledged by the eventual recipient. At the most intimate, visceral level, handing over a tin of food was a material connection to the conflict that other schemes could not replicate – the knowledge that food leaving your hand would make its way to the mouth of a Spanish worker.[84] What TUC leaders failed to appreciate, despite being undoubtedly correct in an abstract economic sense, is that for activism to be sustained over a longer period, emotional connections such as these needed to be nurtured and maintained rather than dismissed. The growing success of Scottish labour movement activism over the course of 1938 reflected their growing appreciation that, for Aid Spain activism to succeed in the long term, it needed to capture people's imaginations.

However, for all that 1938 proved the most successful year in raising money in Scotland for the Spanish Republic, events in Spain were a stark reminder that Scottish shillings could not win the war. Despite a brief window of hope during the initial stages of the Republican Army's Ebro offensive in July 1938, news from Spain was increasingly grim for the Republic's Scottish supporters. Though public opinion was firmly shifting towards the Republic, there appeared to be little prospect of a British diplomatic about-face, and, without external support, the Republican position was increasingly untenable. Though the Scottish labour movement may well have been more forthright – and perhaps in some ways more successful – than many of its counterparts elsewhere in Britain on the issue of Spain, the course of events in the final months of the Spanish Civil War exposed the limitations of transnational solidarity in the face of modern warfare.

Notes

1. The STUC, aside from providing a key forum for labour movement debate and discussion on Spain and Non-Intervention, gave generously from its own funds. In 1937, for instance, the STUC contributed £181 – approximately ten per cent of its total expenditure for the year – to the 'Spanish Workers' Fund'. STUC Annual Report (1937), MML, Box B-4, File Q/8, 172–3.
2. The crucial text is Buchanan, *British Labour Movement*. See also 'Divided Loyalties: the Impact of the Spanish Civil War on Britain's Civil Service Trade Unions, 1936–9', *Historical Research* 65:56 (1992), 90–107; 'The Role of the British Labour Movement in the Origins and Work of the Basque Children's Committee, 1937–9', *European History Quarterly* 18:2 (1988), 115–74; 'The Politics of Internationalism: the Amalgamated Engineering Union and the Spanish Civil War', *Bulletin of the Society for the Study of Labour History* 53:3 (1988), 47–55. See also Mates, *Spanish Civil War*, 61–114.

3. For an overview of alternative institutional approaches, albeit rarely including Scottish perspectives, see Mason, *Democracy, Deeds and Dilemmas*.

4. 'Report and Balance Sheet for Half-year Ended 8th September 1936', p. 21; 'Report and Balance sheet for Half-year ended 9th March 1937', p. 32; 'Report and Balance Sheet for the Half-year ended 7th September 1937', p. 32, NLS, Acc. 11835, File 160.

5. St Cuthbert's Quarterly Reports and Financial Statements, 1937–1939, NLS, Acc. 11835, File 160.

6. On the ISF, see Buchanan, *British Labour Movement*, 137–66.

7. Buchanan, *British Labour Movement*, 141–3.

8. Buchanan, *Spanish Civil War*, 11–12.

9. 'Report on Scottish District', 3 June 1938, RGASPI, 495/14/260/59.

10. Glasgow Trades Council Minutes, 8 September 1936, GCA. At the time of access, the minute books of the Glasgow Trades Council were not present on the Glasgow City Archives' catalogue, though an enterprising member of staff was able to locate them in their collections.

11. Glasgow Trades Council Minutes, 16 August 1936, GCA.

12. Glasgow Trades Council Minutes, 1 December 1936, GCA.

13. *Daily Worker*, 25 August 1936, 6.

14. Glasgow Trades Council Minutes, 12 January 1937, GCA.

15. Glasgow Trades Council Minutes, 23 February 1937, GCA.

16. Glasgow Trades Council Minutes, 9 March 1937, GCA.

17. Edinburgh Trades Council Minutes, 28 July 1936, NLS, Acc. 11177, File 25.

18. Edinburgh Trades Council Minutes, 7 and 25 August 1936, NLS, Acc. 11177, File 25.

19. Edinburgh Trades Council Minutes, 8 September 1936, NLS, Acc. 11177, File 26.

20. Edinburgh Trades Council Minutes, 10 September 1936, NLS, Acc. 11177, File 26.

21. This excludes grants made by the Trades Council directly. See Edinburgh Trades Council Annual Report, March 1937, NLS, Acc. 11177, File 48.

22. Edinburgh Trades Council Minutes, 22 January 1937, NLS, Acc. 11177, File 26.

23. Edinburgh Trades Council Minutes, 5 August 1938, NLS, Acc. 11177, File 26.

24. NAUSAWC Edinburgh Branch Minutes, 28 September 1836, NLS, Dep. 359, File 67.

25. AEU Musselburgh Branch Minutes, 5 March 1937, NLS, Acc. 9853, File 5.

26. Edinburgh Trades Council Minutes, 19 February 1937, NLS, Acc. 11177, File 26.

27. John Holford, *Reshaping Labour: Organisation, Work and Politics in Edinburgh in the Great War and After* (London, 1988), 15.

28. ETLC Annual Report, 1937, NLS, Acc. 11177, File 48, 20–21. This is also reflected in minutes of smaller organisations, e.g. NAUSAWC Edinburgh

Branch, Annual Report and Balance Sheet, 1937, Dep. 359, File 21; AEU Edinburgh District Committee Minutes, 1937, NLS, Acc. 4516, File 17.

29. Buchanan, 'Politics of Internationalism', 47.
30. 'Statement of Donations Received for Quarter Ended 30th June, 1937', TC, 292/946/39/81. See also NUSM Statement of Accounts, 1 June 1938-25 March 1939, NLS, Dep. 227, File 92.
31. AEU Glasgow District Committee Minutes, 30 September 1936, GCA, TD1051; 'Statement of Donations received by the National Council of Labour, 28th July - 30th September, 1936', p. 1.
32. AEU Glasgow District Committee Minutes, 30 November 1938; 'International Solidarity Fund', 20 February 1939, p. 4.
33. AEU Glasgow District Committee Minutes, 14 June 1939, GCA.
34. AEU Glasgow District Committee Minutes, 9 September 1936, GCA.
35. AEU Glasgow District Committee Minutes, 19 August 1936, GCA.
36. AEU Glasgow District Committee Minutes, 14 October 1936, GCA.
37. AEU Glasgow District Committee Minutes, 17 March 1937, GCA.
38. AEU Glasgow District Committee Minutes, 31 March 1937 and 19 May 1937, GCA.
39. AEU Glasgow District Committee Minutes, 4 August 1937, GCA.
40. *Daily Worker*, 22 December 1937, 5.
41. *Daily Worker*, 17 September 1937, 1.
42. AEU Glasgow District Committee Minutes, 19 May 1937 and 23 June 1937, GCA.
43. AEU Glasgow District Committee Minutes, 27 June 1937, GCA.
44. AEU Glasgow District Committee Minutes, 27 April 1938, GCA.
45. SMAC Minutes, 14 September 1938, 2.
46. SMAC Minutes, 5 October 1938, 2.
47. SMAC Minutes, 23 November 1938, 2.
48. Fyrth, *Signal Was Spain*, 270-3.
49. R. Page Arnot, *The Miners in Crisis and War: A History of the Miners' Federation of Great Britain from 1930 Onwards* (London, 1961), 260-70; Francis, *Miners*, 139-53; Mates, 'Durham and South Wales', 373-95.
50. For discussion, see Campbell, *Scottish Miners*, 386-8.
51. FCKMU Minutes, 28 June 1938, NLS, Acc. 4311, File 56.
52. Branson, *History of the Communist Party*, 183.
53. FCKMU Minutes, 22 August 1936, NLS, Acc. 4311, File 55.
54. FCKMU Minutes, 29 August 1936, NLS, Acc. 4311, File 55.
55. FCKMU Minutes, 31 October 1936, NLS, Acc. 4311, File 55.
56. Campbell, *Scottish Miners*, 356.
57. For example LMU Executive Committee Minutes, 5 February 1938; 25 January 1938; 4 March 1938, NLS, Dep. 227, File 74.
58. LMU Executive Committee Minutes, 11 February 1938, NLS.
59. E.g. LMU Executive Committee Minutes, 4 February 1938; 17 May 1938, NLS.

60. NUSM Minutes, 27 July 1938, NLS, Dep. 227, File 92.
61. FCKMU Minutes, 27 August 1938, NLS, Acc. 4311, File 56.
62. FCKMU Minutes, 22 October 1938, NLS, Acc. 4311, File 56; NUSM Minutes, 4 January 1939, NLS, Dep. 227, File 92.
63. NUSM Minutes, 10 October 1938, NLS.
64. FCKMU Minutes, 26 July 1938; 17 December 1938, NLS, Acc. 4311, File 56.
65. LMU Bank Statements, 12 August – 16 September 1938 and 12 November – 14 December 1938, NLS, Dep. 227, File 74.
66. For example 'Dundonald Resolution' in FCKMU Minutes, 22 October 1938, NLS, Acc. 4311, File 56.
67. For example *Daily Worker*, 21 February 1938, 1.
68. Buchanan, *British Labour Movement*, 128.
69. *Daily Worker*, 12 April 1938, 1.
70. Fred Douglas to Wilfred Roberts, 12 April 1938, MML, Box B-4, File Q/7.
71. Alexander Paton to Wilfred Roberts, 12 April 1938, MML, Box B-4, File Q/7.
72. Letter to William Elger, 17 May 1938, TC, 292/946/30/181.
73. William Elger to Glasgow Trades Council, 13 May 1938, TC, 292/946/30/162.
74. See Letter to William Elger, 21 June 1938; William Elger to H. Tewson, 8 July 1938, TC, 292/946/30/115;120.
75. Letter to William Elger, 11 July 1938, William Elger Circular: 'Trades Council Foodship', 15 July 1938, TC, 292/946/30/116;119.
76. NUR Edinburgh 3rd Branch Minutes, 30 October 1938, NLS, Dep. 188, File 9.
77. NUR Edinburgh 1st Branch Minutes, 22 January 1939, NLS, Acc. 4313, File 28.
78. NAUSAWC, Annual Reports and Balance Sheets, 1936–1938, NLS, Dep. 359, Files 20-22.
79. ETLC Annual Report, 1938, NLS, Acc. 11177, File 48, 22.
80. 'International Solidarity Fund', 20 February 1939, TC, 292/946/33/4.
81. 'Scottish Committee and food for Spain', 13 September 1938, TC, 292/946/30/68. For the perspective of the TUC, see Buchanan, *British Labour Movement*, 120-32.
82. William Elger to Robert Leckie, 18 April 1939, TC, 292/946/32/66.
83. Selkirk, *Life of a Worker*, 37-8.
84. A useful comparison here is with Mates's discussion of the Tyneside Foodship campaign of 1938-9, which achieved a similar concentration and escalation of efforts in North-East England. However, a key difference in the Scottish context is the relative absence of humanitarian language and appeals, stemming from its very conception as an 'ammunition ship'. Mates, *Spanish Civil War*, esp. 145-77.

Epilogue: Beyond

The Spanish Civil War ended in defeat for the Republic in April 1939. By this stage, there were few Scots left in Spain – the last of the Scottish prisoners being held by either side were exchanged or released in the final months of the conflict, and had for the most part managed to make their way home by the time the Republic fell. Most volunteers had departed months earlier, after parading one last time through the streets of Barcelona in an emotionally charged farewell, swearing as they left that they would continue their struggle in support of the Republic. It was soon apparent that this would mean working towards the overthrow of a victorious Franco regime, whether through internal revolt or external intervention. The desirability of Franco's overthrow continued to unite the veterans for decades afterwards, with only a small handful abandoning their support of the Republic altogether. Yet beyond this common ground, forging a collective purpose for the International Brigade veterans proved difficult. Only a minority were immediately willing to remain active in political work, although successful campaigns such as the 'International Brigade Convoy' demonstrated how the veterans could speak with authority and impact on Spanish issues.[1]

These Aid Spain efforts continued across 1939, though funds and resources were increasingly devoted towards the refugee question, which became particularly acute as tens of thousands of Republican supporters fled to France as the government position crumbled in early 1939. The indefatigable Murrays – Tom Murray had returned from Spain by September 1938 – were particularly active, seeking to raise funds to secure passage to Mexico for Republican exiles, and sponsoring anti-fascist refugees in coming to Britain. Yet the scale of the crisis seemed insurmountable, especially as Spain faded from public consciousness amidst growing international tension. By May, remaining Scottish SACs had managed to fund the journeys of 22 former Republicans to Mexico, out of 219 such berths sponsored by organisations across Britain.[2] While this achievement reflected the determination and tenacity of pro-Republican activists, it was also starkly illustrative of the scale of the problem and the dwindling resources that could be mobilised for the cause. By the time France fell in June 1940, many thousands of Republican refugees remained in makeshift camps in the south of France.[3] While some escaped to join the French Resistance, many more were captured and sent to Nazi concentration camps.[4]

Over the course of 1939, the focus in Britain shifted from fundraising towards institutionalising the memory and political influence of those who had fought in Spain. The International Brigade Association (IBA) was founded in early 1939, forming a vehicle through which future campaigns could be co-ordinated and the volunteers' legacy defended.[5] Unsurprisingly, the new organisation retained close ties to the CPGB, although, as Tom Buchanan notes, the relationship was at times 'surprisingly complex'.[6] An early attempt to mobilise the political potential of the IBA – in support of the Soviet Union's invasion of Finland – backfired spectacularly in the face of widespread public sympathy for Finnish resistance.[7] The Party had hoped to create a new revolutionary elite, able to speak to wider political issues with an independent, respected voice. Finland demonstrated the impossibility of this vision – they could either be dismissed as a mere mouthpiece for the Party line or limit their campaigning to Spanish issues.

The Second World War came at an awkward moment from the perspective of the IBA. Whilst time might have allowed for enduring organisational structures to be firmly established, war brought upheaval. Many ex-volunteers sought to throw themselves into this new struggle, seeing the chance to continue their fight against fascism, though their acceptance as trustworthy participants in the war effort could be at best conditional in the eyes of the British state.[8] The IBA lost contact with many former volunteers serving in the armed forces, and many of its most active and fittest members were therefore unable to help establish the Association. However, Scotland, with its particularly high concentration of volunteers, was better placed than most districts to establish a somewhat functional branch system during and after the Second World War. The Glasgow IBA branch managed to hold commemorations, reunions and fundraising events on a semi-regular basis during the 1940s, while most other districts outwith London fell into inactivity.[9] In 1944, Garry McCartney reported that 'the IBA in Glasgow, despite its many weaknesses, had become a real live body, recognised and respected amongst wide circles in the city and with a corporate existence of its own'.[10] By 1946, the Glasgow IBA, with 150 members, was in touch with more veterans than any other city or district, including London.[11] These efforts put it at 'the top of the class', according to the IBA secretary Nan Green – of particular significance as the national organisation was nearly insolvent by 1949, and the occasional cheque from Glasgow was immensely welcome.[12]

Not all news from Scotland was quite so welcome. Although the IBA had retreated from politics beyond the Spanish question, this concealed rather than resolved the underlying tension between its links to the Communist Party and its purpose as an overarching group for all Spanish veterans. With the changed political climate of the Cold War, divisions could swiftly resurface. The rupture between Tito and Stalin in 1948 proved to be the catalyst for one such instance. After Yugoslavian International Brigade veterans reached out to the IBA, the Scottish district protested against the decision to denounce the Yugoslavs. Nan Green sent a blistering reply north.

What is Titoism in essence and what is the essential content of the letter which was addressed to us? Its purpose is:
a) To split the working class progressive movement
b) To blacken and destroy confidence in the Soviet Union.
In other words, exactly the same purpose as the Trotskyites ever since the 1930s, and if you have any doubts on the matter or can't see what it has to do with us, we ask you to cast your minds back to the POUM in Spain, whose role was exactly the same.[13]

Green's efforts to invoke the same tropes of Stalinist discourse that had worked well in defending orthodoxy in Spain were less effective in 1949. The secretary and treasurer of the Scottish IBA both resigned, and were replaced by Andy Shaw and Phil Gillan. These two, Nan Green was pointedly reassured, were 'not likely to indulge in heretical or heterodox viewpoints'.[14] Yet although the Party was able to maintain its dominance over the inner life of the IBA, such conflicts served as reminders that the organisation's unity rested solely on Spain. Future events, such as Khrushchev's 1956 denunciation of Stalin and the Soviet invasion of Hungary, would further splinter the political views of the International Brigade veterans. Political diversity, which had been somewhat illusory during their actual service, was now very real.

Over the decades, the IBA's focus shifted steadily towards commemoration and education, including organising trips and delegations to Spain after

Franco's death in 1975. By the war's sixtieth anniversary in 1996, there were few Scottish volunteers remaining to take part in celebrations in Spain, although two still managed to make the journey as part of a commemorative tour across three cities.[15] A favourable political climate compared to previous anniversaries meant that resources were available to support them – veterans had their accommodation, meals and transport paid for, with further financial aid available for the especially needy. The Spanish government also agreed at last to honour a promise made to the volunteers on their departure from Spain: that they would be eligible for Spanish citizenship after the war had been won. Seven Scots completed initial paperwork accepting this offer, but were never able to claim it, as none proved willing to comply with Spanish law requiring that they also renounce their British citizenship.[16] It was not until 2008 that this requirement was removed, by which stage only one Scot – Thomas Watters – remained to accept this offer, though Watters had served as a driver with the Scottish Ambulance Unit rather than the International Brigades.[17] No Scottish International Brigader was ever formally recognised as a Spanish citizen.

However, even as the Scottish International Brigade veterans dwindled, efforts to remember and celebrate their actions have continued apace. Despite occasional Tory reservations, the memorials were built, and have never stopped being built. With memorials came a rich tradition of art, music, theatre and poetry commemorating or taking inspiration from the volunteers.[18] As with memorial building, this process has shown no sign of slowing in recent years, with performances of *549: Scots of the Spanish Civil War* touring – to critical acclaim – across Scotland in 2019. Through the all-important modern metric of social media engagement, the Spanish Civil War remains alive – the 'Scotland and the Spanish Civil War' Facebook group has over 1100 members, and (occasionally inaccurate) tweets about the volunteers often garner hundreds of engagements.[19] Regular commemorations continue to take place at memorials across Scotland, and pilgrimages to Spanish battlefields – usually to Jarama for the anniversary of the battle in mid-February – are still organised each year.[20]

The significance of Scottish involvement in the Spanish Civil War can therefore be measured, in a sense, by the passion and respect it still evokes across the country. The aim of this book, however, has been somewhat broader than contributing to the continuation of such efforts. The goal throughout has been to integrate the Scottish responses to Spain within wider histories, of Scotland in the 1930s as well as the history of the Spanish Civil War more broadly. In particular, the Scottish volunteers reflect wider stories regarding transnational mobilisation and participation in this conflict, highlighting new dimensions to the so-called 'national question' in the International Brigades. In exploring the ways that there could be a distinctive Scottish 'experience' of Spain despite the absence of a dedicated national unit, this accounts joins those of Gerben Zaagsma and Ariel Mae Lambe in seeking to move this debate beyond the formal structures of the International Brigades themselves.[21] More broadly, the goal throughout these pages has been to take seriously Michael Goebel's plea to go beyond simply demonstrating the existence of transnational networks, but tie them to concrete outcomes. The transnational nature of the International Brigades and the networks that underpinned them mattered not only in shaping the decision to go to Spain, but also volunteers' physical, mental and political experiences of volunteering.[22]

Perhaps most significantly, the explanations put forward for the particularly dense recruitment of volunteers for Spain in Scotland lend themselves to further comparative study. Not only are these arguments grounded in the inherently transnational cultures and organisation of interwar communism, lending themselves to comparison across borders in the 1930s, the scope for comparison may extend beyond the Spanish case study entirely. Recent work, pioneered in particular by Nir Arielli, has suggested the fruitfulness of a comparative approach to the foreign fighter phenomenon.[23] These suggestions are far from incompatible with the thesis developed here: the development of ideological subcultures predicated on internationalism, built on tightly knit social and political networks, appears to be a logical basis for understanding other significant mobilisations of foreign fighters across contexts. This argument may even hold true in a digital age, despite the great attention paid to the role of the internet in foreign fighter recruitment across contexts. The recent observation in a Dutch context, for instance, that Islamist volunteers still tended to share real-life connections with one another, suggests that the importance of local, interpersonal connections remains in the twenty-first century.[24]

Alongside contributing – hopefully productively – to ongoing debates in wider fields, this book has sought to explore what responding to the Spanish Civil War reveals about the nature of Scottish politics and society in the 1930s. In doing so, it is occupying a curiously neglected gap in existing history writing. Histories of the pre-Second World War Scottish left tend to fade away towards the end of the 1930s. In terms of the high drama of party politics, the crescendo had peaked in 1932, with the ILP's abortive attempt to establish itself outside of Labour's broad tent. Many such histories take 1932 as their end date, a tacit admission that only an epilogue remained when it came to Scotland's older modes of labour politics. Even for histories that nominally stretch to 1939 or beyond, however, the years leading up to war tend to be neglected. For one, the absence of general election campaigns in the second half of the decade removed a key focus point for popular politics. 1935 was the last election year for a decade, prolonging the ILP's political un-death in parliament but also limiting the extent that local Scottish politics 'mattered' in Westminster beyond occasional by-elections. Extra-parliamentary activism – a fading feature of mainstream political culture in the period – also seemed to have peaked in importance well before 1939. The Hunger Marches against unemployment, the most obvious such form of local activism and a distinctive feature of the interwar period, lost their impetus after 1936, not least due to the slow re-awakening of British heavy industry due to rearmament.

Part of the difficulty in writing Scottish political history in the late 1930s is this looming shadow of war. Increasingly, British politics became concerned with international rather than domestic issues, as Europe lurched once more towards a continental bloodbath. The perennial Scottish problems of the interwar period – unemployment, industrial decline, housing, even nationalism – were all being solved or sidelined by the oncoming conflict. Historians of Scottish politics, therefore, are perhaps doing little more than tacitly acknowledging their cue to leave the stage in the late 1930s: writing a history of 'Scottish' contributions to high diplomacy and imperial defence could be nothing but parochial. Scotland did not confront and help defeat European fascism. Scots may have played their part, but they did so through the auspices of the British state, and, if mainstream analyses of British nationhood are correct, they mostly did so as Britons.

Yet politics in Scotland did not cease with the prospect of global conflict. If anything, the obvious urgency of the international situation demanded a response from the growing numbers of Scots who had correctly diagnosed that fascism inevitably meant war well before 1939. How to understand and respond to the escalating series of international crises was indeed the order of the day, but the mistake is to assume that these debates could have little in the way of local or regional dimensions. Quite aside from intense discussions surrounding very immediate issues such as Air Raid Precautions, international crises were readily understood and responded to within a local context. Locality mattered, not just in terms of understanding what international developments might mean in practice – who might get conscripted, who might get bombed – but also in terms of how to respond proactively. Many Scots who wished to avert, avoid or prepare for war were not content to leave it to their elected representatives, but rather sought to take things into their own hands as best they could.

Of all the crises that rocked Europe in these years, it was Spain that offered the most obvious and enduring outlet for this widespread desire to act against the gathering storm. In this sense, the marginality of the Spanish Civil War in Scottish history writing is even more remarkable: in assuming that local politics and activism largely ceased to matter in the late 1930s, historians have come to neglect one of the most impressive international solidarity campaigns ever undertaken in Scotland. To be sure, pro-Republican activism was a pan-European, even global movement. Yet equally, the conflict's varied and contested meanings were inevitably understood through other lenses, and the activism itself was profoundly shaped by the contours of local politics. Indeed, in so far as this book has one single, overarching argument, it is that much of the variability in responses to the Spanish Civil War, in Scotland and beyond, can be understood only from below. Whilst wider patterns can be noted, and broader conclusions drawn, understanding the way that communities engaged with international politics remains the starting point. In this sense, this study still belongs as much in the sphere of transnational history as Scottish history. The focus throughout has been on how individuals, institutions and organisations sought to escape the confines of the nation, to challenge the assumption that the state should enjoy a monopoly over war and diplomacy. Many Scots – most obviously the hundreds of International Brigade volunteers – assumed the right not just to criticise British policy in Spain but to take corrective action of their own accord.

Notes

1. See MML, Box 40, File A/1–4.
2. 'Spanish Refugee Bulletin No. 1', 23 June 1939, NLS, TMP, Box 2, File 2.
3. For an overview, see Greg Burgess, *Refuge in the Land of Liberty: France and Its Refugees, from the Revolution to the End of Asylum, 1787–1939* (London, 2008), 204–11.
4. David Pike, *Spaniards in the Holocaust: Mauthausen, the Horror on the Danube* (New York, 2000).
5. On the IBA during and after the Second World War, with frequent reference to Scotland, see Tom Buchanan, 'Holding the Line: the Political Strategy of the International Brigade Association, 1939-1977', *Labour History Review* 66:3 (2001), 294–312.
6. Buchanan, 'Holding the Line', 294.
7. Buchanan, *Impact*, 179–81.

8. For discussion, see Fraser Raeburn, 'The "Premature Anti-fascists"? International Brigade Veterans' Participation in the British War Effort, 1939–45', *War in History* (available online ahead of print: https://doi.org/10.1177/0968344518778315).
9. Buchanan credits George Murray with providing this impetus. Buchanan, 'Holding the Line', 297.
10. IBA Bulletin, 1944, NLS, TMP, Box 4, File 1.
11. IBA Executive Committee Meeting Minutes, 14 June 1946, NLS, TMP, Box 4, File 1.
12. Green to Murray, 29 March and 9 May 1949, MML, Box 40, File B/85,88.
13. Green to Murray, 14 December 1949, MML, Box 40, File B/100.
14. Murray to Green, 30 April 1950, MML, Box 40, File B/106.
15. These were Steven Fullarton and Christopher Smith, Archivo Historico Provincial Albacete, International Brigade Collection (AHPA), Box 63190, File 6/110,134.
16. These forms are held in the AHPA, Box 63186.
17. '70 years on, Spain says thank you to British and Irish civil war veterans', *The Guardian* [online], 8 June 2009, <https://www.theguardian.com/world/2009/jun/08/spanish-civil-war-british-irish-veterans> , last accessed 24 January 2018.
18. For example Robert Munro, *The Cry of Spain* (Unpublished script, 1986), MML, Box A-14, File E/1; Hector Macmillan, *A Greater Tomorrow* (Programme, 1997), MML, Box 21, File F/20; *¡No Pasaran!: Scots in the Spanish Civil War*, Album produced by Greentrax (2012).
19. For example *Radical_Glasgow*, 8 January 2018, Twitter [online], <https://twitter.com/Radical_Glasgow/status/950435337712652288>, last accessed 24 January 2018.
20. For example 'Marking the 80th Anniversary of the Battle of Jarama', *IBMT Magazine* 45:2 (2017), 4.
21. Zaagsma, *Jewish Volunteers*; Mae Lambe, *No Barrier Can Contain It*.
22. Goebel, *Anti-Imperial Metropolis*, 291.
23. Arielli, *Byron to bin Laden*.
24. Reinier Bergema and Marion van San, 'Waves of the Black Banner: an Exploratory Study on the Dutch Jihadist Foreign Fighter Contingent in Syria and Iraq', *Studies in Conflict and Terrorism* 42:7 (2019), 636–61. More broadly, see Thomas Hegghammer, 'The Rise of Muslim Foreign Fighters', *International Security* 35:3 (2010), 53–94.

Bibliography

Primary Sources

Archives

Archivo General Militar, Avila (AGMA).
  Ejército Popular, 1936–1941.
  Ejército Nacional, 1936–1942.

Archivo General de Guerra Civil Española (AGGCE).
  PS-Aragon.

Archivo Historico Provincial Albacete (AHPA).
  Documentación de las Brigadas Internacionales.

Glasgow City Archives (GCA).
  TD675 – Amalgamated Union of Building and Trades Workers
  TD 1042 – Edward Brown Papers.
  TD 1051 – Glasgow AEU Records relating to the Spanish Civil War.
  Uncatalogued – Records of the Glasgow Trades and Labour Council.

Hansard.
  House of Commons Debates.

Labadie Collection, University of Michigan.
  Fausto Villar Esteban Papers.

Marx Memorial Library (MML).
  International Brigade Archive.

Imperial War Museum Sound Archive (IWMSA).
804 – Interview with Bob Cooney.
11947 – Interview with James Maley.
12290 – Interview with Chris Smith.

The National Archives, Kew (TNA).
FO Series – Records of the Foreign Office.
HO Series – Records of the Home Office.
KV Series – Records of the Security Service.

National Library of Scotland (NLS).
Acc. 4311 – National Union of Mineworkers.
Acc. 4313 – National Union of Railwaymen.
Acc. 4516 – Amalgamated Engineering Union.
Acc. 4977 – Leith Constituency Labour Party and Edinburgh Socialist
Sunday Schools.
Acc. 5010 – Amalgamated Union of Engineering and Foundry Workers.
Acc. 7656 – Arthur Woodburn Papers.
Acc. 7915 - David Murray Papers.
Acc. 9083 – Tom Murray Papers.
Acc. 9805 – National Union of Mineworkers, Scotland.
Acc. 9853 – Amalgamated Engineering Union, Musselburgh Branch.
Acc. 10481 – Ian MacDougall Papers.
Acc. 11177 – Edinburgh & District Trades Council
Acc. 11835 – Scottish Midland Co-operative Society Ltd.
Acc. 12087 – John Dunlop Papers.
Dep. 188 – National Union of Railwaymen
Dep. 227 – National Union of Mineworkers, Scotland: Lanark Area.
Dep. 359 – Shop, Distributive and Allied Workers Union, Edinburgh.

National Records of Scotland (NRS).
1911 Census of Scotland.
HH1/595 – 'Foreign Enlistment Act'

People's History Museum, Manchester.
CP/IND/POLL – Harry Pollitt Papers.

Russian State Archive of Socio-Political History (RGASPI).
Note on archive access: Two versions of this archive were consulted. 495
was first accessed at the Library of Congress, where a partial digitisation of the archive is available. 545 Fund and part of 495 were accessed

later through a digitisation project run by the Russian Federal Archives agency, and accessible at <http://sovdoc.rusarchives.ru>. The quality of this latter digitisation project was confirmed through reference to the Library of Congress material.

Fund 495 – Records of the Executive Committee of the Comintern (ECCI).
 Inventory 14 – Secretariat of A. Marty.
 Inventory 20 – Bureau of the Secretariat of the Executive Committee of the Comintern.

Fund 545 – International Brigades of the Spanish Republican Army.
 Inventory 1 – Documents of the Military Commisariat of the International Brigades.
 Inventory 2 – Documents of the International Brigade Central Military Commission.
 Inventory 3 – Documents of the 35th and 45th Divisions, 10–15th and 129th International Brigades.
 Inventory 6 – Lists and personal files of International Brigade soldiers and officers.

Tameside Local Studies Archive, Ashton-under-Lyne (TLS).
 Manchester Studies Series (MS).

Modern Records Centre, University of Warwick.
 Trabajadores Collection (TC).

Newspapers and Periodicals

Cowdenbeath and District Advertiser
Daily Worker
Dundee Courier
Dunfermline and West Fife Journal
Fife Free Press
Forward
Glasgow Herald
Glasgow Observer
The Guardian
Kirkcaldy Times
IBMT Newsletter
Lanarkshire Catholic Herald
Nuestro Combate / Our Fight

The Scotsman
Volunteer for Liberty

Printed

Atholl, Katharine Murray, Duchess of, *Searchlight on Spain* (London, 1938).

Caplan, Jack, *Memories of the Gorbals* (Edinburgh, 1991).

Census of England and Wales, 1931, Classification of industries (1934).

Census of Scotland, 1931. Vol. III, Occupations and industries (1934).

Cooney, Bob, *Proud Journey* (London, 2015).

Copeman, Fred, *Reason in Revolt* (London, 1948).

Corkhill, D. and S. Rawnsley (eds), *The Road to Spain: Anti Fascists at War 1936–1939* (Dunfermline, 1987).

Fraser, Hamish, *The Truth about Spain* (Oxford, c.1950).

Gallacher, William, *Revolt on the Clyde: An Autobiography* (London, 1936, reprinted 1978).

Glasser, Ralph, *Growing up in the Gorbals* (London, 1997 (Omnibus edition)).

MacDougall, Ian (ed.), *Voices from the Hunger Marches, Vols I–II* (Edinburgh, 1990).

— *Voices from the Spanish Civil War: Personal Recollections of Scottish Volunteers in Republican Spain 1936–39* (Edinburgh, 1986).

— *Voices from War and Some Labour Struggles* (Edinburgh, 1995).

— *Voices from Work and Home: Personal Recollections of Working Life and Labour Struggles in the Twentieth Century* (Edinburgh, 2000).

McGovern, John, *Terror in Spain: How the Communist International Has Destroyed Working Class Unity, Undermined the Fight against Franco, and Suppressed the Social Revolution* (London, 1937).

McGovern, John, *Why Bishops Back Franco* (London, 1936).

McShane, Harry and J. Smith (eds), *No Mean Fighter* (London, 1976).

Maley, John and Willy Maley, *From the Calton to Catalonia* (Glasgow, 1992).

Orwell, George, *Homage to Catalonia* (London, 1986).

Ryan, Frank (ed.), *The Book of the XVth Brigade* (Madrid, 1938)

Selkirk, Bob, *Life of a Worker* (Dundee, 1967).

Spender, Stephen, *World Within World* (London, 1950).

Thomas, Fred, *To Tilt at Windmills* (East Lansing, 1996).

[Vallejo Nágera, Antonio], 'Psiquisismo del Fanatismo Marxista: Internacionales ingleses', *Semana Médica Española* 27 (September 1939), 308–12.

— 'Psiquisismo del Fanatismo Marxista: Investigaciones biopsiquicas en prisoneros internacionales', *Semana Médica Española* 22 (January 1939), 108–12.

— 'Psiquisismo del Fanatismo Marxista: Investigaciones biopsiquicas en prisoneros internacionales', *Semana Médica Española* 34 (1939), 522–4.

Wintringham, Tom, *English Captain* (London, 1939).

¡No Pasaran!: Scots in the Spanish Civil War, Album produced by Greentrax (2012).

Secondary Sources

Published

Abrams, Lynn, *Oral History Theory* (London, 2010).

Acciai, Enrico, 'Traditions of Armed Volunteering and Radical Politics in Southern Europe: A Biographical Approach to Garibaldinism', *European History Quarterly* 49:1 (2019), 50–72.

Alexander, Bill, *British Volunteers for Liberty: Spain, 1936–1939* (London, 1982).

— 'George Orwell and Spain' in Norris (ed.), *Inside the Myth. Orwell: Views from the Left* (London, 1984), 85–102.

Alpert, Michael, 'The Clash of Spanish Armies: Contrasting Ways of War in Spain, 1936–1939', *War in History* 6:3 (1999), 331–51.

— *A New International History of the Spanish Civil War* (Basingstoke, 2004).

— *The Republican Army in the Spanish Civil War, 1936–1939* (Cambridge, 2013).

Arielli, Nir, *From Byron to bin Laden: A History of Foreign War Volunteers* (Cambridge, 2018).

— 'Getting There: Enlistment Considerations and the Recruitment Networks of the International Brigades during the Spanish Civil War' in Nir Arielli and Bruce Collins (eds), *Transnational Soldiers: Foreign Military Enlistment in the Modern Era* (Basingstoke, 2012), 219–30.

— 'Induced to Volunteer? The Predicament of Jewish Communists in Palestine and the Spanish Civil War', *Journal of Contemporary History* 46:4 (2011), 854–70.

Armitage, David, *Civil Wars: A History in Ideas* (New Haven, 2017).

Arnot, R. Page, *The Miners in Crisis and War: A History of the Miners' Federation of Great Britain from 1930 Onwards* (London, 1961),

Arnott, Mike, *Dundee and the Spanish Civil War* (Dundee, 2008).

Attridge, Steve, *Nationalism, Imperialism and Identity in Late Victorian Culture* (Basingstoke, 2003).

Baldoli, Claudia, '"With Rome and with Moscow": Italian Catholic Communism and Anti-Fascist Exile', *Contemporary European History* 25:4 (2016), 619–43.

Barrett, Neil, 'The Threat of the British Union of Fascists in Manchester' in Tony Kushner and Nadia Valman (eds), *Remembering Cable Street: Fascism and Anti-Fascism in British Society* (London, 2000), 56–73.

Bartie, Angela and Arthur McIvor, 'Oral History in Scotland', *Scottish Historical Review* 92 (2013), 108–36.

Baxell, Richard, *British Volunteers in the Spanish Civil War* (London, 2004).

— 'Myths of the International Brigades', *Bulletin of Spanish Studies* 91:1–2 (2014), 11–24.

— *Unlikely Warriors: The British in the Spanish Civil War* (London, 2012).

Bearman, Peter, 'Desertion as Localism: Army Unit Solidarity and Group Norms in the U.S. Civil War', *Social Forces* 70:2 (1991), 321–42.

Beaven, Brad, 'The Provincial Press, Civic Ceremony and the Citizen-Soldier during the Boer War, 1899–1902: a Study of Local Patriotism', *Journal of Imperial and Commonwealth History* 37:2 (2009), 207–28.

Bergema, Reinier and Marion van San, 'Waves of the Black Banner: an Exploratory Study on the Dutch Jihadist Foreign Fighter Contingent in Syria and Iraq', *Studies in Conflict and Terrorism* 42:7 (2019), 636–61.

Bolloten, Burnett, *The Spanish Civil War: Revolution and Counterrevolution* (Chapel Hill, 1991).

Bowd, Gavin, *Fascist Scotland: Caledonia and the Far Right* (Edinburgh, 2013).

Branson, Noreen, *History of the Communist Party of Great Britain, 1927–1941* (London, 1985).

Braskén, Kasper, 'Making Anti-Fascism Transnational: the Origins of Communist and Socialist Articulations of Resistance in Europe, 1923–1924', *Contemporary European History* 25:4 (Nov. 2016), 573–96.

Brome, Vincent, *The International Brigades: Spain 1936–1939* (London, 1965).

Buchanan, Tom, 'Anti-Fascism and Democracy in the 1930s', *European History Quarterly* 32:1 (2002), 39–57.

— *Britain and the Spanish Civil War* (Cambridge, 1997).

— 'Britain's Popular Front? Aid Spain and the British Labour Movement', *History Workshop Journal* 31 (1991), 60–72.

— 'The Death of Bob Smillie, the Spanish Civil War and the Eclipse of the Independent Labour Party', *The Historical Journal* 40:2 (1997), 435–61.

— 'Divided Loyalties: the Impact of the Spanish Civil War on Britain's Civil Service Trade Unions, 1936–9', *Historical Research* 65:56 (1992), 90–107

— 'Holding the Line: The Political Strategy of the International Brigade Association, 1939–1977', *Labour History Review* 66:3 (2001), 294–312.

— 'Ideology, Idealism, and Adventure: Narratives of the British Volunteers in the International Brigades', *Labour History Review* 81:2 (2016), 123–40.

— *The Impact of the Spanish Civil War on Britain* (Brighton, 2007).

— 'The Politics of Internationalism: the Amalgamated Engineering Union and the Spanish Civil War', *Bulletin of the Society for the Study of Labour History* 53:3 (1988), 47–55.

— The Role of the British Labour Movement in the Origins and Work of the Basque Children's Committee, 1937-9', *European History Quarterly* 18:2 (1988), 115–74.

— *The Spanish Civil War and the British Labour Movement* (Cambridge, 1991).

Burgess, Greg, *Refuge in the Land of Liberty: France and Its Refugees, from the Revolution to the End of Asylum, 1787–1939* (London, 2008).

Buxton, Neil, 'Economic Growth in Scotland between the Wars: The Role of Production Structure and Rationalization', *The Economic History Review* 33:4 (1980), 538–55.

Byrne, Justin, 'From Brooklyn to Belchite' in Peter Carroll (ed.), *Facing Fascism: New York and the Spanish Civil War* (New York, 2007), 72–82.

Cabanes, Bruno, 'Negotiating Intimacy in the Shadow of War (France, 1914–1920s): New Perspectives in the Cultural History of World War I', *French Politics, Society & Culture* 31:1 (2013), 1–23.

Cairncross, A. K. (ed.), *The Scottish Economy* (Cambridge, 1954).

Cameron, Ewen, *Impaled upon a Thistle: Scotland since 1880* (Edinburgh, 2010).

Campbell, Alan, *The Scottish Miners, 1874–1939, Volume Two* (Aldershot, 2000).

Campbell, Alan and John McIlroy, 'The National Unemployed Workers' Movement and the Communist Party of Great Britain Revisited', *Labour History Review* 73:1 (2008), 61–88.

Carroll, Peter, *The Odyssey of the Abraham Lincoln Brigade: Americans in the Spanish Civil War* (Stanford, 1994).

Castells, Andreu, *Las Brigadas Internacionales de la Guerra de España* (Esplugues de Llobregat, 1974).

Celada, Antonio and Daniel Pastor Garcia, *Los brigadistas de habla inglesa y la Guerra Civil Española* (Madrid, 2002).

— 'The Victors Write History, the Vanquished Literature: Myth, Distortion and Truth in the XV Brigade', *Bulletin of Spanish Studies* 89:7-8 (2012), 307–21.

Clavin, Patricia, 'Defining Transnationalism', *Contemporary European History* 14:4 (2005), 421–39.

Cohen, Gidon, 'The Independent Labour Party, Disaffiliation, Revolution and Standing Orders', *History* 86:282 (2001), 200–21.

Cohen, Gidon and Kevin Morgan, 'Stalin's Sausage Machine. British Students at the International Lenin School, 1926-37', *Twentieth Century British History* 13:4 (2002), 327-55.

Collins, Bruce and Nir Arielli (eds), *Transnational Soldiers: Foreign Military Enlistment in the Modern Era* (London, 2013).

Cook, Chris, *The Age of Alignment: Electoral Politics in Britain* (London, 1975).

Cook, Judith, *Apprentices of Freedom* (London, 1979).

Corral, Pedro, *Desertores: La Guerra Civil que nadie quiere contra* (Barcelona, 2006).

Corthorn, Paul, 'Cold War Politics and the Contested Legacy of the Spanish Civil War, *European History Quarterly* 44:4 (2014), 678-702.

Cullen, Stephen, 'The Fasces and the Saltire: the Failure of the British Union of Fascists in Scotland, 1932-1940', *Scottish Historical Review* 87:2 (2008), 306-31.

Cunningham, Valentine, *The Penguin Book of Spanish Civil War Verse* (London, 1980).

— *Spanish Front: Writers on the Civil War* (Oxford, 1986).

Delperrie de Bayac, Jacques, *Les Brigades Internationales* (Paris, 1968).

Dolan, Chris, *An Anarchist's Story: The Life of Ethel MacDonald* (Edinburgh, 2009).

Donnachie, Ian, 'Scottish Labour in the Depression: the 1930s' in Ian Donnachie, Christopher Harvie and Ian Wood (eds), *Forward! Labour Politics in Scotland 1888-1988* (Edinburgh, 1989), 49-65.

Eby, Cecil, *Comrades and Commissars: The Lincoln Battalion in the Spanish Civil War* (University Park, PA, 2007).

Eller, Cynthia, 'Oral History as Moral Discourse: Conscientious Objectors and the Second World War', *Oral History Review* 18:1 (1990), 45-75.

Esenwein, George, 'Freedom Fighters or Comintern Soldiers? Writing about the "Good Fight" during the Spanish Civil War', *Civil Wars* 12:1-2 (2010), 156-66.

Finlay, Richard, 'Continuity and Change: Scottish Politics 1900-45' in Tom Devine and Richard Finlay (eds), *Scotland in the Twentieth Century* (Edinburgh, 1996).

Finn, Michael, 'Local Heroes: War News and the Construction of "Community" in Britain, 1914-18', *Historical Research* 83:221 (2010), 524-35.

Ford, Hugh, *A Poet's War: British Poets and the Spanish Civil War* (Philadelphia, 1965).

Francis, Hywel, *Miners against Fascism: Wales and the Spanish Civil War* (London, 1984).

Fraser, W. Hamish, *Scottish Popular Politics: From Radicalism to Labour* (Edinburgh, 2000).

Fronczack, Joseph, 'Local People's Global Politics: A Transnational History of the Hands Off Ethiopia Movement of 1935', *Diplomatic History* 39:2 (2015), 245-74.

Fry, Michael, *Patronage and Principle: A Political History of Modern Scotland* (Aberdeen, 1987).

Fyrth, Jim, 'The Aid Spain Movement in Britain 1936-1939', *History Workshop Journal* 35 (1993), 153-64.

— *The Signal Was Spain: The Spanish Aid Movement in Britain, 1936-1939* (London, 1986).

Gallagher, Tom, *Glasgow: The Uneasy Peace: Religious Tension in Modern Scotland* (Manchester, 1987).

García, Hugo, 'Transnational History: a New Paradigm for Anti-Fascist Studies?', *Contemporary European History* 25:4 (2016), 563-72.

Gerrard, Jessica, '"Little Soldiers" for Socialism: Childhood and Socialist Politics in the British Socialist Sunday School Movement', *International Review of Social History* 58:1 (2013), 71-96.

Gillespie, Mark, *When the Gorbals Fought Franco* (Glasgow, 2014).

Goebel, Michael, *Anti-Imperial Metropolis: Interwar Paris and the Seeds of Third World Nationalism* (Cambridge, 2015).

Graham, Helen, *The Spanish Republic at War 1936-1939* (Cambridge, 2002).

— *The War and Its Shadow: Spain's Civil War in Europe's Long Twentieth Century* (Brighton, 2012).

Graham, Helen, and Paul Preston (eds), *The Popular Front in Europe* (Basingstoke, 1987).

Gray, Daniel, *Homage to Caledonia: Scotland and the Spanish Civil War* (Edinburgh, 2008).

Grele, Ron, *Envelopes of Sound: The Art of Oral History* (New York, 1991).

Hall, Christopher, *'Not Just Orwell': The Independent Labour Party Volunteers and the Spanish Civil War* (Barcelona, 2009).

Harvie, Christopher, *No Gods and Precious Few Heroes: Twentieth Century Scotland* (Edinburgh, 1998).

Hegghammer, Thomas, 'The Rise of Muslim Foreign Fighters', *International Security* 35:3 (2010), 53-94.

Heppell, Jason, 'A Rebel, not a Rabbi: Jewish Membership of the Communist Party of Great Britain', *Twentieth Century British History* 15:1 (2004), 28-50.

Hodgson, Keith, *Fighting Fascism: The British Left and the Rise of Fascism, 1919-39* (Manchester, 2010).

Holford, John, *Reshaping Labour: Organisation, Work and Politics in Edinburgh in the Great War and After* (London, 1988).

Hopkins, James, *Into the Heart of the Fire: The British in the Spanish Civil War* (Stanford, 1998).

Hughes, Annmarie, *Gender and Political Identities in Scotland, 1919-1939* (Edinburgh, 2010).

Hughes, Ben, *They Shall Not Pass!: The British Battalion at Jarama* (Oxford, 2011).

Hunter, Kate, 'More than an Archive of War: Intimacy and Manliness in the Letters of a Great War Soldier to the Woman He Loved, 1915-1919', *Gender & History* 25:2 (2013), 339-54.

Hutchinson, Iain, *Scottish Politics in the Twentieth Century* (Basingstoke, 2001).

Inglis, Amirah, *Australians in the Spanish Civil War* (Sydney, 1987).

Jackson, Angela, *British Women and the Spanish Civil War* (London, 2002).

Jackson, Gabriel, *The Spanish Republic and the Civil War, 1931-1939* (Princeton, 1965).

Jackson, Michael, 'The Army of Strangers: The International Brigades in the Spanish Civil War', *Journal of Australian Politics and History* 32:1 (1986), 105-18.

— *Fallen Sparrows: The International Brigades in the Spanish Civil War* (Philadelphia, 1994).

Johnston, Ronnie and Arthur McIvor, 'Dangerous Work, Hard Men and Broken Bodies: Masculinity in the Clydeside Heavy Industries, c.1930-1970s', *Labour History Review* 69:2 (2004), 135-51.

Johnston, Verle, *Legions of Babel: The International Brigades in the Spanish Civil War* (University Park, PA, 1967).

Keene, Judith, *Fghting for Franco: International Volunteers in Nationalist Spain, 1936-39* (London, 2001).

Kenefick, William, *Rebellious and Contrary: The Glasgow Dockers, 1853-1932* (East Linton, 2000).

— *Red Scotland! The Rise and Decline of the Scottish Radical Left, c.1872 to 1932* (Edinburgh, 2007).

Kiernan, Victor, 'Foreword' in Ian MacDougall (ed.), *Voices from the Spanish Civil War: Personal Recollections of Scottish Volunteers in Republican Spain 1936-39* (Edinburgh, 1986), v-xi.

Kirschenbaum, Lisa, *International Communism and the Spanish Civil War* (Cambridge, 2015).

— 'The Man Question: How Bolshevik Masculinity Shaped International Communism', *Socialist History* 52 (2017), 76-84.

Knox, William, *Industrial Nation: Work, Culture and Society in Scotland, 1800–Present* (Edinburgh, 1999).

— 'The Red Clydesiders' in Terry Brotherstone (ed.), *Covenant, Charter, and Party: Traditions of Revolt and Protest in Modern Scottish History* (Aberdeen, 1989), 92–104.

Knox, William, and Alan McKinlay, 'The Re-making of Scottish Labour in the 1930s', *Twentieth Century British History* 6:2 (1995), 174–93.

Kowalsky, Daniel, 'Operation X: Soviet Russia and the Spanish Civil War', *Bulletin of Spanish Studies* 91:1–2 (2014), 167–71.

— *Stalin and the Spanish Civil War* (New York, 2004).

Krüger, Christine and Sonja Levsen (eds), *War Volunteering in Modern Times: From the French Revolution to the Second World War* (Basingstoke, 2011).

Labajo, Joaquina, 'La práctica de una memoria sostenible: el repertorio de las canciones internacionales de la Guerra Civil Española', *Arbor* 187:751 (2011), 847–56.

Lambe, Ariel Mae, *No Barrier Can Contain It: Cuban Antifascism and the Spanish Civil War* (Chapel Hill, 2019).

LaPorte, Norman and Matthew Worley, 'Towards a Comparative History of Communism: the British and German Communist Parties to 1933', *Contemporary British History* 22, 2 (2003), 227–55.

Linehan, Thomas, *Communism in Britain: 1920–39: From the Cradle to the Grave* (Manchester, 2007).

Little, Douglas, *Malevolent Neutrality: The United States, Great Britain and the Origins of the Spanish Civil War* (Ithaca, 1985).

McCartney, Helen, *Citizen Soldiers: The Liverpool Territorials in the First World War* (Cambridge, 2005).

MacDonald, Catriona, *The Radical Thread: Political Change in Scotland: Paisley Politics, 1885–1924* (East Linton, 2000).

McGarry, Fearghal, *Irish Politics and the Spanish Civil War* (Cork, 1999).

McIlroy, John, 'The Establishment of Intellectual Orthodoxy and the Stalinization of British Communism 1928–1933', *Past & Present* 192 (2006), 187–226.

Macintyre, Stuart, *Little Moscows: Communism and Working-class Militancy in Interwar Britain* (London, 1980).

MacKay, Ruth, 'History on the Line: The Good Fight and Good History in the Spanish Civil War', *History Workshop Journal* 70 (2010), 199–206.

McKinlay, Alan and R.J. Morris (eds), *The ILP on the Clydeside, 1893–1932: From Foundation to Disintegration* (Manchester, 1991).

McKinlay, Alan and James Smyth, 'The End of "the agitator workman": 1926–1932' in Alan McKinlay and R. Morris (eds), *The ILP on the Clydeside, 1893–1932: From Foundation to Disintegration* (Manchester, 1991), 177–203.

McLennan, Josie, '"I Wanted to be a Little Lenin": Ideology and the German International Brigade Volunteers', *Journal of Contemporary History* 41:2 (2006), 287–304.

McWhirter, Christian, *Battle Hymns: The Power and Popularity of Music in the Civil War* (Chapel Hill, 2012).

Malet, David, *Foreign Fighters: Transnational Identity in Civic Conflicts* (Oxford, 2013).

Mason, Emily, *Democracy, Deeds and Dilemmas: Support for the Spanish Republic within British Civil Society, 1936–1939* (Eastbourne, 2017).

Mates, Lewis, 'Durham and South Wales Miners in the Spanish Civil War', *Twentieth Century British History* 17:3 (2006), 373–95.

— *The Spanish Civil War and the British Left: Political Activism and the Popular Front* (London, 2007).

Matthews, James, *Reluctant Warriors: Republican Popular Army and Nationalist Army Conscripts in the Spanish Civil War, 1936–1939* (Oxford, 2012).

— '"The Vanguard of Sacrifice"? Political Commissars in the Republican Popular Army during the Spanish Civil War, 1936–1939', *War in History* 21:1 (2013), 82–101.

Marco, Jorge and Maria Thomas, '"Mucho malo for fascisti": Languages and Transnational Soldiers in the Spanish Civil War', *War & Society* 38:2 (2019), 139–61.

Miller, Stephen, 'British and Imperial Volunteers in the South African War' in Christine Krüger and Sonja Levsen (eds), *War Volunteering in Modern Times: From the French Revolution to the Second World War* (Basingstoke, 2011), 108–21.

— 'In Support of the "Imperial Mission"? Volunteering for the South African War, 1899–1902', *Journal of Military History* 69:3 (2005), 691–711.

Moradiellos, Enrique, 'The Origins of British Non-Intervention in the Spanish Civil War: Anglo-Spanish Relations in Early 1936', *European History Quarterly* 21 (1991), 339–64.

Morgan, Kevin, *Against Fascism and War: Ruptures and Continuities in British Communist Politics, 1935–41* (Manchester, 1989).

Morgan, Kevin, Gidon Cohen and Andrew Flinn, *Communists and British Society, 1920–1991* (London, 2007).

Morris, R. J., 'The ILP, 1893–1932: Introduction' in Alan McKinlay and R. J. Morris (eds), *The ILP on the Clydeside, 1893–1932: From Foundation to Disintegration* (Manchester, 1991), 1–19.

O'Riordan, Michael, *Connolly Column: The Story of the Irishmen who Fought for the Spanish Republic 1936–1939* (Dublin, 1979).

Palfreeman, Lina, *Aristocrats, Adventurers and Ambulances: British Medical Units in the Spanish Civil War* (Brighton, 2014).

Payne, Peter, 'The Economy' in Tom Devine (ed.), *Scotland in the 20th Century* (Edinburgh, 1996).

Payne, Stanley, *The Collapse of the Spanish Republic, 1933–1936* (New Haven, 2006).

— *The Spanish Civil War* (Cambridge, 2012).

Petrie, Malcolm, *Popular Politics and Political Culture: Urban Scotland, 1918–1939* (Edinburgh, 2018).

— 'Public Politics and Traditions of Popular Protest: Demonstrations of the Unemployed in Dundee and Edinburgh, c.1921–1939', *Contemporary British History* 27:4 (2013), 490–513.

— 'Unity from Below? The Impact of the Spanish Civil War on Labour and the Left in Aberdeen and Dundee, 1936–1939', *Labour History Review* 79:3 (2015), 305–27.

Petrou, Michael, *Renegades: Canadians in the Spanish Civil War* (Vancouver, 2008).

Pike, David, *France Divided: The French and the Spanish Civil War* (Brighton, 2011).

— *Spaniards in the Holocaust: Mauthausen, the Horror on the Danube* (New York, 2000)

Preston, Paul, *Doves of War: Four Women of Spain* (London, 2002),

— *The Coming of the Spanish Civil War: Reform, Reaction and Revolution 1931–1936* (London, 1994).

— *The Spanish Civil War* (London, 2006).

Radosh, Ronald, Mary Habeck and Grigory Sevostianov (eds), *Spain Betrayed: The Soviet Union in the Spanish Civil War* (New Haven, 2001).

Raeburn, Fraser, '"Fae nae hair te grey hair they answered the call": International Brigade Volunteers from the West Central Belt of Scotland in the Spanish Civil War, 1936–9', *Journal of Scottish Historical Studies* 35:1 (2015), 92–114.

— 'Politics, Networks and Community: Recruitment for the International Brigades Reassessed', *Journal of Contemporary History* (available online ahead of print: https://doi.org/10.1177/0022009419865005).

— 'The "Premature Anti-fascists"? International Brigade Veterans' Participation in the British War Effort, 1939-45', *War in History* (available online ahead of print: https://doi.org/10.1177/0968344518778315).

Rafeek, Neil, *Communist Women in Scotland: Red Clydeside from the Russian Revolution to the End of the Soviet Union* (London, 2008).

Rees, Tim, 'Living Up to Lenin: Leadership Culture and the Spanish Communist Party, 1920-1939', *History* 97:326 (2012), 230-55.

Requena Gallego, Manuel, 'Las Brigadas Internacionales: una aproximación historiográfica', *Ayer* 56 (2004), 11-35.

del Rey Reguillo, Fernando, *The Spanish Second Republic Revisited: From Democratic Hopes to Civil War (1931-1936)* (Brighton, 2012).

Richards, Michael, 'Morality and Biology in the Spanish Civil War: Psychiatrists, Revolution and Women Prisoners in Málaga', *Contemporary European History* 10:3 (2001), 395-421.

Richardson, R. Dan, *Comintern Army: The International Brigades and the Spanish Civil War* (Lexington, 1982).

Richet, Isabelle, 'Marion Cave Rosselli and the Transnational Women's Anti-fascist Networks', *Journal of Women's History* 24:3 (2012), 117-39.

Roberts, Elizabeth, *'Freedom, Faction, Fame and Blood': British Soldiers of Conscience in Greece, Spain and Finland* (Brighton, 2010).

Rolfe, Edwin, *The Lincoln Battalion* (New York, 1939).

Roper, Michael, *The Secret Battle: Emotional Survival in the Great War* (Manchester, 2010)

Rust, William, *Britons in Spain: The History of the British Battalion of the XVth International Brigade* (London, 1939).

Scott, George, *Aberdeen Volunteers Fighting in the Spanish Civil War* (London, 2019).

Seal, Grahame, '"We're Here Because We're Here": Trench Culture of the Great War', *Folklore* 124:2 (2013), 178-97.

Seidman, Michael, *Transatlantic Antifascisms: From the Spanish Civil War to the End of World War II* (Cambridge, 2017).

Shelmerdine, Brian, *British Representations of the Spanish Civil War* (Manchester, 2006).

Simkins, Peter, *Kitchener's Army: The Raising of the New Armies, 1914-16* (Manchester, 1988).

Skoutelsky, Remi, 'L'engagement des volontaires français en Espagne républicaine', *Le Mouvement social* 181 (1997), 7-29.

— *Novedad en el frente: las Brigadas Internacionales en la guerra civil* (Madrid, 2006).

Smith, Elaine, 'But What Did They Do? Contemporary Jewish Responses to Cable Street' in Tony Kushner and Nadia Valman (eds), *Remembering Cable Street: Fascism and Anti-Fascism in British Society* (London, 2000), 48–55.

Smyth, James, *Labour in Glasgow 1896–1936* (East Linton, 2000).

— 'Resisting Labour: Unionists, Liberals and Moderates in Glasgow between the Wars', *The Historical Journal* 46:2 (2003), 375–401.

Spiers, Edward, 'Voluntary Recruiting in Yorkshire, 1914–15', *Northern History* 52:2 (2015), 295–313.

Stevenson, John and Chris Cook, *The Slump: Britain in the Great Depression* (Harlow, 2010).

Stone, Dan, 'Anti-Fascist Europe Comes to Britain: Theorising Fascism as a Contribution to Defeating It' in Nigel Copsey and Andrzej Olechnowicz (eds), *Varieties of Anti-Fascism: Britain in the Inter-War Period* (Basingstoke, 2010).

Stradling, Robert, 'English-Speaking Units of the International Brigades: War, Politics and Discipline', *Journal of Contemporary History* 45:4 (2010), 744–66.

— *History and Legend: Writing the International Brigades* (Cardiff, 2003).

— *The Irish and the Spanish Civil War 1936–1939: Crusades in Conflict* (Manchester, 1999).

— *Wales and the Spanish Civil War: The Dragon's Dearest Cause?* (Cardiff, 2004).

Studer, Brigitte, *The Transnational World of the Cominternians* (London, 2015).

Thomas, Hugh, *The Spanish Civil War* (3rd ed., London, 2003).

Thorpe, Andrew, *The British Communist Party and Moscow, 1920–43* (Manchester, 2000).

— 'The Membership of the Communist Party of Great Britain, 1920–1945', *The Historical Journal* 43:3 (2000), 777–800.

Uhl, Michael, *Mythos Spanien: Das Erbe der internationalen Brigaden in der DDR* (Bonn, 2004).

Watkins, K., *Britain Divided: The Effect of the Spanish Civil War on British Political Opinion* (London, 1963).

Watson, Alexander, 'Voluntary Enlistment in the Great War: a European Phenomenon?' in Christine Krüger and Sonja Levsen (eds), *War Volunteering in Modern Times: From the French Revolution to the Second World War* (Basingstoke, 2011), 163–88.

Williams, Colin, Bill Alexander and John Gorman, *Memorials of the Spanish Civil War* (Stroud, 1996).

Wood, Ian, 'Hope Deferred: Labour in Scotland in the 1920s' in Ian Donnachie Christopher Harvie, and Ian Wood (eds), *Forward!: Labour Politics in Scotland, 1888–1988* (Edinburgh, 1989), 30–48,

— 'Scotland and the Spanish Civil War', *Cencrastus* (Autumn 1984), 14–16.

Worley, Matthew, *Class against Class: The Communist Party in Britain between the Wars* (London, 2002).

Young, Hilary, 'Hard Man, New Man: Re/Composing Masculinities in Glasgow, c.1950–2000', *Oral History* 35:1 (2007), 71–81.

Zaagsma, Gerben, *Jewish Volunteers, the International Brigades and the Spanish Civil War* (London, 2017).

— '"Red Devils": the Botwin Company in the Spanish Civil War', *East European Jewish Affairs* 33 (2003), 83–99.

Unpublished

Holloway, Kerrie, *Britain's Political Humanitarians: The National Joint Committee for Spanish Relief and the Spanish Refugees of 1939* (PhD Thesis, Queen Margaret University of London, 2017).

Lambe, Ariel Mae, *Cuban Antifascism and the Spanish Civil War: Transnational Activism, Networks, and Solidarity in the 1930s* (PhD Thesis, Columbia University, 2014).

Index

Printed and bound by CPI Group (UK) Ltd, Croydon, CR0 4YY

15/12/2024

01806472-0004